Philip Larkin: Art and Self

Also by M. W. Rowe

PHILOSOPHY AND LITERATURE: A Book of Essays

HEINRICH WILHELM ERNST: Virtuoso Violinist

Philip Larkin: Art and Self

Five Studies

M. W. Rowe
Senior Lecturer in Philosophy, University of East Anglia

palgrave
macmillan

First published 2011 by
PALGRAVE MACMILLAN

Palgrave Macmillan in the UK is an imprint of Macmillan Publishers Limited, registered in England, company number 785998, of Houndmills, Basingstoke, Hampshire RG21 6XS.

Palgrave Macmillan in the US is a division of St Martin's Press LLC, 175 Fifth Avenue, New York, NY 10010.

Palgrave Macmillan is the global academic imprint of the above companies and has companies and representatives throughout the world.

Palgrave® and Macmillan® are registered trademarks in the United States, the United Kingdom, Europe and other countries.

ISBN 978–0–230–25171–7 hardback

This book is printed on paper suitable for recycling and made from fully managed and sustained forest sources. Logging, pulping and manufacturing processes are expected to conform to the environmental regulations of the country of origin.

A catalogue record for this book is available from the British Library.

A catalog record for this book is available from the Library of Congress.

10 9 8 7 6 5 4 3 2 1
20 19 18 17 16 15 14 13 12 11

Printed and bound in Great Britain by
CPI Antony Rowe, Chippenham and Eastbourne

To Alan Heaven

But o, photography! as no art is,
Faithful and disappointing!

Larkin

Contents

Preface viii

Acknowledgements xi

Note on References xiii

Introduction 1

'Here' by Philip Larkin 6

I. 'Here': Avoiding the Subject 7

II. Larkin/Flaubert 48

'Livings' by Philip Larkin 88

III. 'Livings': Aesthetic Intimations 91

IV. Larkin and the Creepy 124

'Aubade' by Philip Larkin 165

V. 'Aubade': Death and the Thought of Death 167

References 205

Index 212

Preface

The essays in this book have largely been written over the last four years, but my interest in their topics extends much further back.

Like many others, I was introduced to Larkin's poems at school: in my case by Hubert Moore, Head of English at Cranbrook School, Kent. He was a brilliant teacher – wry, engaging, knowledgeable, relaxed – and his feel for poetry immediately suggested it was part of his life as well as his teaching. I soon discovered this was true: I heard him read one or two of his own poems (hints of the wonderfully accomplished work that would follow); saw a copy of the newly published *High Windows* in his hand; and learnt that his father, W. G. Moore, had been the Dean of St John's, Oxford, when Larkin was an undergraduate. The older Moore had become something of a legend in the poet's circle: Larkin imitates his voice on the recording of 'Dockery and Son' ("Dockery was junior to you, / Wasn't he?' said the Dean. 'His son's here now" [CP:152]); and Bruce Montgomery – writing as Edmund Crispin – turned Moore into Gervase Fen, the hero of a famous sequence of detective novels. (The surname, Larkin tells us, was transmuted by way of 'Lead Kindly Light''s 'O'er moor and fen' [FR:124].)

Perhaps this background helped Hubert become an especially expert teacher of Larkin. His expertise certainly became clear in the second or third form when we studied 'Poetry of Departures' and 'Toads'; and several years later I remember him showing what a splendid performance piece 'The Whitsun Weddings' was – so rich, apparently effortless, amused and well observed. But the Larkin experience which stands out most clearly in my mind, was studying 'Afternoons' in one of Hubert's sixth-form lessons just before lunch on a Saturday. In spite of the sunlight, the chill and melancholy of the poem seemed to seep into me; it lingered for several hours into the afternoon, and even the thought of a free day-and-a-half and a visit home could not altogether shake it off. In fact, in some sense, and at some level, I have never quite shaken it off.

While mentioning teachers, I must also thank Cecil Irwin, who was Head of Music and house tutor in my junior boarding house. One or two evenings after prep, he sat at the excellent upright Kemble in the sewing room and played Chopin. Even though it's forty years ago, I can still remember some of the pieces he played very clearly: the E major and 'Black Key' études from op. 10, the A^{b} major study from op. 25, and to round off – and in particularly high style – the 'Revolutionary' study from the earlier book. He was the first really brilliant pianist I'd ever heard at close quarters, and I found both his playing and the music awe-inspiring; indeed, I suspect he helped give me a taste for the glitter and thunder of nineteenth-century virtuoso music which has shadowed me since.

More to the present purpose, he also introduced me to the ghost stories of M. R. James – which I discuss in the fourth essay. From a second-hand bookshop, he had picked up an ancient copy of *Ghost-Stories of an Antiquary* – huge, apparently bound in hessian, and stamped with Gothic lettering – and read us most of it by torchlight in the dormitory. I found these stories utterly gripping – there was something so learned and authoritative about the narrative voice – and even now there are certain parts of the country and certain times of day that I can only experience through the filter of James's consciousness.

Flaubert and his work – the partial topic of the second essay – only entered my life between school and university, when I was working as a clerk in Victoria Street, London. It was a lonely and dismal period: I felt a desperate need for intellectual life and stimulation, and utterly stifled by savourless commercial dullness. The only bright patches were lunchtimes: reading the *New Statesman* in the Shaw Theatre restaurant on Fridays, and browsing on other days in an airy bookshop nearby. This was run by an attractively arty couple – he was plumpish, neatly-bearded, and smock-wearing; she was willowy and slightly exotic – and it was on their shelves that I first came across *Madame Bovary* – quickly followed by *Sentimental Education, Salammbô* and the *Three Tales*. It was just the literature I needed. There was something about Flaubert's forensic chill, his icy aesthetic perfection and exoticism, that seemed to disinfect and partly obliterate the world of fumes, luncheon-vouchers and cold but stuffy trains I then inhabited. I remain profoundly grateful.

Partly influenced by the literature I read at this time, I studied philosophy as an undergraduate and graduate, but Mrs Thatcher's higher-education cuts ensured that no career in this area was possible. Accordingly, I became an English teacher myself, and in my first year at Pocklington School near York, pupils would sometimes tell me about standing next to Larkin in the delicatessen in Cottingham, or the number of bottles that he left outside his house for the dustmen. On his death, one of the national papers reprinted the hitherto uncollected 'Aubade'. I was very struck with it, began to teach his work regularly, and published a short piece on his imagery. A decade later, when I learnt that his papers were fifteen miles away in Hull University Library, I thought the opportunity too good to miss and went to look through them. This was the origin of my taste for archive work, my first proper article on Larkin, and my scholarly engagement ever since.

It was only in 2006, when I was about to leave Pocklington, that I discovered the school had hosted a rare event: an 'informal discussion' about poetry, conducted by Larkin in 1960 ('thereby confirming my opinion that this is one of the least profitable ways to spend an evening' [SL:314]). The enterprising Head of English at this period, Tim Rogers, had close connections with Hull University, and managed to secure a number of distinguished speakers including Herbert Read and Malcolm Bradbury. On this occasion, he wisely held the meeting in his house, and ensured that the hand-picked sixth-formers he'd invited were well briefed beforehand about Larkin's shyness and reluctance [LM:267].

Working on Larkin has been made easier and more pleasurable by the existence of the Larkin Society which, besides many other events, organizes an important conference on his work every five years. I am personally grateful to a number of its members – particularly James Booth, John Osborne and Anthony and Ann Thwaite – for help, discussion and advice. I'd also like to thank some ex-colleagues at Pocklington who talked with me about Larkin (Darrell Buttery, Emma Cunningham, Ruth Donachie, Bryony Marshall, Mike Smith); a number of ex-pupils (Caroline Merson, Rob Milne, Oliver Radley-Gardner, Siân Smith and Aimée Woodliffe come to mind); and the organizers and audience members in various universities to whom I've read sections of these essays (especially Michael Hulse, Chris Miller and Jeremy Noel-Tod). I greatly benefited from two anonymous referees' reports on my work, and they will recognize where I have been able to respond to their points and advice.

The dedication of this book indicates my debt to Alan Heaven. He is that rare thing, a friend who not only reads one's stuff – uncommon enough – but with *the appearance of enjoyment*. Penelope Pelizzon – another excellent poet – has been an unfailing source of encouragement; and Anthony Price was helpfully sceptical about some of my general claims in the Flaubert essay. My wife, Marie McGinn, has greatly improved the book's contents: she was a tremendous help with the essay on 'Here' (particularly the sections on Romanticism, and narrative), and was the person who originally suggested that the affinities between Flaubert and Larkin might bear examination. Finally, I would like to thank my contacts at Palgrave – Paula Kennedy and Ben Doyle – for their flexibility and forbearance.

Mark Rowe, Highgate, October 2010

Acknowledgements

Excerpts from *Required Writing* by Philip Larkin. Copyright © 1983 by Philip Larkin. Reprinted by permission of Faber and Faber Ltd, and Farrar, Straus and Giroux, LLC.

Excerpts from *Collected Poems* by Philip Larkin. Copyright © 1988, 2003 by the Estate of Philip Larkin. Reprinted by permission of Faber and Faber Ltd, the Marvell Press, and Farrar, Straus and Giroux, LLC.

Excerpts from *Selected Letters of Philip Larkin, 1940–1985* by Philip Larkin, introduction by Anthony Thwaite. Copyright © 1992 the Estate of Philip Larkin. Reprinted by permission of Faber and Faber Ltd, and Farrar, Straus and Giroux, LLC.

Excerpts from *Further Requirements* by Philip Larkin, introduction by Anthony Thwaite. Copyright © 2001 the Estate of Philip Larkin. Reprinted by permission of Faber and Faber Ltd, and the Society of Authors as trustees of the Estate of Philip Larkin.

Excerpts from *Trouble at Willow Gables and Other Fictions* by Philip Larkin, introduction by James Booth. Copyright © 2002 the Estate of Philip Larkin. Reprinted by permission of Faber and Faber Ltd, and the Society of Authors as trustees of the Estate of Philip Larkin.

Excerpts from Philip Larkin's manuscript workbook No. 8 (DPL 1/8, the Larkin Archive, Brynmor Jones Library, the University of Hull) appear by permission of the Society of Authors as trustees of the Estate of Philip Larkin.

Excerpts from *Philip Larkin, 1922–1985: A Tribute*, ed. George Hartley. Copyright © 1988 the Marvell Press. Reprinted by permission of the Marvell Press.

Excerpts from *Philip Larkin: A Writer's Life* by Andrew Motion. Copyright © 1993 Andrew Motion. Reprinted by permission of Faber and Faber Ltd, United Agents, and Farrar, Straus and Giroux LLC.

Excerpts from *The Philip Larkin I Knew* by Maeve Brennan. Copyright © Maeve Brennan 2002. Reprinted by permission of Manchester University Press.

"'Aubade': Death and the Thought of Death' (originally entitled 'Larkin's 'Aubade'") from *Philosophy and Literature: A Book of Essays* by M. W. Rowe. Copyright © 2004 M. W. Rowe. Reprinted by permission of Ashgate Publishing Ltd.

Reprinted by permission of the publisher from *The Letters of Gustave Flaubert: Volume I: 1830–1857*, selected, edited and translated by Francis Steegmuller, pp. 40, 41, 48, 73, 74, 75, 78, 79, 89, 132, 148, 156, 161–2, 173, 174, 186–7, 196, 197, 198, 200, 234, Cambridge, MA: The Belknap Press of Harvard University Press, Copyright © 1979, 1980 Francis Steegmuller.

Reprinted by permission of the publisher from *The Letters of Gustave Flaubert: Volume II: 1857–1880*, selected, edited and translated by Francis Steegmuller, pp. 5, 72, 147, 212, 219, 225, 226–7, 257, Cambridge, MA: The Belknap Press of Harvard University Press, Copyright © 1982 Francis Steegmuller.

Excerpts from *Flaubert: A Life* by Geoffrey Wall. Copyright © Geoffrey Wall 2001. Reprinted by permission of the author, Faber and Faber Ltd, and David Higham Associates Ltd.

Excerpt from *Collected Essays: Volume I* by Virginia Woolf. Copyright © 1966 the Estate of Virginia Woolf. Reprinted by permission of the Society of Authors as trustees of the Estate of Virginia Woolf.

Excerpts from *The Invention of Solitude* by Paul Auster. Copyright © 1988. Reprinted by permission of Faber and Faber Ltd, and Carol Mann Agency.

Every attempt has been made to contact copyright holders. Anyone who has not been reached should notify the publishers.

Note on References

Initials in square brackets denote books, long poems and journals; Roman numerals indicate volume or canto numbers; Arabic numerals refer to page, line or paragraph numbers; journals are indicated by the year and issue details. The key to the initials is found in the bibliography at the back of the book, and this is in alphabetical order of the initials. Superscript numbers refer to notes at the end of each essay.

Introduction

When Larkin's *Selected Letters* appeared, they caused consternation. This was largely because many of the earlier ones were so foul-mouthed, and many of the later ones so openly racist and right-wing. But the book's other surprise caused less comment. This was the young Larkin's intense aestheticism, the religious seriousness of his devotion to art, the utter dedication with which he pursued his artistic ideals, and the conscious sacrifices he made in order to achieve them.

Both aspects of his character obliterated the image of the lovably lugubrious cycle-clipped librarian, the genteel author of carefully crafted verses written after work. And both were necessary for his genius – the scabrous side testing the insights of the aesthetic, and ensuring that nothing phony, arty or secondhand survived its jeering. But in some ways it is the aesthetic element which is most important: this, one feels, is the origin of the great poems, and the element lacking in his friends Kingsley Amis and Robert Conquest – ferocious mockers and distinguished figures though they are.

Accordingly, it is Larkin the aesthete on whom this book concentrates; and, even though I don't mention it frequently, the strain in Larkin criticism which I've always found most interesting is Barbara Everett's exploration of Larkin's relationship with French Symbolism, and Edna Longley's work on his connections with *fin-de-siècle* aestheticism.

It's now clear that aestheticism – and its attendant interest in Symbolism – was not simply a phase which Larkin outgrew. The passing of time has made the melancholy Romanticism of *The Less Deceived* seem more closely related to *The North Ship* than Larkin would have us believe. And later in life, he frequently reworked poems he started in the forties and early fifties: thus 'Vers de Société' [1971] is partially based on 'Best Society' [1951?], 'Aubade' [1977] draws on the form of 'The wave sings [...]' [1946], 'Livings I' [1971] revisits 'Negative Indicative' [1953], 'Livings II' [1971] draws on an image in 'Mother, Summer, I' [1953], and so on. Clearly, the Symbolist element in his work is most evident in his last collection *High Windows* ('Sympathy in White Major', 'Solar', 'Money'), and it is significant that although he wrote his version of Baudelaire's 'Femmes Damnées' in 1943, he only published it in 1978. By this date, not only were its contents less shocking, but it blended effortlessly into Larkin's *oeuvre*.

Although *The Whitsun Weddings* is probably the strongest and certainly the most famous of his four collections, it is also the most untypical. The Symbolist element is still present (in 'Water' and the end of 'Here', for instance) but it is more muted, and of all the collections, this is the one which comes closest to satisfying Movement ideals. It is largely clear, uniform and civic: we do not find the obscure private agonizing of 'Dry-Point' or the introspective fantasy of 'If, My Darling' from *The Less Deceived*; and we do not encounter the cultural allusiveness of 'Sympathy in White Major' or the disorientating transitions of 'Money' from *High Windows*. For most of his career, Larkin was a more uneven, more varied, more difficult and in some ways more interesting poet.

The present book consists of five essays. The first, third and fifth are extended examinations of three major poems ('Here', 'Livings' and 'Aubade'); while the second and fourth are studies of more general topics: the affinities between Larkin's life and Flaubert's; and Larkin's feelings for the supernatural. Both studies take what appear to be mere passing comments in the *Letters*, and show just how significant these remarks actually are. Each of the five essays has its own introduction, and examines the central concepts it employs, so I don't want to add too much more introductory material here, but a brief sketch of their subject matters and connections might be useful.

All the studies investigate the interconnections between two ideas: the self and aesthetic experience. The essay on 'Here' argues that one of the major attractions of aesthetic experience for Larkin is that it seems to offer the prospect of release from selfhood. The next two essays remain focused on aesthetic experience but set it in more troublesomely social contexts. 'Larkin/Flaubert' examines two lives devoted to aesthetic ideals, and emphasizes the social and sexual detachment which results from this vocation. The study of 'Livings' investigates the simultaneous discovery of detachment and aesthetic experience, and pursues the latter's connections with freedom, creativity, poetic imagery and the sublime.

The remaining essays are still darkened by the concept of sublimity – with its implications of awe, fear and threat to the individual. 'Larkin and the Creepy' looks at a number of sinister elements in aesthetic experience that normally escape philosophical attention: loneliness, animism, primitivism, the muse, suppressed sexuality, and the presence of the past. 'Aubade: Death and the Thought of Death' examines Larkin's feelings about the end of the self, and considers whether the end of all experience can be an object for aesthetic experience.

There are various ways to think about the book's order. It is built around three poems which are in chronological order of composition; its mood gradually darkens; it begins and ends with dawns, but the first is lambent with imaginative promise, the second blank, stale and deathly.

As this summary makes clear, I sometimes try to show that Larkin explores philosophical issues. This may seem surprising. He was certainly suspicious of philosophical talk, largely because he felt it was likely to be secondhand and pretentious, but in many ways this attitude was a positive philosophical asset. Being a great poet who was preoccupied by life, death, the self and artistic creation, he could not fail to be interested in philosophical questions, but because he was so wary of philosophical *blague* he was forced to formulate questions and answers for himself.

Sometimes, as in 'Aubade', he does this explicitly. That work, after all, is a poem of statement which presents an argument about the nature of death and why we should be afraid of it. On other occasions, he raises rather than states philosophical problems, and gives no apparent answers. In 'Livings', for instance, he highlights a philosophical issue by allowing an apparent lack of connection between things which ought to be connected; in 'Here' he foregrounds a metaphysical difficulty by adopting a form of narrative which seems virtually incoherent.

This practice has many advantages. It raises the problems as if for the first time; it grounds the problems in the concrete facts of human existence; it suggests how such problems fit into the rest of human life; it invites the reader to engage in the thought process; and it avoids any hint of windy pretentiousness. Such poems are genuinely exploratory and probative: they are *doing* philosophy, not merely illustrating philosophical conclusions.

As freshness, concreteness and unpretentiousness are epistemic virtues that promote the discovery of truth, Larkin's explorations have considerable philosophical value. Indeed, as I try to show at several points in the main text, there are moments when his ideas correspond to those of Kant and Schopenhauer. There are two brief mentions of Schopenhauer in Larkin's work [FR:176; AWJ:259], but it is unlikely that he knew either philosophers' writings first-hand, although he had been influenced by authors – Hardy, Mallarmé, Yeats, Joyce – who had read one or both. I also doubt whether Larkin knew he was setting out to explore a philosophical problem when he wrote 'Livings' and 'Here'. But he liked to emphasize that poetry is a matter of unconscious instinct rather than conscious intellect: and sometimes the poem sees more deeply than the poet.

I don't wish to overplay the philosophy. Some of what follows is literary scholarship: the first three sections of the 'Livings' essay trace the origins of the poem's parts; and the opening sections of the piece on 'Aubade' delve into Larkin's manuscript books. A good deal of the material on the three poems is straightforward, often quite detailed, literary criticism; and the essay on Larkin and Flaubert is largely a biographical study. 'Larkin and the Creepy' looks at the superstitious and mystical side to Larkin, and thus investigates not beliefs or theories but superstitions, feelings, emblems, imaginings and ideas entertained for artistic purposes. Clearly, any attempt to claim that Larkin actually believed in the supernatural, or that his views can be reconstructed into a coherent theory, would be absurd, but, as I try to show, there is some logic and consistency behind them.

But why write a collection of essays on the self and aesthetic experience rather than a straightforward monograph? I didn't set out to write a book, or even a series of essays on these subjects; so it was not a matter of conscious choice or intention. I simply started to investigate aspects of Larkin's work which I found strange, resonant or otherwise provoking; and when certain common themes began to emerge, they surprised me as much as any potential reader. Writing about Larkin is unpredictable: a poem often opens out in completely unforeseeable ways; earlier essay-pages always have to be dropped or rewritten scores of times in order to keep pace; and frequently the question or topic I began with had been completely transformed by the end of the process.

In addition, the 40-page essay is a very useful length: short enough to focus on one topic, long enough to investigate it thoroughly. And a book of such pieces gives the author permission not to cover everything, to focus on his interests, and to write only what he wants to write. This should benefit the reader too.

The form, however, has three obvious dangers: repetitions, internal inconsistencies and explanatory gaps. The first is brought about because a book of essays invites two kinds of reader: those who want to start at the beginning and work through; and those who want to sample or read in an unconventional order. Consequently, each essay has to be autonomous to satisfy the reader who samples, but the book must not be too repetitious for the reader who wants to work through. This is quite difficult to accomplish because points in one essay depend on points established in another, and – like every Larkin critic – I keep circling back to certain crucial passages.

I have tried to resolve this difficulty by slightly prioritizing the reader who wants to read from front to back: arguments for conclusions occur before conclusions are assumed, and fuller quotations tend to occur nearer the beginning than the end. However, I have not attempted to avoid repetition altogether: a critical point is only successful if it conforms to or alters a reader's perception of a passage – and this means he has to have the passage in front of him; sometimes quotation is necessary in order for a point carry sufficient weight; and very often a new point is made each time a quotation is discussed.

I don't think there are any internal disagreements, although there are differences of emphasis, but I am conscious of two gaps.

First, this book was originally to have contained six essays and begun with a study I'd already published of Larkin's interest in lesbianism. Unfortunately, the plan had to be set aside, because the resulting book would have been too long, and contained too much previously published material. A slimmer volume has many advantages, but in some ways I still miss the opening study. This is largely because some evidence for what I say about Larkin's sexuality and its connections with creativity can only be found in the lesbianism essay. However, its two parts are easily available, and I can only ask the interested reader to look them up if anything I say on the relevant topics seems less well supported than it should be [NLO:79–96; CQ:Winter/2001:42–58].

Second, the Joyce Estate has prevented me from quoting any material at all from Joyce's published works. In a work on Larkin's aestheticism this is a major problem because Larkin's knowledge of aestheticism, and his theory of poetry, owe so much to Joyce. I have got round this obstacle as best I can by means of paraphrase, but I am very conscious that I cannot provide the kind of detailed analysis and comparison of passages I would ideally like.

However, writing about Larkin is a profound and enlightening pleasure; I hope the reader can share some of this pleasure in the following pages.

Here

Swerving east, from rich industrial shadows
And traffic all night north; swerving through fields
Too thin and thistled to be called meadows,
And now and then a harsh-named halt, that shields
Workmen at dawn; swerving to solitude
Of skies and scarecrows, haystacks, hares and pheasants,
And the widening river's slow presence,
The piled gold clouds, the shining gull-marked mud,

Gathers to the surprise of a large town:
Here domes and statues, spires and cranes cluster
Beside grain-scattered streets, barge-crowded water,
And residents from raw estates, brought down
The dead straight miles by stealing flat-faced trolleys,
Push through plate-glass swing doors to their desires –
Cheap suits, red kitchen-ware, sharp shoes, iced lollies,
Electric mixers, toasters, washers, driers –

A cut-price crowd, urban yet simple, dwelling
Where only salesmen and relations come
Within a terminate and fishy-smelling
Pastoral of ships up streets, the slave museum,
Tattoo-shops, consulates, grim head-scarfed wives;
And out beyond its mortgaged half-built edges
Fast-shadowed wheat-fields, running high as hedges,
Isolate villages, where removed lives

Loneliness clarifies. Here silence stands
Like heat. Here leaves unnoticed thicken,
Hidden weeds flower, neglected waters quicken,
Luminously-peopled air ascends;
And past the poppies bluish neutral distance
Ends the land suddenly beyond a beach
Of shapes and shingle. Here is unfenced existence:
Facing the sun, untalkative, out of reach.

Philip Larkin, 8 October 1961

I
'Here': Avoiding the Subject

Everything that is mortal is dissolved, nothing but light, nothing but freedom [...] no shadow [...] no barrier

Schiller

[The] sky was clear and blue, and I felt disembodied and full of passive ecstasy

Larkin

'Here' doesn't seem to be a philosophical poem. Larkin said it was just a 'plain description' [SL:346], and it certainly appears to be a straightforward account of a journey to the east Yorkshire coast. In this essay, however, I want to argue that the poem is an ambitious attempt to reconcile a profound philosophical tension in his thought.

Larkin loved conscious experience, and yet was oppressed by a sense of self and self-consciousness – the necessity of acting, willing, desiring, and seeing oneself as one amongst others. 'Here' tries to resolve this tension by seeing how close it is possible to come to consciousness without a self, action without an actor, experience without an experiencer.[1] It is a thought-experiment exploring the limits of consciousness.

The poet does not examine these possibilities explicitly and discursively, and he does not argue us into any conclusions. Instead, his method is heuristic: he takes readers on an imaginary journey as a result of which our confidence about the poem's most important structural features are progressively altered and undermined. We come to realize that the precise reference of the title, the grammatical subject of the first three stanzas, the nature of the experiencing consciousness, and the poem's degree of realism are multiply ambiguous and problematic.

And it is only after prolonged reflection on these difficulties that we come to see that most hint at their own solution: a conception of the experiencing subject so minimal that it risks, but does not embrace, incoherence. In the final stanza, this conception of the subject is further thinned and attenuated by dissolving it into a special kind of aesthetic experience – where the subject seems to inhabit a vicarious viewpoint that gradually diffuses itself into nothingness.

I

'Here' belongs to a class of words which philosophers of language call indexicals.[2] Their exact referents depend on a number of factors beyond straightforward word meaning. For example, the referents of many time words – 'past', 'present', 'future', 'now', 'then' – depend on *when* they are said; the precise denotation of indexicals referring to people – 'I', 'me', 'my', 'you', 'your', 'they', 'them', 'their' – depends on *who* says them; and the referents of place words – 'this', 'that', 'these', 'those', 'here', 'there' – depend on *where* they are said. Sometimes, with indexicals denoting people and places, a gesture or gestural device is required to fix the reference as well.

Where does 'Here' refer to in the title of Larkin's poem? Two difficulties in this case are that we have no gestures to guide us, and the narrator so obviously moves. Does 'Here' refer to the beginning of the poem as the narrator begins his eastern swerve? To the 'large town' he arrives at in the second stanza? Or to the countryside and beach he reaches towards the end? Rossen feels that the reference of the title moves once: 'the "here" of the title [...] becomes displaced to the uninhabited area outside the city' [MW:50], while Osborne feels it moves several times, and that the poem might be more accurately entitled, 'Here and now Here and now Here and now Here and now Here' [ICV:148]. Or does the title mean all of these places simultaneously?

It might be thought that looking at the word's appearance in the poem would be helpful. 'Here' is used four times: once, in stanza two, to refer to the large town; and three times in the final stanza to refer to the coastal area. These would therefore seem to focus the title's reference on the final section of the poem. But there is no reason to suppose that the 'Here' of the title must be parasitic on how 'here' is used in the poem. And because the reference of the title is independent, it might very well refer to the town as well as the coast, and to the beginning as well as the middle and end of the poem.

The meaning of many indexicals depends on another element beyond the factors of time, place, person and gesture already mentioned, namely the intellectual context in which the indexical thought takes place. An archaeologist comparing the climate in the Jurassic period with the climate we experience now, does not use 'now' to mean less than a second; whereas the man who shouts 'Now!' to indicate the beginning of an ambush probably does. Similarly, the astronomer who uses 'here' when talking about the planets is probably referring to the Earth; whereas the brain surgeon who asks an assistant to insert a tube 'here' could well be indicating an area no bigger than a few square millimetres.

This reveals a third difficulty with the title of the poem: 'Here' is the first word one sees, and thus the intellectual context of the indexical thought is not specified. As the narrator has probably just travelled from the south of England,[3] the 'Here' of the title could well mean the north or the north-east. In addition, as Simon Petch points out, the poem 'Here' introduces *The Whitsun Weddings*. It depicts the area where Arnold and Mr Bleaney live (or lived), and it sets the scene for many of the incidents which follow [APL:79]. So the suggestion that the title means the north or north-east is quite plausible on at least these two counts.

But the context may be larger. Larkin had previously lived in Northern Ireland and most of his previous collection, *The Less Deceived*, had been written there. Could the emphatic 'Here' with which his next book opens, introducing a poem which celebrates the English landscape, and a collection that was largely written in England, indicate that 'Here' means England? This is certainly how the term is used in 'The Importance of Elsewhere', a poem which occurs later in *The Whitsun Weddings*: 'Lonely in Ireland, [...] / Strangeness made sense [...] / Living in England has no such excuse: [...] // *Here* no elsewhere underwrites my existence' (my italics) [CP:104].[4]

Sometimes, if we broaden the context still further, 'here' can refer to earthly existence, the very state of being alive. Larkin uses the word in just this way in 'The Old Fools': '[...] but then [oblivion] was going to end, / And was all the time merging with a unique endeavour / To bring to bloom the million-petalled flower / Of being *here*' (my italics) [CP:196]. This links hereness with consciousness and flowers, and when it is recalled that Larkin also associates flowers with the sun (it is referred to as 'Single stalkless flower' in 'Solar' [CP:159]), the combination of sunlight, hereness, flowers and flowerings at the end of 'Here' becomes highly significant. They are Larkin's images of conscious life, and suggest that this could be one of the specific meanings of the title.

II

Outside of the poem, Larkin gave three hints about the reference of 'Here', all of them suggesting a slightly different answer.

Writing to Robert Conquest on 9 December 1961, he says: 'Thanks for the kind words about Here. No one much seems to have noticed it [It had first appeared in the *New Statesman* on 24 November], though it is to my mind in direct linear succession to The North Ship – I mean just pushing into a bloodier and bloodier area' [SL:335]. I'm not sure how useful this is. Larkin had a habit of turning against works he had recently completed, and the poem shows the landscape as far from being bloody. But if anything, it would seem to put the emphasis on the northerliness of the area.

His working title for the poem was 'Withdrawing Room' [M:317], a slightly pallid pun on the old name for a sitting room and 'space into which one can withdraw'. This would suggest the main emphasis of the title is on the poem's final stanza. But one cannot just assume that a later title has the same emphasis as an earlier one. Indeed, the emphasis of the old title may have been one reason why Larkin dropped the original and substituted the more neutral existential adverb which now stands in its place.

When, much later, an interviewer asked what the poem was about, Larkin replied: 'I meant it just as a celebration of here, Hull. It's a fascinating area, not quite like anywhere else. So busy, yet so lonely' [FR:59]. These remarks appear to solve one problem (although not in quite the way they first suggest) but immediately open up another.

'I meant it just as a celebration of here, Hull' seems clear enough.[5] But as soon as Larkin thinks of Hull he thinks of its area ('a fascinating area') which he describes as 'so busy, yet so lonely'. 'So busy' clearly applies to all the people and activity in the area; 'so lonely' implies that the area is remote from other centres of population. What makes the area so distinctively lonely is not only the thinly populated land all around, but the vast expanses of sea and sky to the east – and for Larkin, Hull always draws its identity from the east. As he writes in his preface to *A Rumoured City*:

> Behind Hull is the plain of Holderness, lonelier and lonelier, and after that the birds and lights of Spurn Head, and then the sea. One can go ten years without seeing these things, and yet they are always there, giving Hull the air of having its face half-turned towards distance and silence, and what lies beyond them. [FR:128]

Larkin's Hull is inconceivable without its area, and its area is inconceivable without the land, sea and sky beyond. He directs our attention to the whole landscape (and not just the town or the coast) but at the cost of the title's 'Here' expanding infinitely into the unfenced distance and nothingness celebrated at the end of the poem.

III

If we examine the relationship between indexicals and other kinds of description, we can find further connections between hereness and consciousness.

Indexicals function as a system which clusters round the pronoun 'I'. Where this 'I' is will partly determine where 'here' is, where counts as 'there', who counts as 'you', what counts as 'now', and so forth. And as my position in space and time changes, so the referents of this indexical system will change too. The one exception to this is 'I' itself which never changes its reference over a single person's lifetime. This is the reason for choosing it as the fixed point around which the others move.[6]

All these indexical terms invoke the perspective of my subjective experience of the world: they cannot be replaced by objective descriptions which lose this reference to a subject. Because they form a system, indexicals can be used to generate certain necessary truths (i.e. sentences which cannot be false): 'I am not you', 'Now is not then', 'I am here now' and so on. But if we replace the indexical terms in a sentence with objective specifications with the same reference, then we find the sentence's necessity disappears.

If, for example, I say 'I am here' when I am in London, then we can produce an apparently equivalent sentence – 'Mark Rowe is in London' – in which the indexicals have been replaced by names. But closer examination shows that the meanings of the sentences differ in at least three ways. First, 'I am here' is always true, whereas 'Mark Rowe is in London' is often false. Second, someone who is neither Mark Rowe nor in London can truthfully utter, 'I am here'. Third, I am justified in asserting 'I am here' even when I have no idea of my name or place; whereas this is not true of 'Mark Rowe is in London'. We can show the same differences between any other sentence involving indexicals, and an apparently equivalent sentence which uses objective specifications. And this fact demonstrates that the content of the indexical system can never be captured by names, coordinates and measurements.

A creature's ability to use indexical expressions entails not only that it is conscious (i.e. that there is *something which it is like to be* that creature[7]) but that it is self-conscious (i.e. that it is *aware* of itself as a subject of experiences). This form of self-consciousness, which is characteristic of human beings, is expressed in their mastery of the whole system of indexical expressions, including how the use of 'I', 'here' and 'now' differs from the use of names of people, places and times. We can now see that the 'Here' of the title posits the presence of a characteristically human consciousness.[8]

Scientific discourse is the discourse of eternal, objective facts. Scientific explanations do not use indexicals, secondary qualities (tastes, sounds, colours, smells, and sensations of touch and resistance), or emotions (love, anger, nostalgia), because all three introduce the idea, not only of the world, but a subject who experiences it. The explanations of science only employ objectively specified times and positions ('At 18.00 GMT' etc.), and deal with the intrinsic qualities of the natural world: mass, velocity, energy, and so forth.[9] Although we accord scientific explanations enormous prestige, they do not have the monopoly of truth, insofar as they ignore the world as it is experienced from the point of view of a subject. It is this *Lebenswelt*, the world as it appears to a self-conscious subject, which Wordsworth claims to be the ambit of literature, especially poetry:

> The appropriate business of poetry (which, nevertheless, if genuine is as permanent as pure as pure science) her appropriate employment, her privilege and her *duty*, is to treat of things not as they *are*, but as they *appear*, not as they exist in themselves, but as they *seem* to exist to the *senses* and the *passions*. [WW:641]

Thus 'here' implies 'I', 'I' implies self-consciousness, and self-consciousness is the realm of poetry. By using this tiny commonplace word as his title, Larkin suggests the poem will not only be about the places, people and objects it mentions, but about human self-consciousness and the subject matter of poetry itself.

IV

The title 'Here' adds enormously to the power, mystery and complexity of the poem, as we can see if we imagine it retitled 'Hull and Holderness', 'Sunny Humberside', 'To Spurn Head', 'Home', 'My East Riding' or something similar. The last three sections have already supplied two reasons for this: first, the actual title is internally connected to life, consciousness and the poetic; second, and because of this, the title's reference changes according to where we imagine it said, and what the intellectual context of the thought is. The word is more than ambiguous, it is protean, living, shimmering, a play of consciousness over an area.

However, there are further reasons for the title's appropriateness. The use of 'here' implies no objective knowledge of the world that is seen, or any relationship between the world and the subject (apart from position), or any information about the subject at all. It also suggests that the subject has a merely contingent relationship with a particular place (he happens to be here now, but tomorrow he could be somewhere else).[10]

'Hull and Holderness', unlike 'Here', implies objective knowledge of what is seen, and does not imply the presence of an observer. There is thus no suggestion of self-consciousness and literary experience, and this is why the pair of names seems more like a chapter heading from a guidebook than the title of a poem.

'Home' gives no objective description of the area but it does contain an implicit indexical element (it can only be explained with reference to 'I', 'my', 'your' 'their' etc.) which suggests the narrator has a certain kind of tie to the indicated place. 'My East Riding' suggests both knowledge of what is seen and a connection to the area. The indexical element in 'Home' and 'My East Riding' ensures that they are suggestive of literature and the subjective point of view (they could both be first chapters in a certain kind of autobiography) but, by using 'Here' as his title, Larkin intends to suggest no knowledge, ties or history of any kind. Perhaps, like D. H. Lawrence, he wants to be rooted in the world only through being rooted in himself [OSR:96].

V

The poem's indexical title naturally makes us curious about the form of consciousness it posits.

The narrative method of 'Here' differs substantially from that found in 'The Whitsun Weddings' and 'Dockery and Son'. Both of these poems are based on real incidents,[11] and are full of descriptions of trains, railways, passengers and stations. Similarly, both are narrated by the 'I' of a richly characterized narrator: one narrator loses his sense of urgency, is intrigued by the noise outside, welds all the couples joining the train into one event, and then comes to identify with these couples; the other leaves Oxford ignored, eats an awful pie, reflects gloomily on the role of heredity in his life, and then on life itself.

There is no evidence that 'Here' is based on a real event, and the poem does not mention the word 'I'[12] or supply any information about its protagonist.[13] Nonetheless, many critics assume that 'Here' is a realistic account of a journey from the Midlands to the coast undertaken by a protagonist who does not mention himself, his body or his thoughts [PP:149].[14] In addition, some critics believe that the protagonist travels all the way by train. Deborah Bowman, for example, says that 'Here' 'takes the form of a train journey to what's "out of reach"' [MR:175]; while Roger Day argues that 'and now and then a harsh named halt' is a reference to railway halts [L:53]. Critics who endorse this position could also argue that Larkin wrote three other long poems about railway travel; that he had not yet learnt to drive when he wrote 'Here'; and that the rapt contemplation of the landscape is not really compatible with driving a car.

It is possible to make a strong case against the idea of a rail journey. First, before 1964, there were two railway lines running from Hull to the east coast, but each arrived at the coast in the middle of a small town – Hornsea or Withernsea – so a journey to isolated villages, poppies, weeds, quickening waters and solitude would have required at least a long and unmentioned walk. Second, a journey to the coast would have necessitated a change of train and line, but again no such changes are mentioned in the poem. Third, trains to the coast were frequent, and left from the building and station (Hull Paragon) into which trains from the south arrived. Consequently, a change of train would not require a traveller to leave the building, and this seems at odds with detailed description of shoppers, buses, and widely scattered buildings in the town centre, several of which cannot be seen from the station.[15]

Fourth, 'halt' can also mean a pull-in for drivers (the SOED quotes a sentence from Peter Levi: 'A lorry-drivers' halt [...] that served sandwiches until midnight'). Such cafés display their signs clearly, they could easily shield workmen at dawn, and a motorist could well pass a number of them. These too could be harsh-named, perhaps because they take their names from their villages or their owners' surnames.[16] This removes the main piece of evidence in favour of the initial rail journey, and suggests that the protagonist might always be travelling by car. The great advantage of this idea is that it explains how the protagonist can seamlessly travel from the Midlands to Hull, through the centre of Hull, and out to the coast without a change of transport. This also explains why there is no mention of *transferring* to a car or another train.

Fifth, the first hint of a form of transport in the poem is 'traffic all night north' and it is initially natural to assume that the protagonist has been part of this traffic. Sixth, 'swerving' is much more obviously applicable to cars than it is to trains. For excellent reasons, main-line trains do not travel quickly around sharp bends, and the passenger is never conscious of a physical sense of swerving. 'A slow and stopping curve' – which is how 'The Whitsun Weddings' describes travelling on the same line in the opposite direction – seems a much more appropriate description of this experience [CP:114]. If 'swerving' does refer to a train, then the swerving is something intellectually known rather than physically felt: perhaps the protagonist knows from the map how the line branches off to Hull; perhaps he sees from his window the carriages ahead or behind curving round. But this experience seems too decorous to be called 'swerving'.

Seventh, Larkin himself may not have been able to drive when he wrote the poem, but there is no necessity to suppose that he could not recall being a passenger in a car, or that he could not imagine driving, or that he could not create a fictional protagonist who could drive. Eighth, at the end of stanza three, the protagonist has to be travelling by road, and yet this section is every bit as rapt and contemplative as the opening. Lastly, just because Larkin wrote three major poems about railway journeys (if we include 'I Remember, I Remember'), this does not mean that 'Here' has to be a fourth. 'Going, Going', after all, is clearly a poem that concentrates on road transport.

The phrase 'Fast-shadowed wheat-fields, running high as hedges [...]' does not help identify the form of transport used in the later part of the poem. It is not clear that the shadows are caused by transport at all: the rapid passage of cloud-shadows over fields is characteristic of this part of the country. And if the fast shadows are thrown by vehicles, then one of them does not have to be thrown by the vehicle in which the protagonist travels: he could be walking and just observing the shadows cast by passing traffic.

Supporters of the railway hypothesis have objections to these points, of course. The non-railway sense of 'halt' as a specifically named stopping-place is rare and not recognized by the OED: this only lists: 'A small railway station without the ordinary [...] staff.' There are definitely halts on the Hull line, and they definitely have harsh names (Saltmarsh, Gilberdyke etc.), but the supporter of the road hypothesis cannot know for certain what pull-ins existed on the road to Hull in the late 1950s and early 1960s or what their names were.[17] In any case, such places usually have rather cheerful names ('The Welcome Café') or are named after their owners' more euphonious Christian-names – Bob's, Betty's, Rita's. Lastly, since it is absolutely obvious that the narrator has to change his train or method of transport for the final part of his journey, these changes are simply not worth mentioning.

Perhaps the railway hypothesis still has the edge, perhaps Larkin was imaging the journey to Hull by one method of transport and the journey from Hull by another, but the fact that he makes it so difficult to decide may indicate that we are construing the poem in the wrong way. I shall consider an alternative in the next section.

VI

So far, I have assumed that 'Here' has an unmentioned first-person protagonist, but this assumption can be challenged. Given that there is no 'I' in the poem, there is no obligation to assume the journey is undertaken by a protagonist: the perspective in the poem may be entirely impersonal.[18] It may contain no *self* at all.

Such a reading is already implicit in the literature insofar as a number of critics do not posit a protagonist or consider plausible methods of travel, but suggest the poem's point of view is akin to a film-camera, and the poet's role to that of a film director. Andrew Motion, for example, likens the poem's viewpoint to 'a camera in a helicopter' [M:250]; while Simon Petch writes: 'The visual manipulation is cinematic [...] we have a moving camera, the technique being similar to that of a film director who organizes our perception of what he wants to show us' [APL:80. See also L:54]. These analogies with film can provide useful clues to a satisfying alternative interpretation.[19]

The point of view from which something is seen does not have to be *someone's* angle of vision. If we are watching a football match on television, then we naturally assume that at least the cameraman can see what we see, but this doesn't have to be the case. A camera mounted in a pilotless drone shows us the world from an angle no *person* sees, even if someone watches the screen and operates both the drone and its camera. Similarly, when a feature film cuts from a train leaving London straight to its arrival in Edinburgh, we do not assume some watching person has travelled equally quickly between the two cities.

There are literary analogues for this. When, in an impersonally narrated novel, the author describes his characters meeting in a square as if from high above, we do not think to ask whether the author imagines someone sustained at that height by a gantry or helicopter. And when the writer switches from describing a character in Paris to another in Berlin, we do not feel some watching person must make this journey. To assume either of these things would be to confuse the method of representation with what is represented. Such points of view, and changes in point of view, are characteristic of the representational qualities of a medium, and we do not naturally mistake them for characteristics of what is represented by means of that medium.

There is therefore a distinction between imagining moving from one place to another, and imagining *myself* or any other *person* travelling from one place to another. For example, if you ask me how to get from point A to point B in a city I know, I may well arrive at an answer by imagining my point of view passing down certain streets, observing certain landmarks, and turning certain corners. I can obviously do this without imagining my body and overcoming practical difficulties, so questions like 'Did you get hot on the way?' or 'How did you avoid the roadworks?' are clearly irrelevant. Whether I can also abstract away features distinctive of my psychology is a more difficult matter. I can certainly try, but imagining I cannot read the shop signs, or that I like a certain kitsch post-modern building I actually detest, is demanding.

Thus, instead of understanding 'Here' as about an unmentioned protagonist travelling from one place to another, we can think of it as the poet imagining *a point of view* moving from one place to another. In this case, he allows his imaginary point of view to travel through a familiar town and countryside, but this does not *require* him to imagine a method of transport. Imaginary points of view do not need transport, anymore than the novelist needs to imagine a gantry when describing a scene from above. However, it strikes me as quite likely that Larkin initially imagines a point of view occupying the position of a passenger on a train (for example), but that when the poet envisages the town, he simply imagines the point of view moving out to the coast and beyond, all practical difficulties of travel forgotten and irrelevant.

On this reading, 'Here' has no protagonist in the poem; and the viewpoint can consequently have no thoughts, history or personality. The presence of an 'I' is implied by the title but is not in the title; similarly, an 'I' is implied by the poem but is not in the poem. 'Here' still has a controlling consciousness – the poet's – but that consciousness does not inhabit the poem's point of view and is silent throughout, although his tastes and interests still govern what is noticed and how it is valued. In exactly the same way, the man who operates the drone and its camera sees the events from its point of view, can even manipulate that point of view, but has his consciousness elsewhere.

However, there is at least one important relevant difference between watching pictures relayed by a drone, and imaging a place from an imagined point of view, and this is that, in the case of imagination, there is no analogue for the drone itself. Vicarious *perception* requires that the point of view be instantiated in some kind of physical object (a camera or mirror, for example). But if I imagine my point of view passing through streets, then no physical object of any kind (including an imagined physical object) is required to pass through those streets in order to make my imagining possible. In other words, you can imagine a camera's point of view without imagining the camera; you can imagine a person's point of view without imagining the person. Imagining from an impersonal point of view is the most primitive form of imagination; every child is familiar with its capacities; and first-person imagining is actually a more complex process. Impersonal imagining is the *Urphänomen* of the projective imagination, and 'Here', like 'Absences', celebrates its apparently magical powers.

These considerations complicate the earlier discussion of indexicals because we now see that point of view and consciousness can come apart; and that indexicals can be applied to remote realities, fictions and represented realities. The man operating the drone can talk about 'here' and 'there' when pointing to the mountain peaks that appear on his screen; a character can use 'here' to mean Camelot, not the cardboard set where the actor playing him stands; and a poet can use 'here' to denote a place he imagines seeing, not a place he actually sees.

The vague and vaguely contradictory hints about forms of transport in the poem may indicate that the impersonal reading is preferable, and there are a number of other reasons which can be adduced in the interpretation's support.

First, the journey portrayed in the poem is an unlikely journey for anyone to make. Why should someone travel from the Midlands *at dawn* (and if we imagine the train coming from London, several hours earlier) in order to head straight for the beaches of the east coast? One can invent an emergency or an overwhelming desire for peace and quiet, but both of these manoeuvres seem implausibly *ad hoc*.

Second, it is not at all clear that the apparent time-scale of the journey could correspond with real life. In the opening stanza, as the point of view begins its eastern swerve, we are told about 'workmen at dawn' and then, in stanza two, about the cut-price crowd pushing through plate-glass doors to their desires. On the London line, the track branches east at Doncaster, and in the late 1950s and early 1960s *Bradshaw's Guide* shows that most morning trains made the journey from Doncaster to Hull in little over an hour. The poppies and uncut wheat suggest we are probably dealing with the period between early June and late August, and on 21 June, for example, dawn occurs in Doncaster at 5.35 a.m.

(British Summer Time).[20] This means we have to imagine passing from dawn to crowds of shoppers in Hull in a little over an hour, and even if we imagine the shops opening unusually early, and construe 'dawn' very broadly, this hardly seems possible.

On the one hand, the poem's relentless emphasis on swerving suggests something travelling rather faster than the normal train (hence Motion's idea that the point of view is like a camera in a *helicopter*); on the other, the objective times of events described in the poem demand something travelling considerably slower.

Third, in later life, Larkin twice returned to the theme of Humberside: in 'Bridge for the Living' and his already-mentioned preface to *A Rumoured City*. Both of these rework the material of 'Here' and both follow the same expository order. The first section of 'Bridge for the Living' describes the city, as from a distance, and then turns to the plain of Holderness, and finally the sea. In his preface to the anthology, he begins at the station, describes aspects of the city, and then moves on to Holderness and the sea. It is clear that this movement was Larkin's preferred way of thinking about his city, and that the journey in 'Here' could well be an imaginative device for dramatizing these places and making them follow a temporal order. No one speculates about the method of transport used in these later works.

Fourth, imagining 'Here' with an unmentioned first-person protagonist would require a great deal of unnecessary work. Why would the poet imagine a protagonist (and possibly his body, personality and history), and practical solutions to all the transport problems, and then edit them out? As the whole focus of the poem is on the changing landscape, why not simply imagine as much of the journey as is necessary for this?

All these reasons suggest it is better to acknowledge that the poem is not a realistic depiction of a person's trip through Humberside, but a journey through that region which has to take place within the poet's imagination. The poem hints at its own fictionality: this is an idealized journey – albeit based on Larkin's real experiences – made in the mind's eye.

VII

Yet the problem of whether the poem has first-person or impersonal narration, whether it does or doesn't have a protagonist, and whether it shows a realistic or idealized journey, is finely balanced and intended to be so. After all, Larkin could have made the matter clear if he had wanted to. Some of the journeys he portrays are realistic (from Hull to London in 'The Whitsun Weddings'); some of his dynamic narratives are just changes in what the poet imagines (from Hull to Patrington in 'Bridge for the Living'). Neither strikes us as strange or magical. But the journey in 'Here' hovers delicately in between.

One reason the issue is finely balanced is that, although the poem's method of narration does not change, it *appears* to change, and this is because all the poem's initial signals on the matter are deeply misleading. Larkin's two previous long poems about railway journeys all have a full-blown and sharply characterized narrator, and initially this poem gives every sign that it will follow the same pattern. (I shall discuss why this is so in the next section.) We soon realize, however, that this is not the case, and acclimatize ourselves to the idea that it has an unmentioned first-person protagonist.

The poem gives us two separate sets of reasons for thinking this. First, there are the veiled hints about methods of transport especially in the first stanza. Second, the narrative follows the pattern of first-person narration: the point of view appears to be that of someone travelling at ground level; the motion is seamless and without breaks; there is none of the jump-cutting to other places, or impossible angles, which alert us to the use of an impersonal perspective. It is only when we realize that the journey is unlikely, the time scheme does not pan out, a protagonist is redundant, and the hints about transport are vague and contradictory, that we conclude the method of narration has *always* been impersonal, and that our surmises about the presence of a protagonist, although based on hints from the poet, are false. Consequently, our conception of the experiencing self in the poem gradually thins: from a full-blown protagonist, to a suppressed protagonist, and then to only a point of view.

If the poem appeared to be consistent in its form of narration, then the story it tells would seem straightforwardly realistic throughout, i.e. constrained by practical difficulties and the laws of nature. But the apparent change in 'Here' from a first-person to an impersonal point of view produces a destabilizing and slightly magical effect. Initially, still clinging to the idea we are reading a first-person narrative, we envisage someone on a vaguely imagined train journey (for example) to Hull. But once we reach Hull, the momentum of the journey appears to continue, and we seem to follow the movement of a man, or possibly a disembodied consciousness, through the city and out to the coast. By this stage, all thought as to how this journey is accomplished seems both forgotten and irrelevant. In other words, instead of revising our ideas about narration, we revise our ideas about the *realism* of the poem, and feel for a moment that the laws of nature have been suspended. This is deeply mysterious and gives to 'Here' the 'magical quality of a fable' [PL:103]. Gradually, however, we realize that the laws of nature are still in operation, and that we have always, despite appearances, been reading a largely realistic impersonal account of a journey in the poet's imagination.

Again, film makes a useful analogy. Imagine you are watching a realistic film from the point of view of a hand-held camera, and certain obvious clues – the fact that characters speak to this camera in certain ways, the angle of vision, the manner of movement – lead you to believe it represents the first-person point of view of a small boy. Now imagine that, halfway through the film, the camera starts to do things that are physically impossible for a boy – it passes through walls, flies unaided, and so forth. This is very disorientating, and presents us with three alternatives: we can try to show these movements are in fact physically possible; we can decide that the film is not (and possibly never has been) realistic; we can conclude that the camera tracked the boy's point of view for the first half of the film, but we now see that its viewpoint was purely impersonal and should not have been *identified* with the boy's first-person position. 'Here' presents us with exactly the same alternatives, and while most critics choose the first option (and try offering solutions to its practical difficulties), I tend to favour the last.

The moment when we realize 'Here' is not both first-person and realistic, and suddenly wonder if it is first-person and unrealistic, is particularly magical and continues to cast its spell over the rest of the poem. But there are several other factors which lend 'Here' the quality of a dream or fable. Without the distraction and mediation of a narrator, the poem seems completely transparent, and this allows us to see individual things with almost hallucinogenic clarity. But the *relationships* between things are often much less perspicuous than they might be: the grammatical structure is often intentionally hidden, risky or elusive; the punctuation is sometimes misleading; the images occasionally obscure or blurred. When this combination of vivid concrete detail, strange aporias, muddles and elidings, is combined with the apparently disembodied journey described above, the whole experience comes to seem somehow enchanted or dreamlike, so that when we are shown a town which is a 'pastoral', 'ships up streets', luminously-peopled air ascending, and untalkative skies, we are not altogether surprised.

This impression is enhanced by the fact that the journey is so deathly quiet. One would have expected emphasis on the noise of the train, station and crowd of shoppers, and this would have heightened the quiet of the beach and seascape. But the only words to do with sound in the entire poem are 'stealing', 'silent' and 'untalkative', i.e. words that indicate the absence of sound. Similarly, Coleridge[21] once remarked that in his dreams, unlike his life, he was never conscious of seeing one thing and thinking another (perhaps because dreams take place where thought occurs during waking hours), and the lack of thoughts on the part of the poet or protagonist (no 'The mind blanks at the glare' or 'But Dockery, good Lord …' [CP:208,152]) enhances the dreamlike quality.

The poet pretends to be surprised by the appearance of the town and no proper names are used in the poem or title. 'Dockery and Son' has no hesitation about naming Oxford and Sheffield, 'The Whitsun Weddings' feels no embarrassment about naming London, and yet in 'Here' the halts are only 'harsh-named', and the 'large town' is neither called 'Hull' nor a 'city' – both of which Larkin knew it to be. If Larkin had created a protagonist, then this ignorance could easily be explained by saying that this protagonist was either a man new to the area or pretending to be new to the area. But neither of these explanations is available if we think the poem's landscapes are only seen from Larkin's imagined point of view.

Analogies with film can also help here. Isherwood begins the second paragraph of *Goodbye to Berlin* with the line 'I am a camera with the shutter open, quite passive, recording, not thinking' [GB:15]. Larkin, a great Isherwood fan, may be taking up a similar role in this poem, except for the fact that he swaps a camera for a film-camera. This would go some way towards explaining why he brings no special knowledge to bear on his home county, and why he does not overtly reflect or comment on the landscapes. This absence of commentary and expected knowledge is one of the very few hints early in the poem that its narration is impersonal. However, as I suggested in the previous section, suspending your own psychological states while imagining impersonally is more demanding than imagining yourself without a body, and Larkin's suspension of knowledge becomes less obvious as the poem continues.

For someone who feels burdened by the self and self-consciousness, the impersonal but realistic mode of narration has several advantages. Because its point of view is not *in* the scene described, there is no possibility of its being perceived by others, and this avoids any chance of feeling awkward, embarrassed and ashamed. Indeed, the whole envisaged world becomes a kind of private paradise because it is entirely sustained by the poet's imagination. In addition, the point of view cannot *act* in the world depicted, and – so far as possible – Larkin has also ensured that it does not think, remember or know either. He can thus surrender to the passive bliss of imagined perception untainted by experience – the 'million-petalled flower / Of being here' [CP:196].

VIII

The grammar of the poem's first sentence turns out to be misleading in at least two respects.[22] One's first thought is that 'Swerving east ...' is an adjective phrase and that it will be followed by the sentence's grammatical subject and a finite verb. Perhaps 'Swerving east, ... I see the town ... ,' or 'Swerving east, ... the train begins to slow ...'. But reading the first sentence through, no obvious grammatical subject presents itself. One's next thought is that 'gathers', the first word of the second stanza, must be the finite verb, and one looks back to discover *what* 'gathers'. An obvious idea is that all the places, persons, animals and objects mentioned up to now, gather to the surprise of a large town. But this cannot be right either, because these would require the plural 'gather' not the singular 'gathers'. It then becomes clear that, despite first appearances, 'Swerving east' must be the subject of the sentence.

But there are two further problems. First, is 'swerving east' the kind of thing that can gather? Certainly not if 'gathers' is construed intransitively (as a number of people might gather); and only in a rather strained sense if it is construed transitively (as a mother might gather her children). 'Gathers' itself is clearly a metaphor (the very objects mentioned in the opening verse are not literally pushed towards Hull, nor does the swerving push them), and therefore 'Swerving east' can only be the grammatical subject of the metaphor if it is construed metaphorically. Second, we are told of 'the surprise of a large town' but who or what feels this surprise? Can 'swerving east' feel surprise? Or some suppressed narrator? The poet? The train or landscape? Or can there be a kind of objective surprise which exists, as it were, abstractly, without being felt by anybody? From the grammatical point of view, metaphorical attribution to 'swerving east' is most probable; from the metaphysical point of view, the poet suspending his knowledge seems the most likely person to experience the surprise.

Larkin's strategy for hiding the subject is extremely risky because it teeters on the edge of grammatical nonsense. He could easily have made the first sentence make obvious sense simply by changing 'gathers' to 'gather' (which would not harm the rhythm or rhyme), or by adding an obvious subject (although this would require a little more rewriting). It is extremely unlikely that he was unaware of these problems or their obvious solutions, and this suggests that the poem's elusive grammar is deliberate; indeed, that it is an essential part of its meaning and effect.

There would seem to be three main reasons for Larkin's choice of grammatical subject. The first is that it's a wonderful way to emphasize speed: 'swerving' is necessarily abstract, dynamic and elusive – almost as if we were dealing with the phenomenon of speed itself. The second is that everything about the poem is unstable; all its main structural features (its title, narration, genre etc.) balance on the edge of undecidability, and the elusive nature of the grammatical subject is simply of a piece with these larger difficulties. In particular, the hints the poem gives about a protagonist turn out to be deeply misleading; and the same is true of the first sentence's hints about its subject. The third reason is that when the poem finally suggests the travelling subject is a mere point of view, it reveals the most pared-down conception of a subject it is possible to imagine. Similarly, when the subject of the first sentence is found, it is as close to an action without an actor as grammar allows: pure swerving without something that swerves.

Of the three journeys in *The Whitsun Weddings*, 'Here' is the only one narrated throughout in the present tense (indeed, it begins with a present participle). This too hints at the poem's own fictionality because the present tense has intimate associations with the fictional and the visionary. It is the tense in which we narrate what we are currently imagining, and we normally summarize fictions, unlike histories, in the present. Even when we read the present tense in narrations of historical events, we know the tense itself is fictional: there must always be a delay, first between the events and the writing, and then between writing and reading. Above all, the present tense suggests the instability of a vision: nothing is over, nothing is complete, nothing can be viewed as a whole, because it is happening now.

The energy of the three-fold swerving ('Swerving east [...] swerving through fields [...] swerving to solitude') not only propels the enormous first sentence through three stanzas, but seems to monopolize motion in the first of them. It sucks out the verb from the all-night traffic, and reduces the landscape to a frieze of inactivity. The only other verb in the first stanza – 'shields' – suggests stasis; no hothouse flashes, no one '[runs] up to bowl' [CP:114–16]. Instead, we are shown a number of things that cannot move themselves (fields, thistles, halts, skies, scarecrows and haystacks); and a number of things which can move themselves (workmen, hares, pheasants) but which we have no reason to suppose are moving now. It is only at the end of the stanza that we encounter definite evidence of movement: the river's 'slow presence' suggests motion – albeit of a most leisurely kind – and the gull-marked mud gives evidence of recent prior movement.

Each instance of 'swerving' indicates temporal progression and a new aspect of the landscape. The first indicates what have been swerved *from*; the second introduces the fields and halts; the third moves towards solitude. At each stage we seem to pass from a newer to an older landscape, as if going deeper into east Yorkshire were also going deeper into history. Motorized all-night traffic could only have been found in the twentieth century; the halts could have been found during and after the nineteenth; but the scarecrows and haystacks seen after the third 'swerving' could have been found in medieval times; and the hares, pheasants, rivers, clouds and gulls before that.

There is also a movement from the man-made and artefactual to the natural and organic: after the first 'swerving' we find only objects created by man (traffic, roads, industry); in the next four lines we find a mixture (fields and halts, hares and haystacks); in the last two lines only the natural (the river, clouds, gulls and mud). Finally, we can note a movement from the unpleasant to the pleasant: from grim traffic and industry, to thin fields and halts, and then to a rich traditional farmland. Here the marks of man's presence seem to be part of, indeed enhance, the natural landscape.

IX

Stanza two introduces us to Hull, but the fact that the 'large town' is a 'surprise' indicates not only that Larkin is engaging in a pretence, but that the town was never the object of the journey; the aim was either the coast, or some kind of solitude, or simply to get away from thundering all-night traffic.

Stanzas two and three as a whole are clearly designed to assemble variegated impressions of Hull, but when we look closely, we see that Larkin's descriptions are carefully ordered and stratified. He begins by noticing the tall and upstanding objects one might observe at a distance: domes, statues, spires and cranes. In the next line he notices objects at ground level and below – grain-scattered streets, barge-crowded water. The domes and statues suggest civic life and pride; the spires (and possibly domes) the religious life of the town; and the dock cranes, which stand beside barge-crowded water, the commercial life of the city. Grain-scattered streets and barge-crowded water pick up the idea of industry from the cranes, and both places link the town to the prosperous rural landscape described in the last four lines of the first stanza: grain suggests continuity with the haystacks; barges with the river. The picture is civic, well-ordered and prosperous. It is also slightly archaic – there is nothing redolent of the twentieth century in it – and we should notice that the order of the first stanza's movement backwards into history has been reversed: we now move from what could be an ancient landscape to one that could be from the nineteenth century. The stanza's levels of observation – distant and looking up, close and looking down – are not ideal for observing human beings, and consequently none is mentioned.

People and the twentieth century both enter with a vengeance in the last four lines of the stanza:

> And residents from raw estates, brought down
> The dead straight miles by stealing flat-faced trolleys,
> Push through plate-glass swing doors to their desires –
> Cheap suits, red kitchen-ware, sharp shoes, iced lollies,
> Electric mixers, toasters, washers, driers –

The angle of vision is now at the human level, and Platonic old England is disrupted by crowds of unruly desire-driven interlopers. As Stephen Regan points out, Larkin had grown up in the depressed interwar years, and then lived through the Second World War and years of rationing and austerity which followed [PL:100–1]. But by 1957 – the years of Macmillan's 'you've never had it so good' speech – export targets had been achieved, employment levels were high, and credit was widely available for the purchase of consumer goods. Thus within a year or two of Larkin's return from a slightly sleepy Belfast, the consumer revolution was well underway and struck Larkin with enormous force. It is little surprise that the first poem of *The Whitsun Weddings* mentions the mania for buying consumer durables, and that later poems in the collection freely adopt the language of advertising, and frequently cast an amused if disparaging eye on contemporary consumerism, particularly the spread of televisions [PL:100–5].

Larkin can't quite bear to admit to himself at the moment that these people live in the same Hull he has described hitherto, and can only acknowledge them as 'residents from raw estates' who can only get into the centre by being brought 'down the dead straight miles' by 'stealing flat-faced trolleys' (i.e. quietly moving – because electric – flat-fronted trolleybuses). Not only are the things they want of the twentieth century, the artefacts they seek are absolutely of the early 1960s, and they are designed to contrast in every way possible with what has gone before. The crowd's interests extend no further than food and its preparation (red kitchen-ware, iced lollies, mixers, toasters), and clothes and their care (cheap suits, sharp shoes, washers, driers), and neither of these enthusiasms suggests the civic life of the town and rural hinterland. The materials associated with this crowd – plastic, plate-glass – find no place in the old agrarian Hull; and the one colour mentioned – the red of plastic kitchen-ware – is dissonant with the browns, greens, olives, buffs, golds and ochres conjured up by the preceding stanzas.

We should also note that, in contrast to the point of view's imaginary swerve, the journeys pursued by consumers and commerce are straight. The 'rich' of 'rich industrial shadows' suggests money as well as size and darkness, and the traffic is 'all night north'.[23] The cut-price crowd is also brought to its desires down 'dead straight miles', and both of these are clearly intended to contrast with the viewpoint's poetic curve which will ultimately end in aesthetic contemplation.

Larkin describes the shoppers as 'urban yet simple', but otherwise he allows them no individuality and defines them wholly by their purchases: they are a 'cut-price crowd'. However, he captures their manner by a clever manipulation of verbs. In all the preceding lines and stanzas, there has not been a single example of a human agent doing something. It is swerving that 'gathers'; it is the halts that 'shield' (the workmen seem immobile); it is the domes and spires which 'cluster'; it is the trolleybuses which bring down the residents into Hull. Human beings are never presented as active agents, they merely watch and suffer what the world does to them; events either seem to happen of their own accord, or objects do things for people.[24] All this changes with the arrivals from the raw estates: 'And residents from raw estates [...] / Push through plate-glass doors to their desires'. Against the abstract and indirect grammatical background, that 'residents ... *Push through*' seems startlingly direct and forceful. The verb and preposition are strikingly rude. The normal neutral description would have been 'open the plate-glass swing doors' or 'go into/enter the shop', but 'push through' in conjunction with dangerously heavy 'plate-glass swing doors' suggests the body, careless force and indifference to others.

The effect and shock is heightened by two further features. The first is rhythm. The basic metre of the poem is an iambic pentameter (i.e. with a first unstressed syllable), and the two lines about the residents from raw estates are as close as the poem comes to a perfect pair of pentameters:

> And residents from raw estates, brought down
> The dead straight miles by stealing flat-faced trolleys,

˘ – ˘ – ˘ – ˘ – ˘ –
˘ – ˘ – ˘ – ˘ – ˘ – ˘

For the first time in the poem, here are two nearly perfect lines, suggesting ease and untrammelled motion. Consequently, when we arrive at the stressed first syllable of 'Push' our surprise is all the greater:

> Push through plate-glass swing doors to their desires –

– ˘ – ˘ – ˘ ˘ – ˘ – ˘

The second heightener is the immediacy with which the verb arrives. There is no description of the trolleybus stopping; the passengers do not disembark and collect themselves. Instead, we go straight from the bus to barging through the shop doors: '[...] stealing flat-faced trolleys, / *Push* through plate-glass swing doors [...]' as if their appetites were ungovernable. The noun 'desires' rather than the more usual 'wants' or 'needs' suggests an almost sexual element in their fixation. The phrase 'going shopping' hardly captures the determination and goal-directedness of these people.

X

In the next stanza we find that the two Hulls – the unpeopled civic and agrarian vision, and the residents of the raw estates – begin to become one:

> A cut-price crowd, urban yet simple, dwelling
> Where only salesmen and relations come
> Within a terminate and fishy-smelling
> Pastoral of ships up streets, the slave museum,
> Tattoo-shops, consulates, grim head-scarfed wives [...]

The grammar here is hard to follow. The lack of a comma at the end of the second line suggests that we are being told how far the salesmen and relations have come; that 'terminate' is a noun meaning something close to 'terminus'; and that 'within' is used in the sense of 'less than' (e.g. 'within a mile'). But this interpretation degenerates into nonsense if one tries to read further. The sense is much improved if we imagine a comma at the end of the second line after 'come'. This makes it clearer that 'terminate and fishy-smelling pastoral' refers to where the cut-price crowd dwell, that 'terminate' is used as an adjective describing 'pastoral' (like 'fishy-smelling'), and that 'within' is only used in the sense of 'in'.

What does 'terminate' – a word normally used as a verb – mean when used as an adjective? The SOED provides only one sense: 'Limited, bounded, ended, having a definite limit or termination.' Thus the cut-price crowd dwell within a fishy-smelling pastoral with definite limits. It is the kind of place one arrives at suddenly and leaves suddenly. This emphasizes, in contrast to stanza two, that the city centre and the raw estates belong to one town, and the use of 'within' rather than 'in' suggests something cosy and secure.

Moreover, Larkin's use of 'pastoral' seems odd because he is describing the centre of a large town. What does he mean by the word? Part of its sense is that, although sharply distinguished from the area around it, the life of the town and its surroundings interpenetrate one another. Even in the town centre we are aware of the river and the sea it leads to; and the 'grain-scattered streets' point forwards to the wheat-fields of stanza four as well as backwards to the haystacks of stanza one. However, Larkin is probably also thinking of the SOED's sense 1B: 'having the simplicity or natural charm associated with pastureland'. Just as Hull's limits hold both the civic Hull and the estates, so the element of simplicity in 'pastoral' forms links between the civic life, the country, and the 'urban yet simple' cut-price crowd.

Apart from integrating the two Hulls already described, the third stanza introduces a third element – the older, more traditional population of Hull – which now rubs shoulders with the elegancies of civic Hull:

> [...] Ships up streets, the slave museum,
> Tattoo-shops, consulates, grim head-scarfed wives.

But this list also has several other functions. In stanza two, Larkin maintains a pretence of being new to the town, and consequently his descriptions could have been given by someone who had never been to Hull before: they are confined to the appearance of buildings and other public objects, and of people shopping. No background knowledge is assumed. In stanza three, this pretence is largely dropped. We are told that only salesmen and relations go there. This is a joke, to be sure, but it's only funny because it contains an element of truth, and this truth requires a certain amount of background knowledge. The observation in stanza three is on the human level established in the middle of stanza two, but now the *functions* of public buildings are noted – the slave museum and the consulates – and this integrates the buildings and people hitherto kept apart. In contrast to the unlovely crowd of the second stanza, there are now faint hints, as I mentioned in section VI, of enchantment (even the slave museum, in conjunction with 'ships up streets' may suggest the *Arabian Nights*), and there are stronger hints of Hull's national and international role: a ship, unlike a barge, can sail abroad; the contents of Wilberforce House concern Africa, America and the West Indies as well as England; the consulates are owned by foreign governments. It is these places – especially the museum – which allow Hull to be identified from any other large English port, and show that the narrator's disavowal of knowledge has been largely dispensed with.

The tattoo-shops are the first mention of the more traditional population, and they also continue the international theme: in the late 1950s and early 1960s, it should still be possible to remember, tattoos were still associated with sailors and the armed services rather than young consumers. It's unlikely that the 'grim head-scarfed wives' – the only citizens to be described by their appearance – collect red kitchen-ware or have their menfolk in sharp shoes; they are far more likely to have found their husbands amongst the farmworkers of the hinterland, or the sailors, fishermen and dock workers of the port.

I have mentioned the four aspects of Larkin's Hull to be found in the poem: civic Hull, consumer Hull, international Hull, and the older working-class population of Hull. Three of these he also identifies in his preface to *A Rumoured City*:

> When your train comes to rest in Paragon Station against a row of docile buffers, you alight with an end-of-the-line sense of freedom. Signs in foreign languages welcome you. Outside is a working city [...] Unpretentious, recent, full of shops and special offers like a television commercial, it might be Australia or America, until you come upon Trinity House or the Dock Offices. For Hull has its own sudden elegancies. [FR:128]

The only aspect of 'Here' not mentioned in the preface is the older working-class population which also has the most vestigial existence in the poem. Interestingly, neither the poem nor preface mentions the middle-class population of Hull: those who run Trinity House, the Dock Offices, the churches, consulates, museums, the University and its library. This would be the populace Larkin was most aware of in real life, and if he identified with anybody, they would most likely be found amongst the middle-class. By depopulating the city of this stratum of society, he further heightens his sense of solitariness amidst the bustle, and the poem's sense of unreality.

XI

The grammar shared between stanzas three and four is tricky. One sometimes sees the clause 'Isolate villages, where removed lives / Loneliness clarifies', quoted alone, as if 'isolate' were an archaic or poetic adjective meaning 'isolated' [e.g. EP:17; MPG:105]. In 'Bridge for the Living', the word certainly functions in this way ('Isolate city spread alongside water' [CP:203]), but in 'Here' it is a perfectly normal transitive verb, because it is the *wheat-fields* which isolate villages, partly because they run as high as hedges. The slight blurring of grammar now spreads to images. It's quite difficult to dissociate 'running high as hedges' from 'Fast-shadowed wheat-fields' – and one has a slightly vertiginous sense of both the shadows and where they fall moving together. In this context, one has to remind oneself that 'running' comes close to meaning 'as'.

The linguistic texture of the final stanza differs from the others. The full-stop after 'Loneliness clarifies', the first full-stop in the poem, indicates that the colossal sentence which rushes through the first three stanzas has run its course. Such a sentence clearly indicates speed, bustle, clamour, and all these things have now been left behind. The first two words of this stanza also complete an inversion begun at the end of the third ('where removed lives // Loneliness clarifies') when the normal order would be 'where loneliness clarifies removed lives'. This suggests we are about to enter more traditional poetic territory, somewhere untouched by the modern world, and the unusual word order and stanza-break makes us slow towards the full-stop.

The first sentence contains 181 words. The next, to indicate new-found stasis, has only five. This sentence contains the first of the three final 'here's, and it is quite possible that Larkin intends these to balance and neutralize the three 'swerving's with which the poem begins. The relationships between verbs and subjects have tended to simplify as the poem progresses, and here we find simple active verbs related to simple subjects in close proximity to one another. Only one subject and verb is separated by even an adjective: 'silence stands', 'leaves [...] thicken', 'weeds flower', 'waters quicken', 'air ascends'. Thus natural simplicity and directness are reflected in grammar. All the verbs indicate growth, uprightness or movements upward, in contrast with the motion-verbs in the three previous stanzas which tend to indicate horizontal movement: swerving, gathering, clustering, bringing, coming, running.

The opening stanzas are full of fluent alliterations and assonances suggesting speed and ease ('swerving to solitude / Of skies and scarecrows', 'haystacks, hares and pheasants'). But if you try to read the whole poem aloud, you discover the last verse is thistled with impeding consonants ('Here silence stands / Like heat').[25] And whereas the first three stanzas are full of hyphenated compounds ('harsh-named', 'grain-scattered', 'barge-crowded', 'fishy-smelling' etc.) which try to cram almost too much into a line, the additions to words in the last stanza tend to be prefixes indicating absence: unnoticed, unfenced, untalkative.[26] In line with this, all the nouns in the first lines of the stanza are described by adjectives indicating that they are away from human eyes: '[...] leaves *unnoticed* thicken, / *Hidden* weeds flower, *neglected* waters quicken' (my italics).

The sense of 'And past the poppies bluish neutral distance' is improved by imagining a comma after 'poppies' (otherwise there is a tendency to read the phrase as if 'poppies' were followed by an apostrophe). The 'bluish neutral distance' itself is probably a combination of sea and sky, seen from some distance through haze, grasses and shimmer. 'Ends the land suddenly' looks like a poetic inversion of 'the land ends suddenly' but I suspect this is not the case, even though it would harmonize with inversion at the beginning of the stanza. 'Ends' on this construal is intransitive, but it makes better sense to read it transitively, i.e. bluish neutral distance puts an end to the land. This follows Larkin's frequent practice of ascribing active qualities to the apparently least powerful of two objects, and achieves a more striking and unusual effect. It also makes the word order utterly natural.

The next line is obscure: '[...] beyond a beach / Of shapes and shingle'. The shingle is clear enough, but what are the 'shapes'? Cooper [SW:159] and Motion think they are people: 'The few people allowed into this personal Eden are reduced merely to "shapes"' [NC:51]. But this interpretation is not altogether happy; after all, it would be very odd to describe people on a sunlit beach as 'shapes', largely because it is difficult to imagine what shape they could be apart from people-shaped. It is possible that the shapes are rocks, groynes or jetsam, but the most likely solution can be discovered only by looking at these shingle beaches on and towards Spurn Head. Several of these are still covered by rows of Second World War tank-traps, vast cubes of reinforced concrete which, because of erosion and weathering, are now variously discoloured, toppled, semi-buried and any-angled. Mention of tank-traps – with their suggestion of armies, mechanization and death – would be wholly out of keeping with the solitary raptness Larkin celebrates, and abstracting them into 'shapes' seems a brisk and admirable solution.[27]

If we think the poem is seen from the realistic point of view of an unmentioned protagonist then we shall have to imagine his stopping at the coast. If we think of the poem as seen from an impersonal realistic point of view then this does not have to stop at the coast: it can move across the land, over the sea, and then disappear into the clear blue air beyond. For the impersonal imagination, at least, existence is unfenced.

XII

I have not yet mentioned the clause, 'Luminously-peopled air ascends' because it is so obscure it requires a section to itself. What exactly does it mean? What is it referring to?

Regan and Cooper say it refers to insects in general [PL:105; SW:159]; Booth hints at midges in particular [PLW:168]. But neither of these interpretations seems entirely satisfactory. Midges are associated with late afternoon and evening rather than mid-morning; insects – or birds for that matter – don't just ascend; and the language seems too wrought, obscure and magnificent just to be talking about creatures of this kind. Another explanation might be that Larkin is imagining glints from still-moist leaves and grasses, and sparkles off the sunlit sea, viewed through haze and rising heat. This captures the idea that it is the *air* which is ascending rather than things in the air; it explains why the emphasis should be wholly on ascending; and the entire glistening scene comes closer to the grandeur of the language. Yet the fit between language and imagined reality does not seem to be completely perfect: 'peopled', in particular would be an odd way to describe glitterings and sparklings, and the feeling remains that the language exceeds any possible naturalistic referent.

If a naturalistic explanation of the language is not entirely adequate, then it may need to be supplemented by a more historical and symbolic interpretation. As the beginning of such an account, we might note that Larkin often uses seascapes to invoke imagination and the artistic life. Sometimes, as in 'Absences' and 'Livings II', the setting is rough and sublime. At other times, a combination of glittering sea and glistening landscape is used. In a letter to Sutton, he describes the artistic life as 'sitting down on a lonely rock and contemplating glittering loneliness' [SL:116]; and in a lengthy improvisation written in his mother's house, he longs for: '[...] miles and miles of sunlight, the untouched downs, / glistening with dew, / And the hundred untenanted bays where the sea comes sliding in, not / rough [...] [M:182].

It's also striking that 'luminously' and its cognates are not terms which Larkin uses frequently or lightly. 'Luminous' is used fairly neutrally in two early poems [CP:18,277], but it does not occur in his mature poetry; 'luminously' is only to be found at this point in 'Here'. So far as I know, the mature Larkin only used 'luminous' in one other recorded place, and this was when he said to an interviewer: 'I have no enthusiasm for obscurity, except, of course, for luminous and wonder-generating obscurity' [AEY:58]. This inspired phrase suggests he associates luminosity with the mysteries of the poetic imagination, and the experience described comes close to the characterization he gives (via Montgomery) of the moment of inspiration: 'You feel as if the rose or whatever were *shining* at you' (my italics) [MT:127–8].[28]

'Luminously-peopled air ascends' also recalls Coleridge's almost obsessive use of the word 'luminous' in that great dirge to the departing imagination, 'Dejection: A Letter', a work much admired by Movement writers.[29] Here Coleridge describes his imagination as: 'A Light, a Glory, and a luminous Cloud [...]'; 'This Light, this Glory, this fair luminous Mist [...]'; 'Joy is that strong Voice, Joy that luminous Cloud' [C:103–4]. 'Here' certainly contains luminous clouds ('The piled gold clouds'), and if I am right in my suggestion that the final stanza suggests a shimmer of rising heat and morning haze, then a 'luminous Mist' does not seem remote from Larkin's concerns either.

There are further parallels between the two poems. Larkin writes: 'Here leaves unnoticed thicken, / Hidden weeds flower', while Coleridge, describing the happiness he experiences when in full possession of his poetic imagination, says that 'Hope grew round me, like the twining Vine, / And Leaves and Fruitage, not my own, seem'd mine' [C:101]. Larkin observes that 'neglected waters quicken', while Coleridge uses one kind of quickened water to symbolize his own creative powers: without imagination, he says, he may not 'hope from outward Forms to win / The Passion and the Life, whose *Fountains* are within' (my italics) [C:95].

Coleridge, saying farewell to his imagination, watches through a threatening sky as the sun sets over the land in the west. Larkin, showing and celebrating his own imaginative power, watches the sun rising over the sea, in a clear sky, from the east. 'Dejection' was written in partial response to Wordsworth's great ode about *his* departing imagination – the 'Immortality Ode' – and both Coleridge and Larkin knew that in this poem inspiration flows from the ocean ('that immortal sea' [WW:301]), and the sun rising in the east: 'The Youth, who daily farther from the East / Must travel, still is Nature's Priest, / And by the vision splendid, / Is on his way attended' [WW:299].

Even Larkin's mysterious 'shapes' may take additional resonance from Coleridge's work. 'Those lifeless Shapes,' writes Coleridge despairingly, 'around, below, Above, / O what can they impart?' [C:95]. To which the answer is 'nothing' without his '*shaping* spirit of Imagination' (my italics) [C:101]. Finally, Larkin contrasts his final solitude with the bustle of the urban, 'cut-price crowd', while Coleridge contrasts his solitary raptures with the situation of 'that poor loveless ever anxious crowd' [C:103].

'Peopled' is also a word associated with the Romantic imagination. Consider this fragment from Wordsworth:

> When in my bed I lay
> Alone in darkness, I have seen the gloom
> Peopled with shapes arrayed in hues more bright
> Than flowers or gems or than the evening sky [...] [WR:634]

Once again, the similarity with 'Here''s final stanza is very striking. Obviously, Wordsworth mentions that his imagination is 'peopled' by 'shapes', and also invokes flowers, bright colours and the sky. But the analogy is closer yet. The two final lines liken his mental images to gems and the evening sky, i.e. things that are not only brightly coloured, but which seem to emit a light of their own. Thus, as in the final stanza of 'Here', the poet finds his imagination *peopled* by objects which glint, sparkle, radiate and luminesce.

It therefore strikes me as likely that the whole of 'Here''s last stanza is intended to invoke the powers of the poetic imagination. By discovering a congenial place of peace and infinity, the poet surrenders to aesthetic contemplation and all harmful self-awareness disappears. In these moments, the mind enters a state of being where nothing is repressed or forced, and the whole economy of the psyche functions readily, cooperatively and harmoniously. This is the condition in which poetry is written: as Larkin writes to Sutton: 'For me, a poem is the crossroads of my thoughts, my feelings, my imaginings, my wishes, & my verbal sense: normally these run in parallel, but only when they all cross at one point do you get a poem' [SL:173]. Paradoxically, it is the moment when you seem to lose yourself that you become most wholly yourself.

It is utterly fitting that 'Here' should culminate in this way. The title of the poem invokes self-awareness and the ambit of poetry, and the entire poem draws attention to the imagination by using a form of perspective which only imagination can use: impersonal imagining from a fictional viewpoint. Because the whole journey is in the mind's eye, the transformation of Larkin's realistic details into symbols is completely natural. He does not merely project meanings on to the real sea and the real landscape; on the contrary, like the shapes that people Wordsworth's imagination, the sparkling sea and glistening landscape are entirely creations of the mind, imbued through and through with symbolic meaning. The whole vision thus takes on 'the glory and the freshness of a dream' [WW:298]; and it is between land and sea that Larkin rejoices in 'the gleam / The light that never was on sea or land' [W:326]. 'Here', standing at the head of what Larkin considered his greatest collection, is a morning hymn to the creative powers.

XIII

Before approaching the philosophical complexities of the last stanza's final lines, I need to go into more detail about Larkin's attitude to selfhood.

He found his own personality burdensome: 'I suppose I am trapped in my own personality' [M:365]; 'I don't like my character. / I wouldn't back it for twopence, and I don't advise anyone else to do so either' [M:181], and several of his poems can be seen as attempts to evade and dissolve the self. His first significant thoughts in this direction are found in the semi-poetic improvisation, mentioned above, which he wrote while living at his mother's house in 1948:

> [...] I think of the miles and miles of sunlight, the untouched downs, glistening with dew,
> And the hundred untenanted bays where the sea comes sliding in, not rough,
> And then I long to be in a thousand of these places at once, to have a thousand pairs of eyes.
> To be sniffing on a bed in Leicester is not good enough. [M:182]

The mechanism for self-dissolution proposed here – having a thousand pairs of eyes and being in a thousand places at once – is slightly clumsy and of dubious coherence. His later poem 'Absences', while still focusing on the sea, achieves the same end with altogether more elegant means:

> Rain patters on a sea that tilts and sighs.
> Fast-running floors, collapsing into hollows,
> Tower suddenly, spray-haired. Contrariwise,
> A wave drops like a wall: another follows,

Wilting and scrambling, tirelessly at play
Where there are no ships and no shallows.

Above the sea, the yet more shoreless day,
Riddled by wind, trails lit-up galleries:
They shift to giant ribbing, sift away.

Such attics cleared of me! Such absences! [CP:49]

In this poem he discovers the liberating power of the impersonal imagination, and realizes it is not self-contradictory to imagine somewhere where you are not.

'Absences' ends with the sky, and in later poems the sky assumes even greater significance. The close of 'High Windows' for example:

[...] And immediately

Rather than words comes the thought of high windows:
The sun-comprehending glass,
And beyond it, the deep blue air, that shows
Nothing, and is nowhere, and is endless. [CP:165]

'High Windows' has a straightforward narrator, an 'I', who has spent the first part of the poem reflecting on freedom and constraint. And in 'Absences', the line which celebrates Larkin's absence, also includes a reference to himself ('Such attics cleared of *me!* [my italics]). 'Here' attempts a more daring and elaborate experiment in self-dissolution. At the beginning of the poem, we are under the impression that there will be a full-blown narrator; we then come to think there is a suppressed first-person narrator; and gradually we realize we are sharing only a point of view created by the poet. Like 'High Windows', 'Here' ends with a vision of empty sky, but without the presence of a narrator; like 'Absences', 'Here' celebrates the absence of a narrator. But there are three important differences between 'Here' and the other poems: in 'Here' the celebration is shown rather than stated; the viewpoint *moves* as well as changing its angle of perception; and the narrator is absent from the poem as well as the vision:

And past the poppies bluish neutral distance
Ends the land suddenly beyond a beach
Of shapes and shingle. Here is unfenced existence:
Facing the sun, untalkative, out of reach.

This 'bellissiomo niente' [LD:25] allows Larkin to further diminish both the self and the sense of self. To show how this works, I shall examine the nature of aesthetic perception.

XIV

Most things we perceive can be assessed either from an aesthetic or a cognitive point of view. Thus, I can look at something either to acquire knowledge of it (either from disinterested curiosity or from a desire to fulfil a practical project) or because I just enjoy looking at it. In the first case, my interest will lapse as soon as the required knowledge is obtained; but in the second, my looking will only end when my enjoyment ceases or when practical considerations force me to give it up. Where looking is motivated by a desire to gain knowledge, the scrutiny is simply a method – there could well be others – of gaining a desired end. But in aesthetic appreciation, perception is not replaceable by some other method, and contemplation is an end in itself.

If I look at an object because I want to derive knowledge from it, then this is something I *do*; it is an action motivated by beliefs and desires, and there is no particular reason why I should take pleasure in it. But when my attention is held by the aesthetic quality of an object this is not an action which is explained by beliefs and desires; it is something which *happens to me*, and aesthetic pleasure is the natural outcome of this unwilled attention. Thus we cannot just *decide* that certain objects will hold or sustain our unwilled aesthetic attention; this can only be something we find out or discover.

Of course, before taking aesthetic pleasure in an object, I must bring my attention to bear on the object in question, and this is usually an action. But such an act is only a preliminary to the aesthetic attitude not the attitude itself. This is because transferring my attention is merely a means to an end and not wholly intelligible in its own right; whereas aesthetic attention is not just a means to an end and is fully intelligible in its own right. Thus if I say, 'I'm looking at the sky because I love the look of it', then in normal circumstances this does not invite the question: 'Yes, but why are you doing that?'[30]

Larkin evidently does not like, and does not identify with, either the all night traffic, harsh-named halts, and thin and thistled fields of the first stanza, or the cut-price crowd and grim head-scarfed wives, of the second and third. But the landscape of the final stanza is clearly wholly congenial to him. He does not look at the coast and sky because he wants to predict the weather or count the number of visible aircraft.

He looks because it gives him pleasure to look at the scene before him; and he becomes wholly absorbed in the contemplation of that scene. This state therefore fits the specification of aesthetic attention described in the previous paragraphs.

There are three reasons why aesthetic contemplation leads to a diminished sense of self.

First, to take aesthetic pleasure in something is to have your attention held by it and to take pleasure in that absorption. This is precisely the state in which you are completely self-forgetful, and not thinking about yourself or your normal life. Indeed, many of our idioms for pleasure indicate the translation of self: I am taken out of myself or absorbed (like water into a sponge). Of course, you can become absorbed in any kind of activity – football, bell-ringing, stamp-collecting – but the loss of self in these circumstances cannot be complete because they all involve action, and often thinking of myself as one agent amongst others. This is not true in the aesthetic case.

Second, as a prelude to aesthetic contemplation, the mind should be cleared of practical projects, ambitions, thoughts about our lives, competitiveness, bias, ambition and prejudice, and be allowed to contemplate the aesthetic object undisturbed. Thus every thought which is characteristic of ourselves and our lives should be pushed to one side. This blanking process – which, as we've seen, takes place in 'Here' – is partly to allow the object to begin to generate its own thoughts and associations in us. In a similar way, patients undergoing psychoanalysis are required to try to clear their minds before engaging in free-association. What happens in both cases is sometimes described as overcoming the self so that something deeper than the self can make itself felt. A psychoanalyst would say that the Ego must be deactivated in order to make Id-thinking manifest; Matthew Arnold said that the great thing in literary criticism was to 'get yourself out of the way and let humanity decide' [SR:III:227]. Of course, in neither case is our subsequent response impersonal; indeed, it could be described as emerging from a deeper, more personal level of the self, but it *feels as if* our ordinary everyday selves have been put to one side.

Third, and as a consequence of the previous point, if we value an object because it helps achieve a practical goal, then we also know that these practical goals vary between one person and another. Consequently, we do not try to persuade people who do not share our goals to put the same practical value on the things as we do. If I have cut myself, for example, I will place a high value on plasters; if you have not cut yourself, then you won't. But if we are enjoying an object on aesthetic grounds, then instinctively we see no reason why other people should not share our evaluation. Our enjoyment, as Arnold noted, feels like a natural expression of human nature, although we know intellectually that this is not the case. This means that when we encounter aesthetic disagreement we feel the other person *ought* to agree with us, and possibly argue with him, even if we think it most unlikely he will ever agree [CJ:180]. In a sense, practical projects separate human beings, making them more conscious of others and so of themselves, whereas aesthetic absorption reduces the sense of individual difference, and hence of individuality.[31]

All three processes contribute to the complete loss of self in aesthetic experience which is so well described by Schopenhauer in the following passage:

> [We ...] devote the whole power of our mind to [aesthetic] perception, sink ourselves completely therein, and let our whole consciousness be filled by the calm contemplation of the natural object actually present. [...] We *lose* ourselves entirely in this object [...] we forget our individuality, our will, and continue to exist only as pure subject, as clear mirror of the object, so that it is as though the object alone existed without anyone to perceive it, and thus we are no longer able to separate the perceiver from the perception, but the two have become one, since the entire consciousness is filled and occupied by a single image of perception. [...] Thus [...] the person who is involved in this perception is no longer an individual, for in such perception the individual has lost himself; he is *pure* will-less, painless, timeless *subject of knowledge*. [WWR:I:178–9][32]

XV

Clearly, I can become absorbed by the ordinary object – a table, chair, or car – in front of me. There could be a number of reasons for this (it might horrify me, for example), but when the motivation is aesthetic, the loss of self is wholly due to my absorption. But sometimes I can become absorbed by an object which *represents* something else – a mental image of the Eiffel Tower, a picture of a dog, a documentary about jungle warfare – and in this case it is usually the *represented* world which holds my attention. Again, the reasons for absorption can either be aesthetic or non-aesthetic. In circumstances like this, there is a further reason for loss of self: I seem to inhabit a position in an entirely new and possibly fictional world. A daydream or fantasy can sometimes be so absorbing that when someone real speaks to me I am shocked to discover that I am actually sitting amongst my ordinary surroundings; and obviously, one can have a very similar experience with films, books and photographs. In these cases, I have another reason besides absorption for saying I was lost in or transported by what I experienced.[33]

As Larkin is aesthetically absorbed by the landscape he imagines, he experiences a loss of self for both reasons: he is absorbed, and he is absorbed by a represented not an actual landscape. He therefore feels himself to be inhabiting a new perspective and another place. When we read the poem he wrote in order to let us reconstruct and share his experience, we too become lost in the aesthetic experience he provides, and for the same reasons.

There is, however, a third reason why the particular content of Larkin's imaginings and poem can lead to a further diminishment of self. The contemplation of blue nothingness makes the precise position of an imaginary point of view impossible to determine.[34] If we are imagining a point of view, then we can only determine where that imagined point of view is by triangulating from the physical objects around it. But if there are no physical objects to look at – just blue nothingness – then our sense of where the point is vanishes altogether. If we are imagining inhabiting this point of view, then our sense of where we are, and consequently who we are, begins to diminish too. But it is not just a question of not *knowing* where the point of view is. An imaginary point of view can only be defined by its position, and when this is lost, there is a sense in which the point of view has ceased to exist, vanished altogether.

XVI

The sky, sun and stars are remote and easily visible, and these facts make them both ideal aesthetic objects and continual invitations to aesthetic contemplation. At many points in life, therefore, they offer us escape from selfhood and the world of practical projects, ends and means, getting and spending. But there are two further reasons why *aesthetic* contemplation of airy blueness in particular should further reduce our sense of self.

First, contemplation of the sky seems to lift us beyond the human. Many aesthetic objects contain representations of people and normal human environments, and many explore difficult and tragic dilemmas also encountered in real life. It is thus right and proper that they sometimes give rise to painful emotions in the spectator; in particular, the disagreeable emotions of self-assessment: guilt, shame, remorse, bashfulness, inadequacy, embarrassment, shyness and self-consciousness (in the non-technical sense). But the clear blue sky contains nothing to remind us of human life and human dilemmas, and thus leaves us free to enjoy pure beauty untainted by human troubles.

Second, contemplating the sky blocks our usual access to self-knowledge. One is never just conscious, one is always conscious *of* something.[35] Consciousness is a kind of transparency which, although itself unseen, allows us to see through to its objects: I see *the table*, I think of *Jack*, I imagine *the wedding*. Consequently, there is no such thing as being conscious of nothing. And yet Larkin's contemplation of the void does seem to come close to being conscious of nothing. We have the impression that the objects have been subtracted from consciousness and only consciousness itself remains; we seem to be conscious of the undifferentiated blue medium itself, and enjoy awareness without being aware of anything in particular.

Under any circumstances, the conscious self is never directly aware of itself. Wittgenstein, discussing a very minimal conception of selfhood, writes: 'The subject does not belong to the world: rather, it is a limit of the world [...] nothing in the visual field allows you to infer it is seen by an eye' [T:5.632–3]. This is exactly true of 'Here': we are only aware of the subject of the poem and his viewpoint through the limits of his vision; we share his viewpoint as if it were our own. But Wittgenstein's observation can also be applied to richer conceptions of the self which involve our desires, wants, beliefs and personalities: 'man knows himself', wrote Goethe, 'insofar as he knows the world, [...] he only perceives [...] himself in it' [GE:99]. This means, I take it, that we only know ourselves through noting our *expressions* of self – our partners, friends, enemies, home, profession, hobbies, amusements, tastes and so forth – and all of these are found *within* the limits of our vision. But the sky contains no expressions of self – no possession, image, place of work, home or familiar place – and therefore gives us no self-knowledge.

At the end of the poem, Larkin, by coming to inhabit his point of view, and by becoming absorbed in aesthetic contemplation of the airy void, seems to have achieved an impossibly pure form of consciousness, which dispenses both with *what* is conscious and what it is conscious *of*. The distinction between self and world has vanished; the subject has dissipated into what it contemplates; they have become one radiant and undifferentiated state of being. This may or may not be the condition

Merleau-Ponty draws attention to in the following luminously obscure passage:

> When I contemplate the sky I am not *set over against* it as an acosmic object; I do not possess it in thought, or spread out towards it some idea of blue such as might reveal the secret of it, I abandon myself to it and plunge into this mystery, it 'thinks itself within me', I am the sky itself as it is drawn together and unified, and as it begins to exist for itself; my consciousness is saturated with its limitless blue. [PPE:214, quoted in MR:40]

The idea that aesthetic contemplation of the sky produces a particularly pure form of consciousness is an illusion, of course, but a peculiarly attractive and liberating illusion.

XVII

Larkin was haunted by the perpetual fear of death, and longed for light and freedom. The two are separated by the thinnest possible partition. In one sense, emptiness and absence of self is his supreme vision of happiness, liberation and transcendence; in another, it is his overwhelming dread.[36]

Notes

1. Here, and at most other points in the essay, I am using the words 'experience', 'experiencer', 'action', 'actor' and 'agent' in their modern philosophical senses. An experience is defined as a mental state where there is something which it is like to be in that state. Thus, there is something which it is like to perceive, feel pain, have a thought, or entertain a mental image. These, therefore, fall under the concept of experience. But there is nothing which it is necessarily like to have a belief. For example, for many years you have believed that ducks do not eat wolves. Has there been something which it is like to have held this belief for so long? Clearly not; you were completely unaware of it. Thus beliefs of this kind are not experiences. An action is a bit of behaviour motivated by beliefs and desires, and an actor or agent is someone who is thus motivated.
2. For my information about indexicals, I have largely relied on the excellently clear and informative, Colin McGinn, *The Subjective View: Secondary Qualities and Indexical Thoughts* [TSV]. An early and innovative discussion of indexicals can be found in D. Kaplan, 'On the Logic of Demonstratives', in *Contemporary Perspectives in the Philosophy of Language*, ed. P. French et al. [CPPL].
3. It is possible but unlikely that the train is travelling from the north. The fact that the traffic is 'all night north' need not indicate that the narrator is travelling in the same direction, but whereas Larkin had no close links with Scotland, he frequently travelled to London and Oxford. The Midlands is also much more industrial than the Borders and north of England. He is unlikely to be travelling from Oxford because that would be in an easterly direction most of the way.
4. I realize that this way of supporting the objection is vulnerable to the same kind of argument which I brought against using the 'here''s in the poem to determine the reference of the title.
5. Some critics think that Hull rather than the coast is the focus of the poem. Nicholas Jenkins, for example, in his article, 'Auden, Larkin, and the English Question', writes: '[Since] Larkin's poem is about a town very near the sea, it pulls away from buildings and streets and towards the ocean and the sky' [MR:53].
6. For a detailed discussion of the peculiarities of 'I' see G. E. M. Anscombe, 'The First Person' [MPM:21–36].
7. This way of capturing what we mean by saying something is conscious was made famous by Thomas Nagel in 'What is it like to be a bat?' [MQ:165–80].
8. I am arguing that the ability to speak a language, including mastery of its indexical system, is a *sufficient* condition for being self-conscious. In addition, by 'the ability to speak a language' I do not mean the kind of thing parrots and sat.navs can do.
9. Locke says that the existence of secondary qualities depends on the existence of a subject, and that primary qualities (size, weight, shape, speed and number) are intrinsic qualities of the world. (See, for example, Locke 'Some Further Considerations Concerning our Simple Ideas', Book 2, Chapter 8, *An Essay Concerning Human Understanding* [ECH:133–41], and McGinn [TSV:5–22].) However, Locke's conception of the world is Newtonian, and modern physics has largely replaced his 'primary qualities' with other kinds of explanation.

10. For some reflections on the descriptive blankness of the word 'here', and Larkin's attitude to place in general see James Booth, 'From Here to Bogland: Larkin, Heaney and the Poetry of Place' [NLO:190–212].
11. On the origins of 'The Whitsun Weddings' see [RW:75]; for the origins of 'Dockery and Son' see [PLIK:58].
12. 'Here' seems intended to refute Amis's claim that landscape poetry is necessarily egotistical. In his poem, 'Here is Where', Amis sets out on a piece of standard poetic description (*'Here, where the ragged water / Is twirled and spun over / Pebbles'* [...]) and then comments: 'Going well so far, eh? / But soon, I'm sorry to say, / The here-where recipe / Will have to intrude its *I*' [KACP:46]. 'Here', is a here/where landscape poem which manages to avoid an *I* altogether.
13. The poem certainly has an *external* narrator (i.e. the person we imagine speaking the poem) who may or may not be the poet. But I want to argue it does not have an *internal* narrator (i.e. the person from whose point of view the poem is experienced). Thus from this point on, to avoid the ambiguity, I use 'protagonist' to refer to the (alleged) travelling centre of consciousness in the poem.
14. Understandably enough, a number of critics seem to waver or exhibit discomfort about their interpretations. Booth, who has clearly thought hard about the poem, seems to hover between the first-person and impersonal reading. In one place, he writes: 'Though no means of transport is ever named, the poem, while remaining always "here", maintains a continuous momentum: into the city by train and out again, implicitly by car or bicycle, across country to the sea' [PP:149]. This is the passage which makes me say he believes the narrator has an (unmentioned) body. But a page later Booth writes: '[...] a disembodied centre of consciousness travels across the landscape [...]' [PP:150]. But can disembodied centres of consciousness buy train tickets or cycle?
15. I am grateful to staff at the National Railway Museum, York, for supplying me with a copy of *Bradshaw's Guide* 12th September – 6th November 1960, and for information about railway lines to the east of Hull. For details about changing trains at Hull Paragon Station in the days before the Beeching Report, I am grateful to members of the online *LNER Forum*.
16. Even if 'halt' means 'railway halt', it does not follow that the protagonist is travelling by train. The usual interpretation of the poem requires that the traffic be seen from the train. But if the whole journey is by car, then the railway halts could be seen from the car, particularly if the road has level-crossings, or closely follows the line. In both of these cases, it may be possible to read the halts' names from the road; or it may be that the protagonist simply knows the names of the halts. In addition, 'halt' could be used synecdochically to refer to the whole of the village or hamlet in which the halt stands.
17. I mean that these pull-ins' names cannot be discovered without an absurd amount of effort.
18. If the impersonal point of view follows a number of characters, none of whom is referred to by 'I', then it is natural to call this a third-person point of view. The trouble is, that 'Here' lacks any characters of this kind (only the workmen and shoppers could be called 'they'), so 'impersonal narration' seems less misleading than 'third-person narration'. Confusingly, first-person

narration is *from* a first person perspective, whereas third-person perspective is *of* a person referred to in the third-person.

19. Several critics explicitly notice there is something peculiar about 'Here''s point of view. Apart from Booth [PP:150] (see note 14), Cooper says that 'Here' 'contains no self at all' [SW:157]; while Regan observes: 'The absence of any obvious subject or personal pronoun in the opening stanza gives the poem a curiously disembodied effect' [PL:103]. The latter remark does not quite grasp the matter firmly, however, because it does not distinguish between an impersonal realistic reading and a first-person unrealistic reading, and much of 'Here''s enchantment depends on its apparent wavering between the two. See section VII.
20. I am grateful to the Royal Observatory at Greenwich for this information.
21. 'In dreams I do not recollect the state of feeling so common when awake of thinking on one subject and looking at another.' Quoted in [FBA:362].
22. Good discussions of difficulties with the grammatical subject of this sentence can be found in [PP:148] and [OOR:103–4].
23. Although evidence from early drafts needs to be handled carefully, it is striking that one early version of the opening lines reads: 'Swerving east, away from money's shadows / And more important traffic, to fields.' Quoted in [SW:158].
24. Both Booth [PLW: 91–2] and Cooper [SW:157] have interesting things to say about Larkin's grammar and use of passive constructions.
25. Larkin himself drew attention to these two features of 'Here' [FR:59].
26. This is also noted by Booth in [PLW:165].
27. A photograph of a beach on Spurn Head, covered by toppled tank-traps, is shown on the front cover of [AL:4/2007]. James Booth provides the caption 'a beach / of shapes and shingle' (on the back cover), so he clearly has the same interpretation of 'shapes' as I have.
28. 'Via Montgomery' is explained in essay four, section IV.
29. See Michael O'Neill's article '"Fond of What He's Crapping On": Movement Poetry and Romanticism' [MR:278–9]. O'Neill discusses the 'Ode' version of Coleridge's 'Dejection', but since the longer 'Letter' version was first published, with a considerable fanfare, in 1947 [C:145–7], it seems reasonable to assume Larkin knew both.
30. This is not intended to be a full account of the aesthetic attitude. Clearly, I can also look at a picture to work up an appetite, for sexual stimulation, or to motivate myself to take more exercise, but none of these seem directly relevant to contemplating the sky. For fuller accounts of the aesthetic attitude see my 'The Definition of "Art"', in [PALB:148–64], and 'Literature, Knowledge, and the Aesthetic Attitude' [RO:12/2009:377–97].
31. This passage is vaguely Kantian in inspiration but is not intended to be an explication of Kant's views. For more on this topic see my 'The Objectivity of Aesthetic Judgements' [BJA:1/1999:40–52].
32. I am grateful to Ian Dyball for drawing this passage to my attention.
33. For example, the young Richard Church reading *The Swiss Family Robinson*: 'It is an understatement to say that I began to read. I stepped into another life. I was one of that family on the wrecked ship, passing through the barrier of words, enlarging my small suburban experience [...] I heard the sea breaking on the shore [...]' [OTB:78].

34. I have, of course, slightly idealized what the point of view sees in order to make a philosophical point. It is possible that the point of view contemplates empty sky at the end of 'Here' and also in 'High Windows', but to avoid problems with clouds, birds and window-frames I have imagined the condition to which both poems aspire.
35. For example, '[All] consciousness, as Husserl has shown, is consciousness of something' [BAN:xxvii].
36. I adapt this sentence from p.149 of my early article 'The Transcendental Larkin' [E:Summer/1989:143–52].

II
Larkin/Flaubert

If I could talk, I'd be a workless prof, […]. Not old toad: Frank Kermode

Larkin

[I am like] an old toad in his old damp hole

Flaubert

In late 1984, Julian Barnes sent Larkin a copy of his recently published novel, *Flaubert's Parrot,* and soon received an appreciative reply. This briefly mentioned what Larkin felt about the French author:

> It's many years since I tried to read Flaubert (in translation!) and I didn't make much of him, but Steegmuller's *Life* fascinated me & I think I have a selection of his *Letters* that came out about the same time. So Louise Colet and Alfred le P. & co are all familiar to me. [SL:721]

Collins published Francis Steegmuller's *Flaubert and Madame Bovary: A Double Portrait* in 1947; and his *The Selected Letters of Gustave Flaubert* appeared from Hamish Hamilton in 1954. These dates are not 'about the same time', but it's possible that Larkin came across the biography rather late, or that, from the perspective of 1984, the late forties and early fifties seemed about the same time.[1]

Larkin's interest in Flaubert at this period was probably quickened by beginning a relationship with the glamorous Patsy Strang in 1952. Patsy, who was married to a philosopher, had not only studied at the Sorbonne but wrote French poetry, and she sent some of it to Larkin for approval ('It is exceedingly clever: I had to look one or two words up'

[SL:216]). The increased sophistication of both his Francophile lover and the situation in which he found himself, may well have prompted Larkin to start reading Flaubert more extensively; indeed, the fact that Larkin signs a letter to Patsy 'Flo Bear' in October 1954, suggests a degree of amused identification [SL:231].[2]

In this essay, I want to investigate how Flaubert's and Larkin's attitude to art determined the pattern of their lives. One outcome of the inquiry will be an explanation as to why Larkin found Flaubert's life so fascinating, and why he could still describe himself as 'familiar' with its main personalities thirty years after first reading about them.

I

Théophile Gautier published the preface to his epistolary novel *Mademoiselle de Maupin* in 1834. It is a ringing endorsement of *l'art pour l'art*: a passionate defence of the intrinsic value of beauty, which argues that the concept is devalued and denatured if it is supposed to have some use or function:

> Nothing that is beautiful is indispensable to life. If you did away with flowers, the world would not suffer in any material way. And yet who would wish there not to be flowers? I could do without potatoes more easily than roses and I think there is only one utilitarian in the world capable of tearing out a bed of tulips to plant cabbages.
>
> What use is the beauty of women? Provided a woman is medically fit and capable of bearing children, she will always be good enough for the economists.
>
> What is the good of music? What is the good of painting? Who would be mad enough to prefer Mozart to M. Carrel, and Michelangelo to the inventor of white mustard?
>
> The only things that are really beautiful are those which have no use; everything that is useful is ugly, for it is the expression of some need, and the needs of men are ignoble and disgusting, like his poor and infirm nature. The most useful place in the house is the lavatory. [G:23]

The paean to beauty is taken up and amplified by one of the novel's narrators, d'Albert, in several of the long letters which follow, and these make clear that the veneration of beauty has a religious dimension: '[...] Above all things I love the beauty of form. Beauty for me is God made visible, palpable happiness, heaven come down to earth' [G:121].

Like many literary Frenchman of his generation, Flaubert knew much of Gautier's work by heart, and it is therefore no surprise to find Gautier's doctrines developed at greater length in the novelist's own letters, particularly those to his mistress, Louise Colet. Recommending that they 'love one another "in Art," as mystics love one another "in God"' [FL:I:196], he chides her for sullying the purity of Art with considerations of fame, utility and social good: 'You have a genuine love of art, but not the religion of art' [FL:I:89]; 'You adulterate the Beautiful with a mass of extraneous things – the useful, the agreeable, and who knows what else' [FL:I:75]. And he holds up James Pradier, the sculptor, as an example of an artist who does not allow himself to be distracted from his task by moral, religious, political or social issues: 'A man who doesn't let himself worry about anything – not politics, nor socialism, nor Fourier, nor the Jesuits, nor the University. Instead, he rolls up his sleeves like a good workman and is there to do his job from morning till night, desiring to do it well and loving his art. That is everything, love of art' [FL:I:74]. In middle age, Flaubert became friendly with Gautier, and the two could often be found in Parisian salons, growing red-faced over their joint enthusiasm for beauty's autonomy, and decrying the idiocies of a utilitarian age. On the poet's death in 1872, Flaubert could write: 'With him, the last of my *intimate* friends is gone' [FS:286].

Gautier was a more exotic and recherché taste amongst young Englishmen in the 1930s and 1940s, but Larkin had certainly read *Mademoiselle de Maupin* by 1943 because it plays an important role in the story of his early novella, *Trouble at Willow Gables*, and he quotes a passage from it as the epigraph to section iv of chapter 10 [TWG:115]. Larkin's motivation for reading it is clear enough. Many of his early explorations of French literature were brought about by his interest in lesbianism. He produced a version of Baudelaire's 'Femmes Damnées' in 1943, and decided to persevere with reading Proust three years later because 'there are occasional bits about lesbians in it, and I like those bits' [SL:119]. It is thus no mystery that Gautier's novel, which contains some of the longest and most explicit descriptions of lesbian sex (spiced by cross-dressing) that were freely available in the 1940s, should have aroused his interest.[3]

Larkin quotes his epigraph from Gautier in French, and he probably read all or some of the novel in the original language. A full and cheap English translation had appeared as early as 1887, but the publisher was prosecuted, and in the 1930s and 1940s the only available English versions were cheap expurgated editions, or unexpurgated luxurious limited editions, neither of which would have suited Larkin's requirements

[G:xxxv]. Although he later played down his ability at French [SL:277, 658], he was evidently proficient enough in the sixth form and soon after: '[Larkin] was good at languages,' writes his school friend Noel Hughes, '[of] course, he could not master the pronunciation of French, but he could translate into and from it with ease' [MW:55].[4]

Gautier's influence helped develop the kind of aestheticism we find so forcefully expressed in Larkin's early letters. These emphasize that seriousness of moral and political intent is quite irrelevant to artistic quality ('A book concerning the most vital social and political problems may be quite dead except for a description of a man eating a steak pudding' [SL:115]); and express contempt for the mechanisms and consequences of literary success: 'I don't care about putting literature over on the people, which is what most education, literary propagandists, booksellers, publishers, authors, librarians and other gombeen men are doing to earn a living' [M:129]. Art can only be approached with mystical and religious awe: 'I must experience the religion of creation and imagination (to use an old fashioned word)' [SL:52–3]. And even D. H. Lawrence is viewed through the prism of *l'art pour l'art*: 'I have been thinking recently that Lawrence's beliefs are pure (in the sense of utter, most sensitive and refined) aestheticism [...] More & more I believe in the central pavilion of mystery, whose various sides are emblazoned with different emblems' [SL:56–7].[5]

Although these mysteries are private, they can still – as Flaubert felt – be shared with the closest and most sympathetic of friends: 'I need someone who consciously accepts mystery at the bottom of things [...],' Larkin writes to Jim Sutton, 'the kind of artist who is perpetually *kneeling* in his heart – who gives no fuck for anything except this mystery, and for that gives every fuck there is' [SL:106]. His friend, Bruce Montgomery, on the other hand, doesn't 'realize that art is as near to religion as one can get' [M:131]; while Larkin's first girlfriend, Ruth Bowman, doesn't have the necessary Flaubertian interest in *form*: she lacks 'the requisite [...] interest in *style* [...]' [M:131].

Of course, Larkin's aestheticism has other sources, although all of them were influenced directly or indirectly by Gautier's views. It's not clear when Larkin first read some of Flaubert's fiction. His comments to Barnes suggest an early (if unextensive) acquaintance, but Flaubert was not particularly interested in lesbianism, and thus may not have encouraged the young Larkin to continue his reading. A much more likely route for Gautier's indirect influence is through *fin-de-siècle* Irish aestheticism. One such source is Wilde's *The Picture of Dorian Gray*, which also has a famous preface telling us that no artist has ethical sympathies and all art is quite useless [DG:5–6]. Another is the last chapter of Joyce's *A Portrait of the Artist as a Young Man,* particularly the sections when Stephen Dedalus outlines his views on aesthetics, avoids the traps of politics and religion, and becomes a young votary of art. It was probably the influence of these works amongst others which made Larkin describe himself as a 'fin de siècle romantic' [SL:10].[6]

II

Larkin and Flaubert began to publish the work by which they became known comparatively late: Larkin was 33 when he published *The Less Deceived* in 1955; Flaubert was 35 when *Madame Bovary* began to appear in 1856. In their youth, both writers had written fluently and copiously. Larkin finished at least three light-hearted novels and seven booklets of poems while at school; two novellas and about a dozen poems at Oxford; and then published a book of verse and two novels in quick succession in 1945–7. This was followed by a long fallow period caused by writer's block and publishers' rejections of work he did manage to complete. Similarly, the schoolboy Flaubert wrote more than thirty plays; and by the time he finished *Madame Bovary* he had four or five unpublished books – including the autobiographical novel *November*, and the first version of *The Temptation of St Anthony* – in his bottom drawer. At the age of thirty, both felt profoundly depressed about their achievements and prospects: in one case, early promise seemed to have burned out; in the other it seemed to have achieved nothing public at all.

Part of the reason for this comparatively late development is that both writers needed to curb or sublime a form of Romanticism, and, in the process, transmute themselves into fastidious craftsmen. However, their personalities contrast strongly at this point, and their two forms of Romanticism are utterly different.

Flaubert was profligate with money, loathed the bourgeois, and loved the theatrical and dramatic. Plays were his favourite literary form when young, and he and his friends acted them out on the family billiard table. He longed to be a great actor [FL:I:48], wrote one mature play (*The Candidate*), one unstageable drama (*St Anthony*), and a whimsical farce (*Le Château des coeurs*); and conscientiously oversaw the rehearsals of his friend Louis Bouilhet's play *Mademoiselle Aïssé* at the Odéon. There was also a strong theatrical element in his personality: he liked to put on flowing Arab dress while writing; declaimed his works in an impassioned, roaring voice; and occasionally enjoyed playing the buffoon in company.[7]

In line with this theatricality, his Romanticism hankers after the magniloquent, exotic, cruel, Eastern, grandiose and picturesque. This is the impulse which made him speculate that he had, in previous lives, been 'a boatman on the Nile, a pimp in Rome at the time of the Punic Wars, then Greek orator in Suburra where I was devoured by bed-bugs. I died during the Crusades from eating too many grapes on a beach in Syria. I have been a pirate and a monk, an acrobat and a coachman. Emperor of the Orient too perhaps?' [W:274]. He wished for Iroquois blood, regretted that gladiatorial combat was impossible in his garden, dreamed of mattresses stuffed with hummingbird feathers, marvelled at the thought of jewels formed from congealed lynx's urine, and was amused at the prospect of banqueting on hedgehog pâté and tigers' clitorises.

It was unrestrained Romanticism of this kind which made the first version of *St Anthony* such an unmitigated failure, and even now, *Salammbô* and the final version of *St Anthony* tend to attract devotees rather than the general reader.[8] It was only when Flaubert was forced to focus his attention on what he regarded as a sordid local incident (in *Madame Bovary*), and the failure of his own generation's political ideals (in the second version of *Sentimental Education*), that he attained his true stature as a novelist. In these works, Flaubert's Romanticism is not absent: it is present in Emma Bovary's and Frédéric Moreau's persistent dreaming, and in the magnificence of some of the descriptions, but in both cases it is latent, implicit, controlled. When this Romanticism is stifled altogether, as in long stretches of *Bouvard and Pécuchet*, then much of the interest of his writing is stifled too.

Larkin tended to be mean with money; loved the bourgeois virtues (particularly as exemplified by Stafford Cripps and Mrs Thatcher); and never had much time for the stage: indeed, he counted the time when he discovered he could walk out of a play half way through 'as one of the great moments of my life' [RW:55]. He rigidly oversaw his public image, cultivated the soberest clothes (with the exception of colourful socks and the odd bow tie), and suffered agonies of shyness and self-consciousness.

His form of Romanticism is not colourful, exuberant or exotic; it embraces the melancholy greys, blacks and silvers of the Celtic Twilight, and haunts the moonlit sedges, streams and woods of Yeats's early collections. His first published book, *The North Ship* – which he wrote very quickly – displays all these characteristics, and it was only when this urge to the vague and mysterious was overcome – 'the Celtic fever abated and the patient sleeping soundly' [RW:30] as he later put it – that his own voice begins to emerge. From this point on, he is able to write poems about the circumstances of his own life: rented rooms, long-playing records, department stores, myxomatosis, railway stations, advertising posters, abandoned churches, and so forth. The symbolic and Romantic elements have not disappeared; instead, they now sit just below the surface, irradiating the everyday, so that the quotidian details of life seem lit from within. When this Romanticism is altogether absent, as in his weaker political squibs, then some of his characteristic qualities are absent too.

Flaubert's struggle with the prose of *Madame Bovary* – and every fiction which followed – is a matter of legend. The discipline required for the new tone and subject matter caused unforeseen problems: 'I am advancing so painfully, spoiling so much paper, scratching out so many lines! My sentences are slow to come, for it is a very devil of a style that I have adopted. A curse on all simple subjects! If you knew how I torture myself you would have pity on me [...]' [S:242]. A ten-hour day in which one page was written was particularly productive – often he could only manage two or three a week – and the Goncourts ironically noted that he seemed to secrete five words an hour [W:197].

The fluent and copious production of Larkin's youth also slowed to a trickle. Occasionally, even a late poem (like 'Dublinesque') could come very quickly, but generally a long poem would require several years' work, and he would often return to drafts he had abandoned decades before. His three published collections, containing work written between 1946 and 1974, contain 85 poems; so, ignoring his unproductive later years, he averaged about three poems a year.

In spite of profound differences, there is one point at which their mature imaginations converge. Neither author liked his own personality (Flaubert: 'I find my own personality repugnant' [FL:I:198]; Larkin: 'I don't like my character' [M:181]), and at certain climactic moments they both aspire towards ecstatic visions of nothingness, emptiness, and un-selfed objectivity.

For Flaubert, the concept of nothingness, in particular, held a profound attraction. Arriving at Thebes on his journey to the Middle East, he reflects: '[...] it seemed to me I was thinking of nothing: it was a sensuous pleasure that pervaded my entire being' [FE:112]. Delighted to discover that Louise is not pregnant, he writes: 'All the better if I have no offspring. [...] It is an idea I find pleasing, the idea of an absolute nothingness' [W:112]; and he glories in the winter stillness of Croisset; '[...] nothing happening, no sound. Complete objective nothingness' [W:248]. In one famous letter, he even suggests that a book about nothingness is his artistic ideal:

> What I'd like to do is a book about nothing, a book with no external attachment, one which would hold together by the internal strength

> of its style, as the earth floats in the air unsupported, a book that would have no subject at all or at least one in which the subject would be almost invisible, if that were possible [...]. There are no beautiful or sordid subjects and one could almost establish it as an axiom that, from the point of view of pure Art there is no such thing as a subject, style being solely itself an absolute way of seeing things. [W:203]

At religious climaxes in Flaubert's fiction, nothingness and blueness are frequently conjoined in visions of the sky and firmament. Félicité, in 'A Simple Heart', watches the heavens part to receive her through blue incense [TT:40]; and when Saint Julian Hospitator is drawn into heaven, he is described as rising up 'into the blue' [TT:70]. Given the religious significance Flaubert attaches to blue skies, it is fitting that he thinks of Art in the same context: 'Like a star, Art watches undisturbed as the world spins round. Shining in its blue immensity, the Beautiful keeps its place in the firmament' [FL:I:74].

In Larkin, the ideas of nothingness, blueness and aesthetic experience are just as important and even more closely conjoined, and several of his most significant poems end with visions of un-selfed blue immensities:

> And past the poppies bluish neutral distance
> Ends the land suddenly beyond a beach
> Of shapes and shingle. Here is unfenced existence:
> Facing the sun, untalkative, out of reach. [CP:136–7]
>
> [...] And immediately
>
> Rather than words comes the thought of high windows:
> The sun-comprehending glass,
> And beyond it, the deep blue air, that shows
> Nothing, and is nowhere, and is endless. [CP:165]

III

On such a religious conception of art, inspiration cannot be forced; the artist must simply watch and wait. 'One doesn't choose one's subjects: one submits to them', wrote Flaubert [FL:II:72]. Larkin goes into a little more detail: 'The hardest part [of writing poems] is having something to write about which succeeds in drawing words from your inner mind – that is very important, as one can always think of subjects, but they have to matter in that peculiar way that produces words & some kind of development of thought or theme or else there's no poem in either thought or words' [SL:328]. He illustrates the delicate and involuntary nature of inspiration with an illuminating analogy: 'I conceive the creative process as depending on an intricate arrangement of little mirrors inside one, & by continual care and assiduity & practice these mirrors can be cleaned and polished, so that in the end artistic perception is a whole-time & not a part-time thing. It's all mainly instinctive [...]' [SL:87–8].

This aesthetical view of literature led to a form of self-effacement. As Larkin writes to Norman Iles:

> [Your] attitude is predominantly ethical & mine aesthetical [...] you aim at increased positiveness of character while I aim at increased negativeness, a kind of infinite recession in the face of the world [...] I feel that myself & my character are nothing except insofar as they contribute to the creation of literature – that is almost the only thing that interests me now. To increase one's value as a pure instrument is what I am trying to do. [SL:87–8]

For both artists, this meant withdrawal from normal life. Action of any sort, for example, should be avoided: 'The reason I distrust action,' Larkin writes to Sutton, 'is that it clouds the mirror. A very little action now and again will give me food for contemplation. [...] Norman gave me a long harangue on the necessity of "living" – it doesn't convince me. We've had enough living' [SL:111]. Similarly, involvement with people interferes with inspiration: 'I find that with the absence of other people one becomes more sensitive to things that make for poetry' [SL:216].

Flaubert too makes plain that the artist cannot participate in life. He writes to his mother:

> You can depict wine, love, women and glory on the condition that you're not a drunkard, a lover, a husband, or a private in the ranks. If you participate actively in life, you don't see it clearly; you suffer from it too much or enjoy it too much. The artist, to my way of thinking is a monstrosity, something outside nature. All the misfortunes Providence inflicts on him come from his stubbornness in denying that axiom. He suffers from that denial and makes others suffer. Ask women who have loved poets, or men who have loved

> actresses. So (and this is my only conclusion) I am resigned to living as I have lived: alone [...]. [FL:I:132]

Happiness is 'long, shut-in hours [...] silent evenings in the light of the lamp, watching the fire and listening to the blowing of the wind' [S:101]. This scene is distinctly reminiscent of the one portrayed in Larkin's 'Vers de Société', where he describes the setting in which poems should be written: 'The gas fire breathes, the trees are darkly swayed', and time is repaid 'Under a lamp, hearing the noise of wind, / And looking out to see the moon thinned / To an air-sharpened blade [...]' [CP:181].

Larkin became increasingly aware of the cost of his decision. First, he came to realize that withdrawing from life did not prevent life from harming him. 'Send No Money', written in 1962, explains how he 'thought wanting unfair: / It and finding out clash' and so had decided to abstain from life in order to observe it carefully. Nonetheless, life came and damaged him anyway, and the poem glumly concludes: 'What does it all prove? Sod all. / In this way I spent youth, / Tracing the trite untransferable / Truss-advertisement, truth' [CP:146]. Second, he came to fear that the size of his talent may not have been worth the sacrifice. He hints at this worry in a letter to Monica Jones written four years after the poem: 'Of course my external surroundings have changed, but inside I've been just the same, trying to hold everything off in order to "write". Anyone wd think I was Tolstoy, the value I put on it' [SL:387].

In retrospect, this decision to become a spectator of life – and not to have a wife, house or children – came to seem like destiny; something that could not have been avoided. He articulates this thought in 'Dockery and Son':

> [...] To have no son, no wife,
> No house or land still seemed quite natural.
> Only a numbness registered the shock
> Of finding out how much had gone of life,
> How widely from the others. [...]
>
> [...] Where do these
> Innate assumptions come from? Not from what
> We think truest, or most want to do:
> Those warp tight-shut, like doors. They're more a style

> Our lives bring with them: habit for a while,
> Suddenly they harden into all we've got
>
> And how we got it; [...] [CP:152–3]

Flaubert always seems much more confident about the wisdom of his decision, but towards the end of middle age, even he began to have regrets and feel a victim of destiny.[9] He writes to George Sand: 'I wallow in black thoughts. Whether this is the result of over-activity during the last eight months, or whether it's due to the total absence of the feminine element in my life, I've never felt more abandoned, more empty more battered. What you wrote in your last letter about your beloved granddaughters moved me profoundly. Why do I have none of that? And yet I was born with every capacity for affection. But one doesn't choose one's destiny. One submits to it' [FS:334].

IV

The best way to enjoy uninterrupted work, and achieve the spectator's perspective, is to live somewhere provincial that does not contain too many distractions – literary events, people, cliques and fellow writers – and is not attractive enough to summon casual visitors. It is thus understandable that both artists chose to spend most of their lives as 'hermits' in northern industrial towns: Flaubert in Rouen, Larkin in Hull. Their friends often commented on this exile, but when Maxim du Camp made a serious effort to draw Flaubert to Paris, he received a magisterial rebuke:

> I am sorry to see a man like you go one better than the marquise d'Escarbagnas, who thought that "outside Paris there was no salvation for gentlefolk." That judgment seems to me itself provincial, that is, narrow. Humanity exists everywhere, my dear Sir, but in Paris nonsense is more prevalent than elsewhere, I agree. [...]
>
> Anyone raised in Paris who nevertheless becomes a man of real consequence was born a demigod. He grew up straitjacketed and with heavy burdens on his head; whereas one must be born destitute of natural originality if solitude, concentration, and persistent work fail in the end to create you something comparable.
>
> As for deploring so bitterly my "ineffectual" way of life, it is as though you were to reproach a shoemaker for making shoes or a blacksmith for striking his iron or a painter for living in his studio. Since

> I work everyday from one in the afternoon until one in the morning, except from six o'clock to eight, I scarcely see how I can make use of the remaining time. If I led a genuinely provincial or rural existence, devoting myself to dominoes or raising melons, I could understand the reproach. But if I am becoming stultified, you will have to lay the blame on Lucian, Shakespeare, and writing a novel. [FL:I:161–2]

Larkin was equally attached to the provincial life, remarking in his preface to *A Rumoured City*: '[Hull] is still as good a place to write as any. Better, in fact, than some. For a place cannot produce poems: it can only not prevent them, and Hull is good at that' [FR:128]. He gives more reasons for his choice in an interview with Miriam Gross:

> As for Hull, I like it because it's so far away from everything else. On the way to nowhere, as somebody put it. It's in the middle of this lonely country, and beyond the lonely country there's only the sea. I like that.
>
> I love all the Americans getting on to the train at King's Cross and thinking they're going to come and bother me, and then looking at the connections and deciding they'll go to Newcastle and bother Basil Bunting instead. Makes it harder for people to get at you. I think it's very sensible not to let people know what you're like. And Hull is an unpretentious place. There's not so much crap around as there would be in London, at least as I imagine it, or in some other university towns. [...] I very much feel the need to be on the periphery of things. [RW:54–5]

Work is further aided by being as inconspicuous as possible. For men of Flaubert's and Larkin's background and education this meant appearing to be bourgeois; an appearance Larkin adopted willingly (because he thought he was bourgeois), Flaubert with rather less enthusiasm. The novelist described his life as '[...] the most bourgeois, the most obscure life in the world' [FL:I:73]; while acknowledging his was a 'wholly internal life' [B:265] and that he aimed 'to live like a bourgeois, and think like a demigod' [FL:I:197]. Larkin too thought that the creative artist should blend into his background: in the 1940s, he said that the poet should wear the same clothes and smoke the same cigarettes as other men, but was happy to confess that his real life was: 'seven-eighths below the surface, like an iceberg' [M:131]. On another occasion, he develops a more accurate analogy: 'My life is very vapid and servile – ON THE SURFACE. Within, there's a great stirring, like a blacked out war factory on the night shift, with plenty of Graham Sutherland furnaces, and great hammers bonking on clots of white hot metal, and plenty of jolly work men drinking tea and then falling to it again – all done by Breughel – at least it is at the moment, and as long as these moments come sometimes I know all is well' [SL:142].

This attitude to life makes taking up any kind of profession difficult: in this case, one can't simply act and behave as other people do, one has to think, care, be involved, be preoccupied; and this clearly interferes with the creative processes. It was trying to pass his law exams that probably brought on Flaubert's first attack of epilepsy; and Larkin felt he was rejected by the Civil Service because he showed he didn't 'give a zebra's turd for any kind of job' [M:108]: '[They] can't have liked my cheerful determination to be a writah and to use the CS merely as a means of livelihood' [M:107].

The main difficulty for both was that the non-artistic life not only seemed worthless but *inconceivable*: 'I cannot imagine,' remarks Flaubert, 'how people unconcerned with art can spend their time: how they live is a mystery to me' [FL:I:79]. Larkin concurs: 'You see, my trouble is that I simply can't understand anybody doing anything but write, paint, compose music – I can understand their doing things as a means to these ends, but I can't see what a man is up to who is satisfied to follow a profession in the normal way. [...] And all the people who don't think it, what do they do? What are they striving for?' [SL:87–8].

V

Gradually, an absolute and exacting standard of art, solitude and abstinence from life, exacerbated their tendencies to depression, pessimism and rage.

The threat of depression was ever present. 'I have reason to remember just how deep was his gloom and how total his hopelessness', writes Ruth Bowman: it was 'never long before the Black Dog appeared' [M:122, 137]. The same Black Dog recurs in Flaubert's letters: 'the black gloom in my heart is a little blacker' [FS:193]; 'a black melancholy [...] recurs persistently several times a day' [FS:194]; 'I'm mortally depressed' [FS:358].

Flaubert hated life, especially the commonplaces of life, but thought it might occasionally be redeemed by opulence, magnificence or sensual pleasure. He felt he was born into a state of ennui, and the mere thought of action poisoned him with apathy. Only withdrawal into his cave offered any hope of comfort, but even here the relentless and tedious imperatives of existence continued: 'I hate life [...] and whatever reminds me that I must suffer it. I am fed up with having to eat, to dress, to stand up [...]' [B:284]. It was a view which encouraged 'an ever-present longing for death' [FS:367].

Larkin, on the other hand, loved life, even the commonplaces of life, but felt it was darkened by two circumstances: the inevitable eternity of death; and the fact that most people's lives – especially his own – fell woefully short of their ideals. The resulting outlook was almost as bleak as Flaubert's. 'Let me hug defeat like a lover' [M:51], he wrote to Sutton; and as two potential titles for his autobiography – which he had no intention of writing – he considered *Self Inflicted Wound* [SL:499] and *Upon thy Belly* [SL:404]. 'Dockery and Son' ends with a famous summary of his outlook:

> Life is first boredom, then fear.
> Whether or not we use it, it goes,
> And leaves what something hidden from us chose,
> And age, and then the only end of age. [CP:153]

'What I like about Phil,' he remarks to Wain, '[is that] he always cheers you up' [SL:710].

Naturally enough, given that both men enjoyed comfortable and privileged lives, several friends felt that such gloom was cultivated and wilful. Montgomery complained: 'You set out with the idea that [something's] going to be beastly, become resigned, and not unnaturally discover that it *is* beastly. [...] More willpower, Philip!' [M:111]; and late in Flaubert's life, Sand wondered if he wasn't self-indulgent in his pessimism [FL:II:225]. He replied hotly: 'I don't "go in for desolation" wantonly: please believe me! But I cannot change my eyes' [FL:II:226–7].

Larkin's rage had any number of objects: applying for jobs ('I boil and spit fury' [M:108]); his landlady ('If the bastard landlady won't bring any bastard coal, why won't the bastard bring me my bastard supper?' [SL:97]); his mother ('I feel *full* of rage [...] What a bloody awful sodding life. Suicidal murder' [M:369–70]); or people at large: 'I HATE anybody who does anything UNUSUAL at ALL, whether its make a lot of MONEY or dress in silly CLOTHES or read books of foreign WORDS [...] BECAUSE THEY ARE USUALLY SUCH SODDING NASTY PEOPLE THAT I KNOW IT IS 1000–1 THAT THEY ARE JUST SHOWING OFF. – *and they don't KNOW it but I know it*' [SL:119].

Flaubert's rage could be triggered by the demands of his art ('I'm constantly bursting with suppressed anger and indignation' [FL:II:227]); financial matters ('Why does the mere sight of an "account" send me into a rage? It borders on madness' [FS:269]); his publisher ('I had a violent quarrel with the great Michel Lévy [...] Never before had the Maison Lévy received such a drubbing' [FS:268]); or his contemporaries generally: 'There are days when I can hardly breathe for sheer anger. I long to drown my contemporaries in the latrines. Or at least to bring torrents of abuse and cataracts of invective down on their noodles' [FS:251].[10]

But the main object of their rage was the political state of their country. Almost wholly absorbed with aesthetic preoccupations, and remote from centres of power, neither developed much grasp of practical politics: Flaubert, for example, was confidently predicting in 1868 that Prussia would never invade France (it invaded in 1870) [STD:199]; while Larkin was prepared to admit that his ignorance of politics was complete: 'I know bugger all about politics' [SL:34]; 'I don't know anything at all about anything [political], and it's no use pretending I do' [SL:115]. Even so, neither felt inhibited about giving vent to his views, although both were happy to own that their opinions were expressive rather than diagnostic. Flaubert, having second thoughts about a political letter he'd published in a newspaper, conceded it was rather brutal but '[what] the hell! I have spat out my bile. It's a relief' [W:319]; while Larkin acknowledged that '[my] political opinions are really no more than gouts of bile' [SL:650].

Both men were profoundly misanthropic. Flaubert was quite prepared to issue general condemnations of mankind: 'Why are you so sad?' he wrote to George Sand after the debacle of the Paris Commune, 'Mankind is displaying nothing new. Its irremediable wretchedness has embittered me ever since my youth. So I am not disillusioned now' [FS:240]. Larkin never summarized his outlook in a statement of this kind, but his letters contain disparaging remarks about virtually every kind of person he encountered: men, women, friends, relations, parents, children, students, academics, librarians, writers, and a particularly rich selection from 'filthy abroad' [SL:533]: Americans [SL:67], Soviets [SL:115], Jews [SL:141], Greeks [SL:293], Puerto Ricans [SL:303], Caribbeans [SL:339], 'the frog and the hun' [SL:461], Scots [SL:510], Africans [SL:567], 'niggers and wops' [SL:590], Pakistanis [SL:699–700], Orientals [SL:704], Indians [SL:703], and the Welsh [SL:758].[11]

This is not to say that some groups didn't enrage more than others. Larkin is frequently disparaging about coloured immigrants (e.g. SL:719, 755); Flaubert sometimes gives way to anti-Semitism (e.g. FS:196–7,

201). But to both, socialists were objects of special scorn. I shall examine why in the next two sections.

VI

'Socialism,' said Flaubert, 'seems to me a pedantic horror that will spell the death of all art and morality' [B:350], and he develops his views in several letters to Sand: 'The general reverence for the fetish of universal suffrage revolts me [...] Do you think that if France, instead of being governed, in effect, by the mob, were to be ruled by the "Mandarins", we'd be where we are now?' [FS:208]. Flaubert did not think of himself as a Mandarin, but he certainly felt that he and his political views should be treated with proper respect, remarking that 'I am worth 20 other Croisset voters' [STD:223].

His particular solutions to the tide of *panmuflisme* ('universal yobbery' [FS:275]) sweeping his country were a firm central authority, a strong sense of justice, and severe punishments for delinquents. 'Our only salvation now lies in a *legitimate aristocracy*, by which I mean a majority composed of something more than mere numbers' [FS:228–9]; 'In my opinion the entire Commune should have been sent to the galleys, and the bloodthirsty fools chained by the neck like common criminals [...]' [FS:247].

Although Larkin never had to face an invasion or the bloody consequences of a failed revolution, he was equally appalled by socialist ideas, failings amongst the ruling classes, and 'the cast of crooks and tarts' [CP:190] that seemed to be taking over the country. 'There will never be another Conservative government. What there will be is a series of Labour governments that will bankrupt the country so that we are all starving, at which point the Russkies will step in ("I am sure all members of the House will join me in extending a welcome to Mr Breznev" [*sic*]) and we shall be run as a satellite Soviet state' [SL:544]. And, because of their proximity, he had a particular dislike of radical students ('subsidised socialist sods' [SL:530]) and their leaders: 'You'll be glad to know,' he told Colin Gunner, 'that four young swine have been "rusticated" for a year for disrupting Senate here – Socialist Workers Student Organisation – unfortunately "rusticated" doesn't mean flogged with rhinoceros hide whips dipped in brine, but supported by you and me through taxes. Heigh ho, ho hum' [SL:666].

Ordinary members of the working classes did not escape, and Larkin's solutions to political problems usually contained a vision of himself being treated with proper respect: 'My simple cure for "unemployment" (no such thing really) is to abolish unemployment benefits. If you don't want chaps to do a thing then don't pay them to do it. In the nineteenth century men used to *run behind* your station growler, following you home to earn a few pence for unloading your luggage. I'd like to see Authur Scargill doing that' [SL:646–7]. He had put his views into rhyme five years earlier:

I want to see them starving,
 The so-called working class,
Their wages weekly halving,
 Their women stewing grass,

When I drive out each morning
 In one of my new suits
I want to find them fawning
 To clean my car and boots. [SL:541–2]

Like Flaubert, he fantasized about ferocious punishments: not only rhinoceros whips for student leaders, but 'Prison for Strikers, Bring back the cat, Kick out the niggers, How about that?' [SL:432].

This variety of aesthetic misanthropy ('I have always tried to live in an ivory tower,' wrote Flaubert, 'but a sea of shit is beating up against its walls' [FT:71]) caused problems with more liberal-minded friends. Flaubert's friendship with Sand survived, despite the fact that he found her 'too good, too full of vain talk, too democratic' [FT:69]; Larkin's friendship with Sutton, whom he found 'fuller and fuller of windy philosophical tosh about mankind', did not [M:205].

VII

Why were they so right-wing? The aesthete is profoundly selfish because he is solely interested in realizing his own artistic vision, and consequently appalled by having to sacrifice his time or liberties to social causes. He is even more appalled by being required to make his thoughts conform to the requirements of a political party, or make his art subservient to social goals. These demands would mean sacrificing his intellectual individuality, and judging his work by the standards of propaganda.

Flaubert therefore felt that any attempt to make artists and the masses join in common cause was doomed to failure: '[mankind] hates us: we serve none of its purposes; and we hate it, because it injures us' [FL:I:196].

Furthermore, socialism appeared to have implications of instruction, regimentation, mediocrity and uniformity that reminded both writers of the schoolroom. 'For me it is almost certain,' wrote Flaubert, 'that at some more or less distant time [society] will be regimented like a college. Teachers will be the law. Everyone will be in uniform' [FE:212]; Larkin felt the same: 'I regard [the left-wing *Guardian*] as a paper written *by* comprehensive schoolteachers *for* comprehensive schoolteachers' [SL:752].

The aesthete, of course, is interested in the beautiful – in Flaubert's case the magnificent and exotic, in Larkin's the solitary and evocative – and the cause of the majority rarely ministers to this taste. Democratic politics is about lobbying, committee work, rhetoric, administration, organization, money-raising and effective action – the very idea of which can only fill the aesthete with weariness and disgust. And the kind of changes democratic politics aims to bring about – fuller employment, better health care, improved schooling – are not likely to gladden the heart of one who seeks out the splendid or the strange.

There is certainly an internal relation between aestheticism and cruelty – because other people are only of interest insofar as they are pleasing to the senses. Gautier's d'Albert wonders why a woman doesn't commit suicide when she reaches 30; declares that if a woman is beautiful he can do very well without intelligence or a soul [G:120–1]; and is quite open about how his tastes have undermined sympathy and morality:

> You know how ardently I have sought physical beauty and what importance I attach to external form, and how I love the visible world. That is how I am; I am too corrupt, to blasé to believe in moral beauty or pursue it for very long. I have completely lost all sense of good or evil and am so depraved I have reverted almost to the ignorant state of a child or savage. [...] My conscience is both deaf and dumb. Adultery seems to me the most innocent thing in the world and I find it quite natural for a young girl to turn to prostitution. I believe I could betray my friends without feeling an ounce of remorse and if I were walking with them along a precipice and they annoyed me, I shouldn't have the least scruple about kicking them over the edge. [G:160]

Similarly, Flaubert said that he worried more about a line of verse than about any man [FL:I:74], and there was undoubtedly an element of sadism in his character: he loved the Marquis de Sade, considering him a great comic writer [W:134], and Sainte-Beuve was not the last critic to find openly sadistic passages in *Salammbô* [SB:298–99].

Larkin is less extreme. On the question of sympathy he is slightly heterodox in that he sees sympathy and aestheticism as closely aligned. 'Do you remember in [Lawrence's] essay on Whitman,' he writes to Sutton, 'where he defines "sympathy" as "the soul judging for herself and preserving its own integrity". Now, what is this but aestheticism, judging everything by its beauty?' [SL:56]. Moreover, the sadistic element in his personality is much more muted: it only shows itself in a few fantasized punishments, his taste in pornography [M:266; SL:308], and a couple of moments in work he chose not to publish [e.g., TWG:88].

But there may be a deeper reason why aesthetic ideals should lead to right-wing views. In Hazlitt's essay on *Coriolanus*, there is a passage designed to show that literature – he takes the example of poetry – has an essentially right-wing bias:

> The cause of the people is indeed but little calculated as a subject for poetry: it admits of rhetoric, which goes into argument and explanation, but it presents no immediate or distinct images to the mind, 'no jutting frieze, buttress, or coigne of vantage' for poetry 'to make its pendant bed and procreant cradle in.' The language of poetry naturally falls in with the language of power. The imagination is an exaggerating and exclusive faculty: it takes from one thing to add to another: it accumulates circumstances together to give the greatest possible effect to a favourite object. The understanding is a dividing and measuring faculty: it judges of things not according to their immediate impression on the mind, but according to their relations to one another. The one is a monopolizing faculty, which seeks the greatest quantity of present excitement by inequality and disproportion: the other is a distributive faculty, which seeks the greatest quantity of ultimate good, by justice and proportion. The one is an aristocratical, the other a republican faculty. The principle of poetry is a very anti-leveling principle [...] It puts the individual for the species, the one above the infinite many [...] [HSW:284–5]

The expression in this essay is compressed and epigrammatic, and its arguments are often run together, but it is nonetheless possible to tease out a number of separate strands. One of these is that the imagination is always attracted by what is dramatic and striking. Another is that the imagination loves what is glittering and aristocratic rather than what is drearily uniform and poverty stricken. Another is that both writers and readers like to engage in wish-fulfilment fantasies and thus identify with the powerful. All of these may in general be true, but it's not hard to think of exceptions. Wordsworth, for example, is undoubtedly a great and imaginative poet, but his sympathies are most deeply engaged by the non-aristocratic, undramatic and weak, as we can see in his portrayals of the discharged soldier, leach-gatherer and old Cumberland beggar. One of Hazlitt's arguments, however, does seem to be rooted in the nature of the psyche, and this is his implicit claim that certain emotions cannot deal with large numbers of people. Let me try rationally to reconstruct this.

The emotions are more closely tied to the perceptual and quasi-perceptual than they are to abstract knowledge. A case of suffering which emerges in front of us is liable to create a much more immediate emotional reaction than a case which is merely known. Similarly, a case of suffering which is faithfully represented in art or journalism, and which can therefore be experienced in all its evocative detail, always has a far more direct and immediate effect on our emotions and actions than an example which is merely acknowledged in the abstract. These forms of representation have the capacity to let us take up other – often remote – perspectives on the world, and thus to extend and enlarge our powers of sympathy and identification. This would seem to be wholly beneficial.

However, while some emotions have no difficulty in engaging with large numbers of human beings – awe and amazement at the size of a crowd, for example, would seem to increase with the number of people looked at – sympathy, empathy, identification and understanding need to focus on individuals and small groups. As the characteristic power of the arts is to show individuals rather than characterize the mass, dramatize rather than describe conceptually, present an image rather than convey in the abstract, they naturally minister to such emotions. But this causes problems when art has to deal with multitudes.

If a representation only presents us with *one* pitiable case then we should have no difficulty in sympathizing with the individual, but we cannot experience (although we can be told) that the case exemplifies a problem suffered by millions of people. If a representation tries to show us a large number of cases at the same time, then clearly our ability to feel for the people involved will decline as our attention fragments. If we are shown a long sequence of cases one after the other, then our sympathies will soon become exhausted. If a representation shows little detail, and tries to present us with schematic human beings who symbolize many others, then it is unlikely that our sympathies will be engaged at all; we feel emotional about concrete human beings, not schematic types or symbols. There is thus no way to sum such emotional reactions to images, and this entails that multiplying the number of cases deadens rather than enhances our sympathies. This is the truth in Stalin's remark: 'A single death is a tragedy; a million is a statistic' [BTQ:690].

From the point of view of the understanding this way of approaching mass suffering is absurd, because it suggests that the *more* common and widespread a problem is, the *less* impact it will have on the imagination and emotions, and the *less* disposed we will be to alleviate it. For the understanding, the true significance of pain has nothing to do with how well we can imagine or sympathize with it, but only how terrible it is for the people suffering. And a million deaths is *not* a statistic: a million deaths are very much worse than one death, and the millionth death is every bit as terrible as the first. To appreciate these points requires elementary notions of consistency, fairness and justice; relying *solely* on the imagination and immediate emotional reactions can only guarantee the most false and harmful conclusions.

This is the argument which Hazlitt presses most strongly in the quoted passage. He argues that literature provides us with 'immediate or distinct images' that provoke instant emotional reactions, but 'the cause of the people' cannot be fairly represented because 'the infinite many' cannot be presented by any image that hopes to achieve an appropriate emotional reaction. The infinite many, according to Hazlitt, can only be comprehended by the understanding, the 'distributive faculty which seeks the greatest quantity of ultimate good, by justice and proportion'. Thus one of socialism's most powerful arguments – its emphasis on the sheer magnitude and quantity of suffering – can only be nullified, indeed inverted, by imaginative literature.

Socialists are often accused of sacrificing those around them in order to benefit the unseen masses. In *Sentimental Education*, for example, Flaubert says of the Republican, Sénécal: '[He] governed them harshly. A man of theory, he respected only the masses and was merciless towards individuals' [SE:199]. But Flaubert and Larkin seem to have suffered from the opposite vice. There is every indication they were deeply emotional men who responded strongly to real and fictional individuals. But their letters indicate that they had very little sympathy with people conceived as classes or in the abstract (workers, students, the bourgeoisie, Jews, immigrants); and they detested socialism, the form of political theory intended to improve the conditions of the masses.

The discussion of Hazlitt's argument allows us to see that this limitation in their moral and political outlook, and their outstanding ability as creative artists, are rooted in the same cognitive bias. They are not men of theory; they are not abstract or conceptual thinkers. Instead, their approach to the world is imaginative: it is concrete, quasi-perceptual and emotional. This explains why they favour individuals over the masses, and it is exactly the disposition of mind we would expect to discover in great creative writers. We can, therefore, no longer think of their political views as aberrations, merely contingent facts, which have nothing to do with their literary abilities.[12]

In fact, both writers simply exemplify a general trend in late nineteenth- and twentieth-century literature long ago identified and discussed by Lionel Trilling in *The Liberal Imagination*:

> I know that I will not be wrong if I assume that most of us here [at this lecture] are in our social and political beliefs consciously liberal and democratic. And I know that I will not be wrong if I say that most of us, and in the degree of our commitment to literature and in our familiarity with it, find that the contemporary authors we most wish to read and most wish to admire for their literary qualities demand of us a great agility and ingenuity in coping with their antagonism to our social and political ideals. For it is in general true that the modern European literature to which we have an active, reciprocal relationship, which is the right relationship to have, has been written by men who are indifferent to, or even hostile to, the tradition of democratic liberalism as we know it. Yeats and Eliot, Proust and Joyce, Lawrence and Gide – these men do not seem to confirm us in the social and political ideals which we hold. [LI:283][13]

As Trilling implies, modern writers of the very *front* rank tend to have little sympathy with socialism; it is those in the ranks below who tend to be committed.[14] Clearly this is a contestable value-judgement, but I don't think it's too contentious to say that Flaubert, Yeats, Proust, Joyce and Eliot – all of whom are hostile or indifferent to socialist ideas – are amongst the very greatest writers; while Zola, Brecht, Orwell, Auden and Pinter – to pick the best of the socialists – fall a little below. Given that the theoretically minded and university-based critical establishment leans to the left, the political views of the literary geniuses of the past 150 years can only cause a certain amount of self-deception, misunderstanding and pain.

This leads to a larger issue: if the understanding has a tendency to overlook individuals (and therefore lean to the left), and the imagination a tendency to overlook the mass (and therefore lean to the right), where should we turn for truth? The answer is that not all knowledge of humanity can be conveyed by the imagination through art, and not all knowledge of humanity can be conveyed by the understanding through philosophy. We need to use both; and be sceptical of both.[15]

VIII

At this point it might be objected that my analogy between the two writers' lives hardly holds: after all, one was a full-time novelist with private means who never took a profession; and the other was a part-time poet without private means who worked as a librarian. This is perfectly true, but overlooks the fact that each viewed the other's life as a road not taken; an entirely imaginable and possible form of life, contemplated in one case with envy, in the other with alarm.

In his late twenties, Flaubert had considered the idea of taking up a profession and writing in his spare time, but emphatically rejected it: 'When one does something one must do it wholeheartedly and well. A mongrel existence in which one sells tallow all day long and composes verse after dinner is made for the banal intelligence equally hopeless in harness or saddled, being unfit to pull a plow or leap over a ditch' [B:249]. Fortunately, no career was required because, with the death of his father, he inherited a substantial private income. But by the mid-1870s he had ran into financial problems, and by 1878 faced disaster. His beloved niece Caroline had married a timber merchant named Commanville, and he had been ruined by a combination of unsound investments and the Franco-Prussian War. Flaubert, who had urged the marriage on his unwilling niece, used all his capital and sold off his land in an attempt to satisfy Commanville's creditors, but the couple's debts remained massive, and Flaubert had no option but to look for a position or pension.

What kind of job would suit him best? A *librarian*, he decided: '[...] since my life is going to be restricted,' he wrote to his friend Agénor Bardoux, 'if you can find me a post worth three or four thousand in a library, along with a lodging [...] I think that would be good for me. We might think about it and keep your eyes open [...]' [FL:II:219]. Like Larkin, he evidently felt that librarianship – especially as it existed in Third Empire France – was the profession least likely to interfere with his creative processes. After all, it had seemed to suit his friend, the poet Louis Bouilhet, rather better than any of his other careers.

Unfortunately, the kind of position Flaubert wanted, which supplied a lodging and salary but required no work, had largely disappeared, and Guy de Maupassant wrote to tell him the distressing news in March 1879:

> I inquired about the various libraries. Unfortunately there is none now, of the kind you want. Pensions for men of letters are taking the place of that kind of sinecure; and librarians are now required to be residents of Paris and to be in their offices every other day. You can see that this wouldn't suit you. Regular attendance is required at Sèvres, at the Beaux Arts, etc. – in all the small libraries, which for that reason are better paid than the large ones. [FL:II:257]

At this point Flaubert decided the envisaged new career was no longer possible, and accepted an official pension in 1879.

Although Flaubert did more than any other writer to raise prose to the level of poetry, he did sometimes feel that poetry was still the higher calling: 'There is something faulty in my character and in my vocation. I was born a lyricist and write no poetry' [FL:I:200]. And he envied poets their freedom to express their feelings and personalities: 'You are lucky, you poets; you have an outlet in your verse. When something troubles you, you spit out a sonnet, and that relieves you. But we poor devils, writers of prose, who are forbidden (myself in particular) any expression of personal feelings – think of all the bitterness that remains in our souls, all the moral mucus we gag on' [FL:I:200].

Flaubert's thoughts about being a poet were purely whimsical, and his contemplation of librarianship involuntary and short-lived, but Larkin's ambition to lead the independent life of a full-time and successful novelist was protracted and serious. When he was asked in an interview if he had any regrets about his writing life, he answered: 'Sometimes I think, Everything I've written has been done after a day's work, in the evening: what would it have been like if I'd written in the morning, after a night's sleep? Was I wrong?' [RW:62]. And he is quite clear that for most of his young adult life, he wanted, above all else, to write prose fiction: 'I wanted to "be a novelist" in a way I never wanted to "be a poet", yes. Novels seem to me to be richer, broader, deeper, more enjoyable than poems' [RW:63]. In one of his last works, 'The Life with a Hole in it', he returns to this youthful vision of himself, and it turns out to have a remarkably French inflection:

When I throw back my head and howl
People (women mostly) say
But you've always done what you want,
You always get your own way
– A perfectly vile and foul
Inversion of all that's been.
What the old ratbags mean
Is I've never done what I don't.

So the shit in the shuttered château
Who does his five hundred words
Then parts out the rest of the day
Between bathing and booze and birds
Is far off as ever, but so
Is that spectacled schoolteaching sod
(Six kids, and the wife in pod,
And her parents coming to stay) ... [CP:202]

Perhaps the daily word-count makes us think of Maugham rather than Flaubert, but the latter did consider his house at Croisset to be a shuttered château [W:220] – and there was a certain amount of bathing, a good deal of boozing, and even the odd seduction.

IX

If a commitment to aestheticism meant that other people had to be held at a distance, then this was especially true of women. Art and love are incompatible: 'I have never been able to accommodate Venus and Apollo,' wrote Flaubert, '[for] me it is always one or the other – being, as I am, a creature of excess, given over entirely to what I'm engaged in' [FL:II:147]. There was no question that love might triumph or that the two might alternate; love was firmly relegated into second position. He makes his views ungallantly plain in a letter to Louise:

> For me, love is not and should not be in the foreground of life; it should stay in the background. There are other things in the soul, it seems to me, which are nearer the light, closer to the sun. So, if you

consider love as the principal dish of existence, my answer is no. If as seasoning, yes. If you mean by 'loving' to be exclusively preoccupied with the loved one, to live only in her, to see, of everything there is to see in the world, only her, to be full of the idea of her – to feel, finally, that your life is bound up in her life and that that has become the organ of your soul, then no. I have never felt the necessity of the company of anyone. The desire, yes. The need, no. [S.111]

Age did not moderate his opinion. Late in life he wrote: 'The feminine has never fitted into my existence. And then I am not rich enough, and then, and then [...] I am too old [...] And then I am too sensitive to inflict my person on anyone in perpetuity' [W:324].

Larkin is characteristically less confident, and more specific about the psychological processes which make art and love incompatible. He describes the problem to Sutton:

> What mainly worries me [...] is the strengthening suspicion that in my character there is an antipathy between 'art' and 'life'. I find that once I 'give in' to another person, as I have given in not altogether voluntarily, but almost completely, to Ruth, there is a slackening and dulling of the peculiar artistic fibres that makes it impossible to achieve that mental 'clenching' that crystallizes a pattern and keeps it while you draw it. It's very easy to float along in semi-submerged way, dissipating one's talent for pleasing by amusing and being affectionate to the other – easy because the returns are instant and delightful – but I find myself, that this letting-in of a second person spells death to perception and the desire to express, as well as the ability. Time & time again I feel that before I write anything else at all I must [...] shake myself dry and sit down on a lonely rock to contemplate glittering loneliness. Marriage, of course (since you mentioned marriage), is impossible if one wants to do this. [SL:116]

Indeed, marriage to Larkin had always seemed 'a revolting institution, unless the parties have enough money to keep reasonably distant from each other [...]' [SL:63]; '[...] If I think of myself married it is always during the stage when I have managed to get my wife out of the picture and am myself again' [SL:118]; 'I have also learned how *bad* living can be, and am sure that no man should ever run the risk of being married to a complaining, nagging or otherwise unserviceable wife. There is no hell like marriage. The hell of loneliness, while still hell, is not so bad as the hell of marriage. And all for what, eh, you tell me that? Christ fuck! To put forward all one's self-control & resilience *just to go on living with someone* – by God' [SL:166].

Flaubert too was appalled by the very idea of marriage, and despaired when he heard about the wedding of his friend Alfred le Poittevin. 'So there is one more lost to me' [FL:I:41], he remarked bitterly to Ernest Chevalier, and could barely bring himself to mention the marriage in what should have been a letter of congratulation to Alfred:

> Not having asked for my advice, it would be proper for me to give none. So we won't speak about that. There are many things which I foresee. Unfortunately, I am farsighted. I think you are deluded, enormously so [...] Are you sure, oh great man, that you'll not end up becoming a bourgeois? In all my artistic hopes, I was at one with you. It is that aspect that distresses me. [FL:I:40]

Even Alfred's early death did not lessen Flaubert's sense of outrage and betrayal. Eighteen months after the funeral, Flaubert wrote: 'For me, marriage would be an apostasy; the very thought terrifies me. Alfred's death has not erased the memory of how shocked I was by his marriage – as pious folk react to the news of a great scandal caused by their bishop' [FL:I:132]. And when Chevalier himself announced he was getting married, Flaubert could only write jeeringly to his own mother: 'When will the wedding be, you ask me, apropos of the news of Ernest Chevalier's marriage. When? Never I hope. [...] Good old Ernest! There he is, married, established – and a magistrate to boot. What a perfect bourgeois and gentleman! How much more than ever he'll be the defender of order, family, property! But then he followed the normal course. He too was an artist' [FL:I:132–3].

Soon after the revival of Flaubert and Louise's affair in 1851, Louis Bouilhet – who had been acting as a go-between – communicated some very unwelcome news: 'It is certain that the Muse [Louise] wants – hopes – to become your wife. I have thought so for some time, without daring to formulate the idea to myself' [S:298]. This was more than enough for Flaubert to decide that 'little by little, very quietly' [S:298] the affair must end. He reminded Louise of the rigour of the artistic life; he hinted that she was coming to see him as he really was and that, for this reason, was beginning to love him less; he began to suspect he was becoming sexless. But Louise was not the kind of person to take hints, or once having taken them, appreciate their implications, and a series of violent rows ensued. In the last of these, she struck out wildly, and he had to run from the room in case the desire to murder her with a flaming fire-log overwhelmed him [S:299].

Larkin and Flaubert formed close male friendships involving much drinking, swearing, talking about art, sharing of unacceptable opinions, and concocting on-going charades (the Garçon, the Yorkshire Scholar); but the two seem to have thought about these groups in slightly different ways. In Larkin's case, when a friend got married, he did not automatically assume that this was an end to their friendship or that the friend had given up all pretensions to the artistic life. Marriage just didn't suit *him*: 'I think of [marriage] as a marvellous thing for other people, like going to the stake' [SL:372]. But Flaubert regarded a friend's marriage not only as a betrayal of the group's loyalty, but as a signal that he was giving up all artistic ambitions by joining the bourgeois.

The children marriages tended to produce were also unwelcome. Larkin had a single niece, to whom he liked sending amusing notes, but he regarded children as a threat to the artistic life, and had little use for childhood in his work. His own early years were a 'forgotten boredom' [CP:33]; his youth was 'unspent' [CP:81]. He liked to skip the opening chapters of biographies (which he found tediously uniform) [FR:47]; and the most ingenious imaginary punishment he could invent for a treacherous ex-colleague was to 'put an advert in his local paper saying he is willing to give a good home to a couple of feeble-minded boys of school age' [SL:171]. When he was asked to review the Opies' *The Lore and Language of Schoolchildren*, he felt free to expand on the reasons for his dislike:

> It was that verse about becoming again as a little child that caused the first sharp waning of my Christian sympathies. If the Kingdom of Heaven could be entered only by those fulfilling such a condition I knew I should be unhappy there. It was not so much the prospect of being deprived of money, keys, wallet, letters, books, long-playing records, drinks, the opposite sex, and other solaces of adulthood that upset me (I should have been about eleven), but having to put up indefinitely with the company of other children, their noise, their nastiness, their boasting, their back-answers, their cruelty, their silliness. Until I began to meet grown-ups on more or less equal terms I fancied myself a kind of Ishmael. The realization that it was not people I disliked but children was for me one of those celebrated moments of revelation, comparable to reading Haeckel or Ingersoll in the last century. The knowledge that I should never (except by

deliberate act of folly) get mixed up with them again more than compensated for having to start earning a living. [RW:111][16]

As a young man, Flaubert had confessed 'I do not even know how to play with a child' [S:118], and although he enjoyed a close relationship with *his* niece – indeed, for thirteen years he acted as her tutor – he showed no great interest in childhood or children either. When Louise wrote to tell him that she was not, as they'd feared, pregnant, his reaction was ecstatic, not because he had avoided scandal or the trouble of a child, but because the very idea of creating another life appalled him: 'The idea of bringing someone into the world fills me with *horror*. I would curse myself if I were to become a father. A son! Oh, no, no, no! May my flesh perish utterly! May I never transmit to anyone the boredom and ignominies of existence!' [FL:I:174]. Foreseeably, children play an utterly negligible role in his fiction, even in his naturalistic descriptions of more or less contemporary life.

X

This attitude to cohabitation, marriage and domesticity created problems. The most obvious of these was how to fulfil sexual desire, especially as for both of them, sexuality and artistic productivity were closely related.

Flaubert's imagery for the creative process is often sexual. *Madame Bovary*, he wrote, was a 'long, painful coitus' [B:322]; and after making little progress with *Salammbô* he was pleased to report: 'Finally I'm beginning to have an erection. That's the important thing. How hard it's been to get it up! Will it stay?' [FL:II:5]. Larkin implies that sexual difficulties will also cause creative difficulties: 'The [poetic] vision has got something to do with sex. I don't know why, and I don't particularly want to know. It's not surprising because obviously two creative voices would be in alliance. But the vision has a sexual quality lacking in other emotions such as pity [...] Ovid, for instance, could never write unless he was in love. Many poets have been and are the same. I should think poetry and sex are very closely connected' [M:80].

One solution to sexual frustration was masturbation. The young Flaubert indulged in 'melancholic orgies' [W:154–5] of this kind, but more extended daydreams about women also played an important role in his psychology. He was inclined to dream and muse on women he'd once been in love with. 'I'd lie down and watch the wind brush the grass and the surf pound the sand,' he writes in one characteristic letter, 'and I'd think of her and reconstruct in my heart every scene in which she acted or spoke. These memories were a passion' [B.85]. As his biographer, Frederick Brown, comments: 'Gustave loved to embrace absences. [...] He would always feel most himself in the fastness of indefinitely unconsummated love, of longing, of bereavement' [B:85].

Erotic dreams of girls entered his creative work, especially *St Anthony*, where the saint is frequently tormented by visions of gorgeous women: 'Another woman – young and marvellously beautiful. At first he takes her to be Ammoniara. But she is taller, blond as honey, very plump, with paint upon her cheeks and roses upon her head. [...] her fleshy lips are sanguinolent; and her somewhat heavy eyelids are so drowned in languor that one would almost take her to be blind' [TSA:174].

But prostitution was an acknowledged part of middle-class male life in mid-nineteenth-century France, and it clearly offered a solution to a highly sexualized man who did not want to cohabit. Flaubert soon came to love every aspect of it. As a youth, Alfred le Poittevin had encouraged him to visit the brothels on Rouen's rue du Platre and rue du Cigogne, and prostitutes were a regular feature of his stays in Paris. Louise received a prose-poem on the pleasures they offered:

> It is perhaps a perverse taste, but I like prostitution – and for its own sake, independently of what lies underneath. My heart has never failed to pound at the sight of one of those provocatively dressed women walking in the rain under the gas lamps, just as the sight of monks in their robes and knotted girdles touches some ascetic, hidden corner of my soul. Prostitution is a meeting-point of so many elements – lechery, frustration, total lack of any human relation, physical frenzy, the clink of gold – that a glance into its depths makes one giddy and teaches one all manner of things. [...]
>
> Yes, that man has missed something who has never awakened in an anonymous bed beside a face he will never see again, and who has never left a brothel at sunrise feeling like throwing himself in the river out of pure disgust for life. [FL:I:186–7]

The Middle East also offered the prospect of sex with boys: 'Here', he wrote to Bouilhet, 'it is quite accepted [...] You reserve the bath for yourself (five francs including masseurs, pipe, coffee, sheet and towel) and you skewer your lad in one of the rooms' [FE:84]. Initially no opportunity presented itself, but six months later Flaubert could write to Bouilhet: 'you ask me if I consummated that business at the baths.

Yes – and on a pockmarked young rascal wearing a white turban. It made me laugh, that's all. But I'll be at it again. To be done well, an experiment must be repeated' [FE:203–4].

The social status of prostitution in post-war Britain was entirely different, and using prostitutes was unthinkable to someone of Larkin's fastidiousness, guarded respectability, and timidity.[17] Accordingly, masturbation (and later pornography) played a much larger role in his life than it did in Flaubert's. The youthful Larkin felt onanism had several advantages: 'Sex is too good to share with anyone else' [M:119]; 'Re sexual intercourse: always disappointing and often repulsive, like asking someone else to blow your own nose for you' [M:119]. In addition, masturbation was free, quick, and left time for yourself: 'I don't, I *don't* want to take a girl out and spend *circa £5* when I can toss off in five minutes, free, and have the rest of the evening to myself' [M:62]. And it summoned up the sexual pleasure of women without the trouble that came with them: 'pocking Miss Jane Exall wouldn't be nearly so nice in reality as it is in my imagination WHEN I'M TOSSING MYSELF [...] It seems to me that while pocking Miss Jane Exall is infinitely desirable, preparing Miss Jane Exall to be pocked and dealing with Miss Jane Exall after pocking is not at all desirable – and that pocks do not exist in the void' [SL:135–6].

Larkin's fantasies also took a literary form. While at Oxford in 1943, he conjured up an entirely feminine world and wrote five works under the name of Brunette Coleman: two vaguely lesbian novellas (*Trouble at Willow Gables*, and *Michaelmas Term at St Brides*), a fragment of autobiography ('Ante Meridian'), a collection of poetry (*Sugar and Spice*), and an essay giving advice on how to write schoolgirl fiction ('What Are We Writing For?'). His interest in imaginary women continued after university: first in *Jill*, a novel about a man who fantasizes about a fictional woman; next in *A Girl in Winter*, a novel about the experiences of a foreign girl in England; and finally in an unfinished lesbian story entitled 'The Sauvage Victory' [SL:124, 126].

Like many fantasists, Larkin found his early experiences with real girls less than satisfactory, and a particular source of complaint was the money expended without any tangible result: 'Don't you think it's ABSOLUTELY SHAMEFUL that men have to pay for women without BEING ALLOWED TO SHAG the women afterwards AS A MATTER Of COURSE? I do: simply DISGUSTING. It makes me ANGRY. Everything about the re-lay-shun-ship between men and women makes me *angry*. It's all a fucking balls up. It might have been planned by the army, or the Ministry of Food' [M:143].

These problems, he mused, could be solved by putting sexual relations on a sound financial footing, and he spent some time hankering after exactly the kind of relationships Flaubert repeatedly enjoyed. Better than either marriage or unsatisfactory socializing was '[a] lonely bachelorhood [of] buggery and strictly monetary fornication [...]' [SL:63]; or the more settled arrangement he suggested to Jean Hartley: 'Sex is so difficult. You ought to be able to pay for it monthly like the laundry bill' [M.267]. 'Strictly monetary fornication' had a further advantage: it could not only be taken up at will, it could be ended at will. Apropos Winifred Arnott, recipient of the lovely 'Latest Face', he scrawls in a notebook: 'Not love you? Dear, I'd pay ten quid for you: / Five down, and five when I get rid of you' [M:237]. Much of this anger and despair is simply a young man reflecting bitterly on his lack of success, but even in his fifties, having enjoyed several long-term relationships with women, the sight of investment statements brings the thought of all the sex he might still have:

> Quarterly, is it, money reproaches me:
> 'Why do you let me lie here wastefully?
> I am all you never had of goods and sex.
> You could get them still by writing a few cheques.' [CP:198]

XI

Dreaming of women led to imagining the feelings of women, and this led to imagining being a woman. Early on, this is largely motivated by envisaging the thrill of being beautiful: 'I would like to have been a woman for the sake of her beauty,' writes the young narrator in Flaubert's early autobiographical novel, *November*, 'to be able to admire myself, strip myself naked, let my hair fall down to my heels and gaze on my reflections in the streams' [N:25]. Later on, this expanded into an interest in young women's psychologies. He devoted many hours to imagining the reveries of the adolescent Emma Bovary: 'For two days now I have been trying to enter into the dreams of young girls, and for this have been navigating in the milky oceans of books about castles, and troubadours in white-plumed velvet hats' [FL:I:156]; and when he read the ten volumes of George Sand's autobiography, he particularly relished the chapters about her early convent education [W:272–3].

As the years passed, Flaubert's interest took on a darker hue. Reflecting on the likely effects of *Madame Bovary*, he emphasizes how well he understands the fate of constrained and unhappy women: 'If my book is any good, it will gently tickle many a feminine wound. One or two will smile when they recognize themselves. I will have known your sufferings, poor obscure souls, damp from your stifled sorrows, like your provincial back yards, where the moss grows on the walls' [W:230]. In spite of the novel's satirical intent, some women felt that Flaubert had indeed analysed the female psyche with unerring skill. Mademoiselle Leroyer de Chantepie, for example, wrote Flaubert an early fan letter:

> How I understood the sadness, the boredom and the sufferings of that poor lady [...]. From the beginning I recognized her and loved her as though she were a friend. I so identified with her experiences that it was just as though she was me. [...] Where have you acquired your perfect knowledge of human nature [...]? [W:230]

This sympathy with disappointed feminine lives is even clearer in 'A Simple Heart', but here the story follows Flaubert's protagonist into neglected old age. Written late in his career, and partly influenced by the advice and example of Sand (who did not live to see it published), he was keen to emphasize that the story was not written in a satirical spirit:

> [It] is quite simply the tale of the obscure life of a poor country girl, devout but not given to mysticism, devoted in a quiet sober way and soft as newly baked bread. One after another she loves a man, her mistress's children, a nephew, an old man she nurses, then her parrot; when the parrot dies she has him stuffed, and when she is on her deathbed she takes the parrot for the Holy Ghost. It is in no way ironic (though you might suppose it to be so) but on the contrary very serious and very sad. I want to move my readers to pity, I want to make sensitive souls weep, being one myself. [TT:xx]

The youthful Larkin was even more interested than the young Flaubert in schoolgirls and their fantasies, and the idea of being beautiful was certainly part of the attraction. Brunette Coleman is described as '[very tall] [...] and beautifully dressed' [TWG:229] and there are moments in her writings when Larkin imagines what it is like to be beautiful in the way that a girl is beautiful: '"Oh!" Myfanwy's gentle soul was quite overwhelmed at the prospect of her own slim brown legs in silken underwear' [TWG:32]; 'She was rather surprised to find herself quite naked, and [...] she remained standing before the mirror for a few moments, studying the lissom lines of her body. Clasping her hands behind her back, she stood on tiptoe, arching herself prettily, and cocking an inquiring eye into the mirror. Yes, she reflected with an unfamiliar thrill of satisfaction, I really am *quite* beautiful' [TWG:80].

The desire to be a girl can still be found in *The North Ship* published in 1944, particularly in the poem 'I see a girl dragged by the wrists'. But here it is less the girl's beauty than her impulsiveness, playfulness and delighted surrender that make him long to be her, although fulfilling this desire is now acknowledged to be beyond possibility:

> I see a girl dragged by the wrists
> Across a dazzling field of snow,
> ....
> [...] snow smudged in her hair
> As she laughs and struggles, and pretends to fight;
> ....
> So I walk on. Perhaps what I desired
> - That long and sickly hope, someday to be
> As she is – gave a flicker and expired; [...]
> ....
> To be that girl! – but that's impossible. [CP:278–9]

Gradually, even the memory of wanting to be a girl fades. Much of Larkin's work in the forties and fifties focuses on the feelings of young women in their own right. Katherine, the protagonist of Larkin's last completed novel, *A Girl in Winter*, is treated with intense seriousness and sympathy, and several poems in *The Less Deceived* – 'Wedding-Wind' and 'Deceptions', for example – depict the extremes of young women's emotions. But from the time of *The Whitsun Weddings* onwards, many of his most moving poems focus on the plight of older women: 'Reference Back', 'Love Songs in Age', 'Faith Healing', and 'Heads in the Women's Ward'.

Throughout their careers, both writers were more than prepared to acknowledge that their personalities possessed highly developed feminine elements. Flaubert enjoyed playing the role of a housewife as he walked through the fair at Rouen with Louis Bouilhet [B:533]; he famously admitted that 'Madame Bovary, c'est moi, d'après moi' ['Madame Bovary is myself – drawn from life'] [FL:I:234]; and writing to Sand in the 1870s, he says: 'Dr Hardy [...] calls me "a hysterical old woman" – an observation I find profound' [FL:II:212]. Larkin too acknowledged that he contained a 'female side' [SL:550], and that a 'passionately-sentimental spinster [...] lurks within me' [SL:199].

XII

Of course, Flaubert and Larkin enjoyed longer-term relationships with women: Flaubert with Louise Colet and Juliet Herbert; Larkin with Monica Jones, Maeve Brennan and – more briefly – his secretary, Betty Mackereth. But in all cases, both authors went to considerable lengths to prevent the formation of a conventional household, and frequently used similar means to achieve it.

Both writers undoubtedly loved their mothers: Larkin felt he might have a mother complex [M:204], while Flaubert, immediately after his mother's death, wrote: 'I have realized that my poor dear mother was the person I loved most. It feels as though a piece of my guts [has] been ripped out' [W:321]. But the needs of a widowed mother often provided a convenient excuse for holding other women at bay.[18]

Sometimes Flaubert used his mother's emotional state to prevent him from visiting Louise: 'My mother needs me, [her] sufferings impose an endless unimaginable tyranny on me [...]. I'm as weak as a little child and I give in because I don't like reproaches and plaintive sighs' [W:115]. Sometimes the alleged *froideur* of his mother's personality was used as a way of stopping Louise visiting him: 'No doubt my mother would have been perfectly affable had you happened to meet in one way or another, but as for being flattered to meet you (and don't take this for a gratuitous brutality), I must tell you that she is flattered by nothing whatever' [S:268].

Because Eva Larkin did not live with her son, Larkin occasionally had to make more elaborate manoeuvres. When Monica's parents died, and there was some thought that she might move in with him, he began an affair with Maeve Brennan [M:287], and this affair was renewed when Larkin's own mother had to go into a home [M:413]. When it looked as if Maeve herself might become more demanding, Larkin began an affair with Betty [M:451]. Only in his sixties, when he realized that in all probability his creative life was ending, did he consent to cohabitation with Monica.

These manoeuvrings placed a considerable strain on all the girlfriends, and both writers were frequently accused – with justification – of being thoughtless, selfish and self-serving. This involved the writing of many long explanatory letters intended to dissipate hurt feelings.

Flaubert is usually implacable and unpersuadable. After his affair with Louise restarted, he wrote:

> Poor child! will you then never understand that things are as I declared them to be? You accuse me of being mean or at least egotistical, inconsiderate of others, loving only myself. But in that respect I am no worse than others, and I would even say less a sinner than most if praising oneself were allowed. You will, I'm sure, give me credit for being straightforward. [...] You should not have fallen for a man like me, worn by the excess of solitude, with nerves as delicately strung as a swooning woman's, harried by supposed passions, full of doubt. I love you as best I can; badly, not enough, I know – my God do I know it! Whose fault is that! [B:278]

Larkin is less sure of himself: more apologetic, introspective and agonized. He writes to Monica:

> I never know what you think about me – whether you think I'm loving or selfish – indifferent or what, or whether I just 'use' you, or if you think it's all rather unsatisfactory but better than nothing – I know you are always very delicate in not blaming me for the way I seem to leave you to yourself for years and years, apparently content with seeing you about once a month, and of course I'm grateful [...] and remorse[ful] for the sort of stalemate I have brought into your life – and mine! [M:339]

In many ways, Larkin and Flaubert preferred to conduct their relationships by post, and grew to love the postman for this reason. Flaubert wrote to Louise: 'I was waiting for the postman on the quay, looking unconcerned and smoking my pipe. I love that postman!' [FL: I:78]. While in a poem about writing letters to women, Larkin admitted: 'I know / None better, / The eyelessness of days without a letter' [CP:69].

XIII

I hope it is now possible to see two things. First, how a shared attitude to art led both writers to acquire a similar outlook and manner of life. Second, why Larkin found Flaubert's life so fascinating. I imagine he first read Steegmuller's biography, and some of Flaubert's writings, with dawning recognition: this was how he thought about art, this was how he thought about work, this was what he thought about politics, this was what he thought about women and marriage. In short, these were his problems and his preferred solutions. And later, it is not inconceivable that he allowed some recollection of Flaubert's life to serve as a guide and template for his own.

Notes

1. The first British edition of Steegmuller's *Flaubert and Madame Bovary* was issued by R. Hale in London in 1939, but for some reason it was published under the pseudonym 'Byron Steel'. I assume, therefore, that Larkin is talking about the new edition issued under Steegmuller's own name in 1947. This is also closer in date to the first edition of *The Selected Letters of Gustave Flaubert*, edited by Steegmuller, and published by Farrar, Straus and Young in New York in 1953. Again, it seems more likely that Larkin saw the British version published by Hamish Hamilton in 1954. The earliest reference to Flaubert I have been able to find in Larkin's writings is from late June, 1951 [LM:46].
2. Larkin may have been struck by some more detailed parallels. Louise Colet was a married French poet whose long-term partner was the philosopher Victor Cousin.
3. Gautier's continuing influence on Larkin can be seen by the fact that 'Sympathy in White Major', written in 1967, echoes the title of Gautier's 'Symphonie en blanc majeure'. On this relationship see [PITT:230–57].
4. For a detailed account of Larkin's knowledge of French and French poetry see Graham Chesters' articles: 'Larkin and Baudelaire's Damned Women', 'Tireless Play: Speculations on Larkin's "Absences"', and 'Larkin's Books: Sidelining French Literature' [MC:81–92; CT:47–59; FSB:LX,100,2006:72–5].
5. Larkin's aestheticization of Lawrence is pointed out by Edna Longley in 'Larkin, Decadence and the Lyric Poem' [NLO:30]. I have found the whole article [NLO:29–50] very helpful.
6. Amongst *fin-de-siècle* Irish writers, the influence of George Moore and Yeats should also be taken into account.
7. Julian Barnes disputes the idea that the theatrical element in Flaubert was important; see [STD:244–5].
8. The shorter 'St Julian Hospitator' and 'Herodias' have retained a non-specialist readership, but they have never been as popular as 'A Simple Heart'.
9. In respect of essays three and four, it's worth pointing out that Flaubert did not own the house he lived in, and had imbibed a healthy respect for the supernatural from his nurse Julie [TT:xv].
10. Perhaps the contrast between their rage and consciousness of creative power, together with their sense of morbid vulnerability, is represented by their emblematic choice of animals. On the one hand there were large and powerful mammals. Larkin was fond of Guy the Gorilla [LM:244] and kept a photograph in his office; Flaubert liked to think of himself as a bear, considered buying a picture of a bear, and often lay on his bearskin rug to read and write [FL:I:132]. On the other hand, both characterized themselves as tiny, cold, slithery, vulnerable creatures. Flaubert said he lived 'the life of an oyster' [W:29], and '[like] a snail afraid of touching something unclean on the sand or of being crushed underfoot, I retreat into my shell' [FL:I:148]. Larkin frequently suffered from the 'trodden worm' feeling [LM:307], and likened his inner self to a snail or a sea-anemone: 'Once more / Uncontradicting solitude / Supports me on its giant palm; / And like a sea-anemone / Or simple snail, there cautiously / Unfolds, emerges, what I am' [CP:56–7].

Once, while writing of Béranger to Louise, Flaubert explicitly said that he liked 'geniuses who are a little less agreeable to the touch' [S:108], and it is significant that he and Larkin both chose the toad as a symbol of their public personae. Both described themselves as old toads [SL:496,588; STD:212], and both kept ornamental toads on their desks.

11. A sedentary life devoted to art, and punctuated by depression and rage, was not conducive to health. Already tall and prematurely bald, Flaubert's and Larkin's manner of living increased their physical similarity. Both ate, smoked and drank immoderately, and despite enjoying exercise when young (Flaubert as a walker, Larkin as a cyclist) shunned it in later years. In consequence, they became seriously unfit and overweight; aged unusually quickly (in their fifties they both write like men twenty years older); and died comparatively young of conditions associated with their lifestyle.
12. The ruthlessness, individualism, honesty and willingness to give offence we find in the writers' letters may well be qualities of mind which helped make them great artists. Most men would not be prepared to admit, let alone commit to paper, the fact that they admire ancient slavery, or find their mothers snivelling pests, or dislike children, want to be women, bugger boys, whip schoolgirls, masturbate, napalm their enemies' offices and machine-gun the sprinting torches, prefer the smell of lemon-groves to be tinged with that of rotting corpses, and love every aspect of prostitution. But the ability to recognize exactly what you feel rather than what you ought to feel, and the courage to admit it, are surely virtues – possibly even necessary virtues – in an artist.
13. Trilling, of course, uses 'liberal' in the American sense of 'socialist'.
14. Given so few words, I intend my argument to be stimulating rather than watertight, but one obvious objection needs to be answered. I have outlined an entirely general and a-historical argument intended to suggest that literature cannot take account of one of socialism's most powerful arguments. Why therefore do we find a predominance of right-wing opinions amongst the greatest European writers only in the late nineteenth and twentieth centuries? How can we explain the social consciences of the greatest English writers of the late eighteenth and early nineteenth centuries: Wordsworth and Coleridge (during their most creative periods), for example?

The rise of Modernism might provide some explanation. The eighteenth century was quite happy for literature to contain abstract statements, and encouraged the idea that it should be general in content and further moral improvement. After the 1810s, and starting in France, we find critical writings spreading the idea that literature should show not state, that it should dramatize not generalize, that it should present particular images not abstractions, and it should have no moral purpose whatever. Hazlitt's account of literature in his essay on *Coriolanus* mentions no moral purposes, and is concerned only with the way it presents concrete incidents and characters. His account of literature therefore fits Modernist literature better than the literature of his own time; and his argument seems truer now than when he wrote it. However, one can see signs of the Modernist sensibility, especially its emphasis on minute particulars, in Coleridge and Dorothy Wordsworth (amongst others), and Hazlitt may be sensing this change of direction early.

15. This is a particular case of the subjective/objective problem articulated by Thomas Nagel: how can I make sense of the world *sub specie aeternitatis, and* make sense of the world from my lived perspective? The truths (or 'truths') available from both viewpoints may not be compatible or reconcilable. The same problem is touched on in the tension between the two ways of describing the world – the indexical and the scientific – discussed in the first essay of this book. See Nagel's article 'Subjective and Objective' [MQ:197–213].
16. Anthony and Ann Thwaite have pointed out to me – in conversation – that Larkin's unkind remarks about children were part of a gloomy *performance* and had little correspondence with reality. Larkin stayed with their family many times, made a great fuss of their children, and clearly loved playing with them.
17. Larkin tries to work out an answer to his sexual difficulties in 'Round Another Point' [TWG:485–97], especially pages 487–92.
18. There are certain structural similarities between the two writers' families. Their fathers were considerable local figures: expert administrators who were a little too self-determined, free-thinking and uncompromising to make their way in the capital, and who were still formidable and sardonic at home. Their sons learnt a great deal from their book collections, and both fathers died in their early sixties when their literary sons were in their mid-twenties. Along with an older sibling – with whom they felt they had little in common – these sons had to look after their widowed mothers who were nervous, inclined to migraines, and lived well into old age. Thus, for most of their adult lives, the two writers' immediate families consisted of a widowed mother, a distant older sibling, and a niece of whom they were fond.

Livings

I

I deal with farmers, things like dips and feed.
Every third month I book myself in at
The ------ Hotel in ---- ton for three days.
The boots carries my lean old leather case
Up to a single, where I hang my hat.
One beer, and then 'the dinner', at which I read
The ---- *shire Times* from soup to stewed pears.
Births, deaths. For Sale. Police Court. Motor Spares.

Afterwards, whisky in the Smoke Room: Clough,
Margetts, the Captain, Doctor Watterson;
Who makes ends meet, who's taking the knock,
Government tariffs, wages, price of stock.
Smoke hangs under the light. The pictures on
The walls are comic – hunting, the trenches, stuff
Nobody minds or notices. A sound
Of dominoes from the Bar. I stand a round.

Later, the square is empty: a big sky
Drains down the estuary like the bed
Of a gold river, and the Customs House
Still has its office lit. I drowse
Between ex-Army sheets, wondering why
I think it's worth while coming. Father's dead:
He used to, but the business now is mine.
It's time for change, in nineteen twenty-nine.

16 October 1971

II

Seventy feet down
The sea explodes upwards,
Relapsing, to slaver
Off landing-stage steps –
Running suds, rejoice!

Rocks writhe back to sight.
Mussels, limpets,
Husband their tenacity
In the freezing slither-
Creatures, I cherish you!

By day, sky builds
Grape-dark over the salt
Unsown stirring fields.
Radio rubs its legs,
Telling me of elsewhere:

Barometers falling,
Ports wind-shuttered,
Fleets pent like hounds,
Fires in humped inns
Kippering sea-pictures –

Keep it all off!
By night, snow swerves
(O loose moth world!)
Through the stare travelling
Leather-black waters.

Guarded by brilliance
I set plate and spoon,
And after, divining-cards.
Lit shelved liners
Grope like mad worlds westward.

23 November 1971

III

Tonight we dine without the Master
(Nocturnal vapours do not please);
The port goes round so much the faster,
Topics are raised with no less ease –
Which advowson looks the fairest,
What the wood from Snape will fetch,
Names for *pudendum mulieris*,
Why is Judas like Jack Ketch?

The candleflames grow thin, then broaden:
Our butler Starveling piles the logs
And sets behind the screen a jordan
(Quicker than going to the bogs).
The wine heats temper and complexion:
Oath-enforced assertions fly
On rheumy fevers, resurrection,
Regicide and rabbit pie.

The fields around are cold and muddy,
The cobbled streets close by are still,
A sizar shivers at his study,
The kitchen cat has made a kill;
The bells discuss the hour's gradations,
Dusty shelves hold prayers and proofs:
Above, Chaldean constellations
Sparkle over crowded roofs.

Philip Larkin, 10 December 1971

III
'Livings': Aesthetic Intimations

With the possible exception of 'Sympathy in White Major', 'Livings' is the poem in *High Windows* which has caused commentators most difficulty [CP:186–8]. Each individual part[1] has its problems. Clive James, for example, writing of the second, says: 'The narrator's situation is not made perfectly clear. While wanting to be the reverse, Larkin can on occasion be a difficult poet, and here, I think, is a case of over-refinement leading to obscurity' [EN:6/1974:68]. However, the most significant difficulty is how the three parts relate to one another. Larkin himself thinks that they have very little in common, and that the sequence was terminated rather than completed: 'I thought I was going to write a sequence of lives, or livings, little vignettes, but it petered out after three. They haven't got any connection with one another, or meaning, but are supposed to be exciting in their separate ways' [SL:653].

Many critics are puzzled not only by the apparent lack of unity or meaning, but also by the absence of the poet from his poem. In one of the first books on Larkin, Simon Petch writes that '[it] is virtually impossible to locate the poet in 'Livings,' the longest and most disparate poem in *High Windows*. [...] [The] speakers of the three parts of this poem may be implicitly commenting on each other, but the objection remains that it leaves us with three poems under a single title. As a whole it is elusive; and elusiveness is rarely this poet's most successful mode' [APL:104]. And nearly twenty-five years later, Richard Bradford, in his biography of Larkin, is still puzzled by exactly the same issues: '[Larkin] produced for *High Windows* a sequence of pictures which are versatile in their avoidance of matters connected directly with their author. [...] 'Livings' is intriguing in that it is comprised of three sections with no apparent thematic or tonal continuities, unless one regards them as demonstrations of the different ways in which a writer can remain aloof from his text' [FBTF:230].

With these obscurities unresolved, of course, the overall purpose and hence success of the poem remains in doubt. Accordingly, the purpose of this essay is to clarify each section (sometimes by looking at its origins); to show how the three parts relate to one another; to suggest a meaning for the poem; to say why 'Livings' should be thought of as a complete work of art; and finally to say something about how it reflects some of Larkin's deepest concerns – freedom, aesthetic experience, dwelling and sexuality.

I

In the late-sixties and seventies, Larkin would sometimes revisit and rework poems he had abandoned in the forties and fifties. Characteristically, he would seek to preserve the aesthetic pressure of the earlier work (he sometimes worried he felt this less intensely in later life) but give the poems greater point and impact by removing all traces of the vague and the arty.

This process occurred with the poem which became 'Livings I'. There were two immediate sources of inspiration. The first was a speech by Saville Bradbury at Pembroke College, Oxford in February 1971. This included the remark, 'I deal with farmers, things like dips and feed.' Larkin turned to a friend and said 'That would make a good first line of a poem' [M:415]. The second source was a holiday spent with his mother at King's Lynn six months later; this, he told Barbara Everett, was the origin of the poem's setting [MW:134]. But we can also see that Larkin allowed both place and line to mingle fruitfully with a poem he had abandoned unfinished nearly twenty years before:

Negative Indicative

Never to walk from the station's lamps and laurels
Carrying my father's lean old leather case
Crumbling like the register at the hotel;
Never to be shown upstairs

To a plain room smelling of soap, a towel
Neatly hung on the back of a rush chair,
The floor uneven, the grate choked with a frill,
Muslin curtains hiding the market square;

Never to meet the lame girl who lives three doors
Down Meeting-House Lane – 'This pile is ready; these
I shall finish tonight, with luck' – to watch, as she pours
Tea from a gold-lined jubilee pot, her eyes,

Her intelligent face; never, walking away
As light fails, to notice the first star
Pulsing alone in a long shell-coloured sky,
And remember the year has turned, and feel the air

Alive with the emblematic sound of water –[2]

28 December 1953 [Unfinished] [CP:79]

There are clearly close similarities between the contents of the two poems: a square, visiting a hotel, carrying a case, looking at a beautifully described sky as evening turns to night, a first hint of optimism – a feeling that something has changed or will change for the better. There is also a similarity in the way the poems are narrated: both are concerned with places and scenes where Larkin is not, and both are concerned to show these scenes are in the past.

However, 'Livings I' represents a considerable advance on the earlier poem. 'Negative Indicative' suffers from three main ambiguities. First, the use of 'never' seems to imply that it is not Larkin himself, but someone known to Larkin, who has stayed in the hotel, visited the lame girl etc., and that he himself is never going to. But the loving particularity of the perceptual detail appears to suggest that he *has* stayed at the hotel and so forth, but that now he is never going to go there *again*. Second, it is not at all clear how Larkin feels about the scenes and events he describes. Is he bored by the routine he sketches, and is he thus glad to get away (as the last line would seem to imply)? Or does he feel some nostalgia for the girl with her intelligent face and gold-lined teapot as, once again, the loving detail of the description would seem to imply? Third, what exactly has happened to prevent Larkin returning to this scene? Is it just the passing of time or has something more significant occurred? The poem seems to give no hint at all. These three ambiguities raise a question about the aim of the poem – what point is he trying to make about these things he will never do? – and may well simultaneously provide an answer as to why he abandoned it.

'Livings I' solves many of these problems: the speaker and his situation are utterly clear-cut and cause the reader no puzzlement. Here, the personal distance and sense of the past are achieved by creating a character, a small businessman, who is not Larkin, and who is set firmly in a dateable historical period.[3] How he feels about the scene described in the hotel is equally clear. The helpful and intelligent girl from the earlier poem has disappeared and been replaced initially by solitary reading and then by a group of men whose conversation is stale and predictable:

> One beer, and then 'the dinner', at which I read
> The ----*shire Times* from soup to stewed pears.
> Births, deaths. For sale. Police court. Motor spares.
>
> Afterwards, whisky in the Smoke Room: Clough,
> Margetts, the Captain, Dr Watterson;
> Who makes ends meet, who's taking the knock,
> Government tariffs, wages, price of stock.

The names and setting give us a fourth source for the poem: a group of men Larkin remembered from wartime Warwick. He described them at the time to Kingsley Amis:

> About the only place I haven't described to you is the Crown Hotel, a 'family' hotel with quite a pleasant public bar. It is the regular customers that interest me, well-to-do business and local government people, and doctors, with their wives. My public enemy number one is a captain with a silly pock-marked face and a cockney accent. [...] [He] makes the most *absurd* remarks. [...]
>
> ([John] Margetts [the auctioneer] is used to not understanding what people say. He is a huge man in red velvet waistcoat, and breeches, and his hair is cut very short. He wears a habitual expression of fierce, insolent non-comprehension. He looks at the captain with a crafty, puzzled grin.) [SL:76]

The loving aesthetic particularities of 'Negative Indicative' disappear with the girl, and are replaced by mentioning *types* or *kinds* of object that are of no interest to the regulars:

> Smoke hangs under the light. The pictures on
> The wall are comic – hunting, the trenches, stuff
> Nobody minds or notices. A sound
> Of dominoes from the Bar.

The commonplace usualness of these men and their context ensure that the last stanza about the sky has significance. In 'Negative Indicative' the description of the sky uses exactly the same kind of observant detail as that of the girl, and the sky is mentioned as being just one more thing not to be seen again. But in 'Livings I' there is a palpable sense of relief as the small businessman escapes from the company; a carefully observed description of a beautiful sunset replaces the commonplaces of the Smoke Room; and fresh air and a broad vista of nature take the place of stuffiness and confinement. We can have no doubt it is this experience which makes the narrator feel, while drowsing between ex-Army sheets, 'It's time for change.'

The hint of optimism at the end of 'Negative Indicative' is caused by the turn of the year and the feeling that the air is '[alive] with the emblematic sounds of water'. Again, this is rather arty and opaque. It is hard to imagine that Larkin really sees or hears water, so the water must be purely emblematic or symbolic, and it is also not obvious how the turn of the year will improve or at least change the scenes he has described. Is it just the arrival of spring? In 'Livings I', nature still has a symbolic value, but this time the sunset is something the businessman really sees, and we can understand exactly how his decision will change his circumstances: these regular visits will end.

One feature found in 'Livings I' which is not found in 'Negative Indicative' is the use of blanks. The device is puzzling as Larkin uses it nowhere else. Why does he write 'The ------ Hotel in ----ton for three days', and 'I read / The -----*shire Times*'?[4] Petch suggests that the blanks are designed to imply the poem could be set anywhere [APL:103], but this does not consort easily with the names (Clough, Margetts, Dr Watterson), the very specific geographical details (the estuary, the Customs House), and the precise date (nineteen twenty-nine).

I think it far more likely that, as in 'Livings III', Larkin is using a certain kind of style to suggest a certain kind of sensibility and period. The use of blanks is hardly characteristic of writing during and after the First World War. But it is typical of Victorian and Edwardian prose, particularly that found in middle-brow mystery stories and thrillers where the author pretends to be protecting his sources. Bulwer Lytton (*The Coming Race*, 'The Haunted and the Haunters') and Conan Doyle (*Tales of Terror and Mystery*), for example, use the device extensively. In nineteen twenty-nine the use of blanks would suggest the poem is narrated by an older man brought up on this kind of literature; and their use, although apparently middle-brow and prosy, is one of Larkin's most inspired and evocative touches.

A clue contained in 'Negative Indicative' confirms this idea of an older man, and perhaps hints at a more precise age and character for the narrator. Both this poem and 'Livings I' are haunted by the presence of absent fathers. In 'Negative Indicative', this is shown by the narrator's use of the phrase 'my father's lean old leather case'. Does the narrator's use of it show that his father is dead? Is there some implication that the father used it on just such occasions as this, and therefore laid down a pattern for his son? These unclarities are characteristically resolved by 'Livings I' which moves the scene a generation back: 'The boots carries my lean old leather case / Up to a single', and 'Father's dead: / He used to [come], but the business now is mine'. One can't help feeling that the same 'lean old leather case' is being referred to. Is the narrator of 'Livings I' therefore not only someone of mature years in 1929, but someone close to the age and character of Larkin's father? Always an avid reader, Sydney Larkin's sensibility was soaked in Victorian and Edwardian stories, and as he was born in 1884, this would suggest the narrator is a man of forty-four or forty-five. This would certainly be late to embark on a new career, but it would also make the change more urgent and significant.

II

In the 1940s, Larkin took on the persona of a schoolgirl and wrote a good deal of material under the pseudonym 'Brunette Coleman'. 'Livings II' appears to have its origin in a fragment of Brunette's autobiography entitled 'Ante Meridian'. Imagining being a woman, or imagining the emotions of a woman, often allowed Larkin to give full rein to his Romantic impulses, and this particular piece of writing also allowed him to replace and negate his own over-ordered childhood in the Midlands:[5]

> The real sound of the sea – or the sea that I used to hear on the Cornish coast – is thunderous, like distant explosions [...] Let the reader [...] lie, as I did, on the top of one of the cliffs, and stare down at the sea breaking against the rocks. The rocks are uneven like broken teeth, but they are all of the same foundation and give the impression of being able to endure for a thousand years. The sea gathers into a huge wave, and comes running full tilt at the shore. You imagine that nothing can withstand it – and smash! the impact seems to make the ground tremble under you. Spray flies twenty feet in the

> air, and the black rocks are submerged by a swelter of white foam; will they ever emerge? Yes, they reappear, not a bit altered, exactly as they were, ready for the next murderous assault. [TWG:235]

Both this passage and 'Livings II' are about watching from a height as waves batter rocks, and both liken the sound of the breakers to explosions. Later, there is a parallel description of a cosy inn surrounded by storm and blackness outside: 'Fires in humped inns / Kippering sea-pictures'; '[Only] the inn blazed light, where the fishermen were spending the evening in an attempt to forget the raging world outside' [TWG:237].

It is possible that Larkin came across 'Round and Round', Thom Gunn's poem about a lighthouse keeper, while reading for the *Oxford Book of Twentieth-Century English Verse*. But although Gunn touches on, as he could hardly fail to do, a number of topics also mentioned by Larkin (e.g. 'Waves [...] are beam-caught / Running below his feet, wry salt, / When, in a calm, the rocks are safe') the whole poem is so fey and whimsical that it is hard to imagine Larkin being interested, even to the extent of feeling he could do better [AL:Autumn/2004:18]. In any case, being a lighthouse keeper was a fantasy of long standing. In 1966, he wrote to Maeve Brennan: 'Oh for Christmas in a lighthouse! Wouldn't it be lovely? The boom of the sea [...] the cry of the gulls [...] the wireless. I wonder how one gets to be a lighthouse keeper?' [M:416].

The image of grape-dark clouds comes from a poem about his mother written in 1953 but never published. Here we discover that his mother hates what the keeper loves:

Mother, Summer, I

> My mother, who hates thunderstorms,
> Holds up each summer day and shakes
> It out suspiciously, lest swarms
> Of grape-dark clouds are lurking there [...] [CP:68]

Larkin's treatment of his sources and inspirations in 'Livings II' has one noticeable similarity with his treatment of sources in 'Livings I': the female element is carefully removed and smoothed over. The paragraph about Cornish breakers is supposed to be written through the consciousness of a girl; the passage about wanting to be a lighthouse keeper is written to a woman; and the image of clouds is taken from a poem about his mother. It's also worth pointing out that the aspect of Christmas he particularly disliked, as a most eloquent photograph from the mid-seventies attests, was having to spend the holiday with his mother in her house [M:illus.47]. It was this, more than anything else, which inspired the wish to be a lighthouse keeper, and the poem's final vision of rapturous male solitude.

'Livings I' makes creative use of order, routine, slackness and staleness by taking a most traditional stanza form – eight lines of iambic pentameter – and using it with deliberate imprecision. Each of the three stanzas has a different rhyme scheme (abcdbaee, abccbaee, abccabee), and the rhythmic pattern is treated with similar freedom: there are several inverted feet at the beginning of lines; and a number of lines have nine syllables (line 7 of stanza one) or eleven (line 6 of stanza two). It is striking, however, that when the narrator reaches his decision to change his life three lines from the end of stanza three, the rhythm from there until the end of the poem is exact and unimpeded.

In contrast, and appropriately, the form of 'Livings II' is remarkably free. The six five-line stanzas look neat and slight enough on the page, but perhaps the form is more ordered to the eye than the ear. The stanza-breaks frequently do not follow changes of subject matter: a new topic ('Radio rubs its legs', for example) is introduced just over halfway through stanza three, and continues through stanza four until the first line of stanza five ('Keep it all off!'). There is no rhyme-scheme and no fixed rhythm beyond maintaining two or three beats to a line. All this gives a fine sense of normal forms and categories collapsing before the onslaught of the wind and waves. There is no earlier poem quite like it in Larkin's oeuvre, but the metre of Donald Davie's *The Forests of Lithuania* may have been at the back of his mind. Reviewing that collection in late 1959, he wrote: 'All I can say is that [Davie] has devised a most telling metre – a varying two or three stress unrhymed line – in which to set out his descriptive passages and episodes' [FR:220].

To compensate for this lack of formal poetic devices, the poem makes extensive use of the more primitive and elemental features of poetry – imagery and verbal music. Metaphor is omnipresent ('Relapsing *to slaver* [...] Rocks *writhe,* [...] Mussels, limpets, / *Husband* their tenacity, [...] By day, sky *builds* [...] Radio *rubs its legs* [...]'). The weaker and more formal simile ('like hounds,' 'like mad worlds') is reserved for the human world which the keeper currently abjures. In all these images, the normal distinctions between the human, the natural and mechanical pass unnoticed as everything is smashed together and mingled by the power of the storm. Larkin also places tremendous emphasis on the sounds of his words. Sometimes this is obvious, as in the alliterations ('snow swerves') and assonances ('O loose moth world'). Sometimes it is less so: to establish a contrast between the advancing and retreating wave, for example, the second stanza contains eight long and short 'i' sounds – perhaps to suggest hissing – whereas the first contains only two.

Continuing his emphasis on the primitive, Larkin's use of apostrophizing ('Running suds, rejoice! [...] Creatures, I cherish you!') brings the poem close to a prayer or invocation. He tends to use the device in other poems about raw nature and the elemental. It occurs at the end of 'Absences', his only other poem about a rough sea ('Such attics cleared of me! Such absences!' [CP:49]); and in 'The Card-Players' ('Rain, wind and fire! The secret, bestial peace!' [CP:177]). The latter poem, like the descriptions of the inns in 'Ante Meridian' and 'Livings II', contrasts a place of fire, warmth and society, with the rain, dark and wind outside.

The one real obscurity in the poem is in its final lines: 'Lit shelved liners / Grope like mad worlds westward'.[6] Why are the liners like mad worlds? One reason might be that they are attempting to make progress in such a powerful storm. Another might be that liners, uniquely amongst ships, are the vessels which aim to give an impression of normal social life, or perhaps a luxurious enhancement of it, continuing: dinners are eaten, bridge played, people introduced, books read, dances attended and so forth. Liners make every attempt to minimize their passengers' sense of isolation, danger and the elements, and for this reason the lighthouse keeper regards them as mad: they are looking for happiness in the wrong place; they can never know the solitary ecstasy he knows.

Could the phrase 'mad worlds' have suggested the word 'Master' in the next line of the triptych, through dim recollection of Middleton's 1608 play-title, *A Mad World, My Masters*? Perhaps this also prompted the idea of setting a poem in the seventeenth century.

III

Like 'Livings II', there seems to be no direct precedent for 'Livings III' in Larkin's work, although the two terms he spent at All Souls Oxford preparing the *Oxford Book of Twentieth-Century English Verse* in 1970–1 were clearly crucial for his choice of subject matter. The setting, however, is not Oxford but Cambridge. We can tell this from the use of 'sizar' denoting a student who has to do menial duties in return for reduced fees (the word was not used in Oxford) and the reference to Snape.

There are several Snapes in England but the one intended is clearly the village between Cambridge and Aldeburgh. This had been much in the news in the late sixties and early seventies since it was the site of Benjamin Britten's concert hall, the Maltings, which burnt down in June 1969, two years after its construction, and was reopened with much publicity in June 1970 [BBAB:489–500]. Larkin completed this part of his poem in December 1971. Wood featured heavily in the news reports. The quantity of dry wood in the structure was held partially responsible for the fire, and as it was rebuilt more or less exactly (although with better fire precautions), huge quantities of seasoned wood were used in the reconstruction [BBAB:492–3].

The date of the setting is rather harder to pin down. There were sizars in Cambridge from the end of the sixteenth century to the middle of the nineteenth. Most of the other words, even the rare words, do not help much either: 'advowson' (an ecclesiastical living in the gift of a college), 'jordan,' 'bog' and 'butler', for example, are all Middle English words and could have been used well into the nineteenth century.

The best clue, and one which gives us an earliest cut-off point, is the appointment of Jack Ketch (actually christened John Ketch) to the position of executioner in 1663. He was exceptionally barbaric, and became well known through his execution of Lord Russell in 1683 and Monmouth in 1685. He died the following year. The latest cut-off date is surely the beginning of Queen Victoria's reign. This is suggested by the use of candles rather than lamps; and the expression 'rheumy fevers' is surely an anachronism by 1837. The public manners also seem too ungoverned for the second half of the nineteenth century: oath-enforced assertions may just have been allowable, but the use of a screened jordan while others are drinking at the table is surely unthinkable.

Exactly when, between the two dates of 1663 and 1837, is the most likely time this conversation could have taken place? Regicide would be most topical immediately around the trial and hanging of the regicides of Charles I in 1661, and the poem's rather extraordinary collection of topics also seems characteristic of the late seventeenth century. Firstly, there is Christianity (Judas, resurrection, prayers); secondly, there is the reference to 'constellations' and 'proofs' which suggests astronomy and maths (although the proofs could also be theological); thirdly, there is ancient astrology whose most obvious manifestation is 'Chaldean', a word which refers to the ancient Babylonian astrologers.

All of these interests are embodied in Cambridge's most famous sizar, Isaac Newton, who first came to Cambridge in 1661 (as a sub-sizar) and received his BA in 1665. Although he is now most celebrated for his epoch-making work on maths and physics (especially cosmology and optics), he wrote far more about alchemy, astrology, ancient history and Christianity; and several of his works (for example, *The Chronology of the Ancient Kingdoms Amended* and *Observations upon the Prophesies of Daniel, and the Apocalypse of St John*) discuss the Chaldeans. Someone like Newton would have known that it was the Chaldeans who first divided the hour into sixty minutes each with sixty seconds. Perhaps this is why 'the hour's gradations' put the speaker in mind of the Chaldeans two lines later.

But these considerations are hardly conclusive. There is no reason why nineteenth-century dons should not be discussing Ketch or seventeenth-century regicide. And in an era which includes the madness of George III, the gluttonous wastrel George IV, the undignified and frequently absurd William IV, and alleged designs on the throne by the appalling Ernest Augustus Duke of Cumberland, a discussion of contemporary regicide is a distinct possibility too. On the other hand, if the scene were intended to be early nineteenth century, one would expect a discussion of the life sciences, geology, royal eccentricity and excess, Catholic emancipation, Napoleon, revolution, sedition or some other central preoccupation of the day. Since *none* of these appears, the late seventeenth century seems much more likely.

However, there are also two factors which make the late seventeenth century slightly less probable. Until 1703, French claret was normally drunk after dinner. But at the end of that year, Lord Methuen's treaty with Portugal ensured that Portuguese wines were subject to a third less duty than French wines, and port began to replace claret as the standard after-dinner drink [THJ:3,2,1960:103–24].[7] This does not mean, of course, that the dons could not have drunk port at an earlier date: port was simply less common in England before 1703, not unavailable. The other reason which makes the late seventeenth century less likely – although once again the consideration is not decisive – is to do with the history of Punch and Judy shows, and this is more appropriately discussed in section XI of the next essay. But Larkin was probably not well informed about the history of either port-importing or Punch and Judy shows, and he could well have intended to describe a late seventeenth-century scene without realizing he was portraying a couple of improbabilities.

Consideration of the style Larkin adopts cannot establish the date depicted either. The style is evidently a tribute or parody, but of what exactly? No poem between the seventeenth and early nineteenth century could have quite Larkin's detailed subject matter and lack of obvious moral point, so these aspects of the poem cannot help determine the period Larkin intends to suggest. The verse-form he adopts is eight lines of iambic tetrameter with alternating feminine and masculine endings, which produces alternating nine and eight syllable lines. This is not characteristic of the Augustan or mid-eighteenth-century period (which tends to use regular iambic pentameters or tetrameters rhymed in couplets) but it could have been used in either the late seventeenth or early nineteenth century.

I have not been able to discover any example of a poem which uses exactly Larkin's metre. Herbert's 'Jordan' (not in Larkin's sense of the word) has the same four stresses in a line, and alternates masculine and feminine endings, but here the feminine endings come second:

> Who says that fictions onely and false hair
> Become a verse? Is there in truth no beautie?
> Is all good structure in a winding stair?
> May no lines passe, except they do their dutie? [OBSV:367]

It is possible to find seventeenth-century examples where the masculine ending comes first, but then the second line with the feminine ending tends to be shortened.

> Gather ye Rose-buds while ye may,
> Old Time is still a flying:
> And this same flower that smiles today,
> Tomorrow will be dying. [OBSV:308–9]

Generally, in the seventeenth century, the use of alternating endings is rare, and usually only encountered in light verse, songs and religious meditations – all of which are very remote from the tone of 'Livings III'.

Some early nineteenth-century verse resembles Larkin's. Again, I have not been able to discover any exact matches for Larkin's form and metre, but there are some close analogies in Praed – a poet Larkin admired. In his 'Confessions,' for example, we find:

> In youth, when pen and fingers first
> Coined rhymes for all who chose to seek 'em,
> Ere luring hope's gay bubbles burst,
> Or Chitty was my *vade mecum*,
> Ere years had charactered my brow
> With the deep lines, that well become it,
> Or told me that warm hearts could grow
> Cold as Mont Blanc's snow-covered summit - [WMP:235]

This has Larkin's eight lines and alternating endings, but the feminine endings occur on the even numbered lines. One of Praed's best known poems, 'Good Night to the Season', has the masculine endings on the even numbered lines, and alternating lines of nine and eight syllables, but it uses a twelve-line verse, and the rhythm is amphibraic:

> Good night to the Season! – 'Tis over!
> Gay dwellings no longer are gay;
> The courtier, the gambler, the lover,
> Are scattered like swallows away[.] [WMP:178]

However, Praed's geographical subject matter and his manner of treating it seem rather closer to Larkin than the work of any seventeenth-century poet. In Praed's collected works, for example, we find poems entitled 'Written under a Picture of King's College Chapel' [WMP:259] and 'A Discourse delivered by a College Tutor: At a Supper Party, July 1st, 1825'. This includes a sketch of dons at dinner: 'Ye halls on whose dais the don of to-day is / To feed on the beef and the benison, / Ye common room glories, where beneficed Tories / Digest their belief and their venison[.]' [WMP:144].

There remains the possibility that Larkin was influenced by later pastiches of an earlier style or a later poet writing about an earlier date. Into the first group would fall Betjeman's 'Winthrop Mackworth Redivivus' – in trimeters with alternating feminine and masculine endings [JBCP:209–11]. Into the second would fall much of Browning's work, and it is significant that when Larkin thinks of monologues by fictional characters he tends to think of Browning. Writing to Anthony Thwaite about the latter's collection of monologues, *Victorian Voices*, Larkin wrote: 'I suppose Browning must have hovered over your shoulder a good deal – trying to avoid him, glad of his example?' [SL:629]. And writing to C. B. Cox, he described 'Livings' itself as 'miniature derivatives of Browning's dramatic lyrics' [SL:453].

There is one moment in 'Livings III' which echoes a Browning poem.[8] In the second stanza of 'Soliloquy of the Spanish Cloister', the speaker reports and then fiercely parodies his enemy's tedious conversation:

> At the meal we sit together:
> *Salve tibi!* I must hear
> Wise talk of the kind of weather,
> Sort of season, time of year:
> *Not a plenteous cork-crop: scarcely*

> *Dare we hope oak-galls, I doubt:*
> *What's the Latin name for 'parsley'?*
> What's the Greek name for Swine's Snout? [RBSP:27]

If we compare this to the second half of 'Livings III''s first verse, then we can observe several parallels:

> Topics are raised with no less ease –
> Which advowson looks the fairest,
> What the wood from Snape will fetch,
> Names for *pudendum mulieris*,
> Why is Judas like Jack Ketch?

Browning's speaker, like Larkin's, is a member of an enclosed clerical community; he is eating at table with the others; typical conversational topics are raised; there is a certain amount of Latin in italics; both poems raise a question involving Latin; and both stanzas end with a question.

On the balance of probabilities, my overall conclusion is that Larkin intended to portray a late seventeenth-century scene (and I shall refer to it from now on in this way); but that he described it in what he intended to be a pastiche of an early nineteenth-century style (although there are hints of Browning in his use of a dramatic speaker).

There could be two reasons why Larkin allows the ambiguity described above. The first is that he wants to portray life in late seventeenth-century Cambridge, but, realizing that no seventeenth-century verse form offers a suitable vehicle, simply adopts a style which suggests something vaguely antique. The second is that he wants to portray a form of life which is so changeless (and possibly reactionary) as to be almost dateless. His ambiguity then allows us to imagine the scene and conversation taking place at any time between the two limiting dates.

IV

The meaning of the poem can only be discovered by considering the differences between the parts. But the easiest way to discover these differences is by trying to identify the common factors which all the sections share.

Let me begin with the obvious: all the parts are in the first person and they are all narrated by anonymous men. They all appear to belong to the middle stations of life. There is no reason for thinking them particularly old or particularly young, they do not seem especially rich or poor, and they all have jobs which suggests they belong to the middle classes. Lacking names, they seem largely defined by their careers, and it is natural to think of them as the businessman, the lighthouse keeper, and the don.

In a variety of ways, these men are detached from those around them, and this set of circumstances becomes clearer when we consider the activity in which they engage. In the course of each section, all three eat their dinners; and meals – especially dinners in our society – usually have pronounced social and personal functions.[9] Formally, they play a central role in christenings, weddings, anniversaries, leavetakings and funerals; less formally, they are part of courtship, form a focus for family life, and cement and confirm friendships.

From the personal point of view, there is something unsatisfactory about the dinner in 'Livings III'. Initially, the talk at High Table is precise, erudite, suggestive and paradoxical; it is clever but characteristically bloodless and impersonal. Later, when the fire grows hotter and the drinking begins in earnest, the dons' loud and fuddled aggression is caught by Larkin's thumping alliterations. The don narrating the poem does not discover more about his companions or further his relationships with them; and a meal where the participants fail to bond, far more than the absence of a meal, encourages feelings of detachment and alienation.

The don at least is a member of a community and dines with them. The businessman in 'Livings I' is either an adjunct to a community or passing through a community. He listens to, and possibly contributes to, discussion of a few stale and familiar topics in the Smoke Room, but he seems to drink his pre-prandial beer by himself. He certainly takes 'the dinner' alone as he reads the newspaper, but there are probably other people in the dining room to whom he does not speak. It does not seem an enlivening occasion.

It is significant that neither the businessman nor the don gets drunk with his companions. The businessman carefully measures his drink ('One beer') before taking his after-dinner whisky in the Smoke Room. And although the port has been round several times, the don, unlike several of his colleagues, does not seem the worse for wear. Nothing about the precise observation of the last verse suggests drunkenness.

The lighthouse keeper dines completely alone. Again, this meal lacks a social dimension, but the keeper embraces his solitude, and the meal prompts no dissatisfactions. He is the only narrator who is intoxicated, although he is the only one who does not drink.

Observing what the narrators notice clarifies this feeling of detachment. In 'Livings II' the narrator has no companions, but the narrators in parts I and III show remarkably little interest in the people they are talking to.[10] In his early letter about the hotel bar, Larkin said '[it] is the regular customers who interest me', and he then describes them at length [SL:76]. But in 'Livings I' the narrator barely seems to notice his fellow drinkers. We hear a good deal about the setting, the content of the newspaper, and the general topics of conversation, but the characters in the bar, although named, are not described or characterized. Again, in part III, the don pays attention to what is drunk, what is discussed, and those absent from the table (the Master, the butler, the sizar), but there is no description of his companions at all. He simply apprehends them as a hubbub of incisive voices, a blur of rubicund complexions, without even the names which give the businessman's companions separate existences (if not personalities).

The businessman and the don find their life routine-governed and confining, and during their narratives discover the possibility of a larger, more emancipated existence. For the businessman the discovery entails giving up the life he inherited from his father and striking out in a new direction on his own. For the don it means reconnecting with a larger, grander universe beyond the routines of college life. Unlike the businessman, he has as yet formulated no plans for escape. The possibility of change is in the air, the materials are to hand; nothing further.

Once again, the lighthouse keeper is different. He does not need to discover anything during the poem because he already has what the other narrators want (or are just becoming dimly conscious of wanting): an overwhelming sense of freedom; a life lived alone, in accordance with desire, and in permanent communion with elemental nature. The central panel of the triptych shows what life ought to be; the two side-panels show men beginning to realize that this should be their goal. This, surely, is the meaning of the poem[11] and a reason for the 'excitement' Larkin found in all three parts.

All the narrators may be members of the middle classes but their sense of freedom is in inverse proportion to their class status. The keeper, who has a skilled trade, enjoys the excess of it. The businessman, who theoretically has greater wealth and independence, has just become conscious of his desire. The don, whose education and profession place him in the upper reaches of the middle classes, merely feels detached from his colleagues and intensely attentive to what happens in the cold and the darkness. The higher their ranking within the class, the heavier custom lies upon them.

These hints of freedom are symbolized by the poem's settings, with their contrast between inside and outside, the artificial and the natural, light and darkness, day and night. The don begins his section by socializing in a lit public room, largely unaware of the darkened vistas beyond, but ends it by himself, contemplating the star-illuminated natural world outside.[12] The businessman begins his narrative in a similar way. He is socializing in a public room probably lit by a combination of natural and artificial illumination ('Smoke hangs under the light'), and he ends it by contemplating the sunset. The distinction between the lit interior and the darkening exterior is not so marked as in 'Livings III', but there is still a clear contrast between what is human, known, social and limited, and what is natural, mysterious, individual and unlimited.

As we might expect, 'Livings II' is different. The keeper is absorbed by the tempestuous natural world beyond from the very first, and although the change from day to night is noted, natural and artificial light play an entirely different role. During the day, sunlight illuminates both the outside world and the lantern chamber; at night, the light from the tower illuminates both the chamber and the natural world outside. At no point, therefore, does either form of light make the keeper feel cut off from the natural world; on the contrary, at least as regards sight, they are what allow him to be aware of it.

The more a narrator has to discover, the greater the contrast between the natural and the artificial, inside and outside, daylight and lamplight. In 'Livings II', the interpenetration within each pairing represents the freest possible relationship between man and nature.

All three narrators consult the sky, but the keeper's interest is distinct from that of the other two. The businessman and the don contemplate it at night or during the evening, and they have no practical reason for looking. But the lighthouse keeper watches the grape-dark clouds building up during the day, and is largely interested in them as a sign of what is to come. He is not struck or rapt, and there is no element of longing in his gaze.

This contemplation of the sky links the businessman and the don to narrators in other Larkin poems who find the night sky suggestive of alternative lives. In 'Dockery and Son', the protagonist is preoccupied with the fact that the course of our lives seems to be determined by something outside us and beyond our control. The contrast between actual constraint and imagined freedom is neatly symbolized when he notes how, at the end of the station platform, 'the ranged / Joining and parting lines reflect a strong // Unhindered moon' [CP:152]. And in 'Sad Steps', it is again the moon which prompts the ageing Larkin to recall 'the strength and pain / Of being young; that can't come again, / But is for others undiminished somewhere' [CP:169]. There is something peculiarly levelling about the appearance of the sky, moon, stars and other heavenly bodies. They can be seen by nearly all human beings in a region; they look the same to virtually every one of them; and, although their appearances vary in the short term, they do not change with our age, wealth, popularity or success. The sky is always a constant throughout and between lives, and thus suggests the (erroneous) thought that all lives, and all stages of life, are permanently open to us.

This sense of freedom, in all three parts of the poem, is heightened by the absence of the usual authority figures. In part I, the father is dead and the son can decide for himself what he wants to do; in part III, the Master is absent and no doubt the conversation is freer (if only because the dons can now say unpleasant things about the Master); in part II, the radio, which presumably sometimes gives the keeper his instructions, now only tells him 'of elsewhere'.

With freedom and the absence of authority comes risk, and the unlimited night-time world beyond the confines of a building hints at both excitement and danger. Indeed, Richard Murphy suggests that all three narrators 'seem faintly threatened in mysterious ways' [PITT:230]. The threat comes in two forms: the threat to the individual and the threat to his way of life. And its degree is directly proportional to the degree of freedom and self-knowledge the narrator has achieved: it is clandestine and mild in the case of the don, obvious and severe in the case of the lighthouse keeper.

In part I, the threat is purely to the individual: 'It's time for change', we are told, 'in nineteen twenty-nine', the implication being that, with the Great Crash about to happen, the narrator's bid for freedom will end in his ruin. The threat to the don is to his whole way of life. This kind of conversation between these kinds of people took place for nearly two hundred years, and even just prior to Victoria's reign there was no reason to suppose it would swiftly cease. But high moral seriousness and the continued advance of science quickly put an end to Fellowships of exclusively ordained bachelors, candles, the last vestiges of astrological belief, the cosy certainties of prayers and proofs, and such careless autonomy and ungoverned manners. The dons' beliefs and behaviour now belong firmly and irrecoverably to the past. The lighthouse keeper is threatened both as an individual and as a way of life. As an individual, he is threatened by the sea and the destructive power of the storm, and also, he feels, by society on shore. His very profession is also dying out because even in 1971 it was clear that lighthouse keepers would soon be replaced by automatic lights. There are now no lighthouse keepers in the British Isles.

V

The world of 'Livings I' is routine-governed and practical. The farmers' work is dictated by the seasons, and the salesman returns to the hotel every third month. It is a world where money has to be earned and saved, cars repaired, and animals dipped and fed. As relaxation from these tasks, men play dominoes, eat, drink, gossip and read the papers. It is not a milieu much given to refection or the arts. Even the one set of objects intended for aesthetic contemplation – the pictures on the wall – are ignored and reduced to a mass-term: they become 'stuff / Nobody minds or notices'. The intellectual world of the dons is larger. Although they too are concerned with their own affairs (advowsons, the wood from Snape) there is also room for disinterested curiosity and cleverness – political and religious debate, esoteric information, smut and riddles. But their lives are even more governed by rules and routines than the people in the bar, and aesthetic contemplation cannot easily coexist with heated complexions and oath-enforced assertions.

When taken to extremes, the practical point of view can be profoundly limiting. If you only see objects and people as items for some purpose, means to an end, items in a category, then in a sense you cease to see them at all. The point is made, eloquently and poignantly, in Paul Auster's memoir of his father, *The Invention of Solitude*:

> Implicit in his attitude [to money] was a kind of perceptual primitivism. All distinctions were eliminated, everything was reduced to its least common denominator. Meat was meat, shoes were shoes, a pen was a pen. It did not matter that you could choose between chuck and porterhouse, that there were throwaway ball points for thirty-nine cents and fifty dollar fountain pens that would last for twenty years. The truly fine object was almost to be abhorred: it meant that you would have to pay an extravagant price, and that made it morally unsound. On a more general level, it translated itself into a permanent state of sensory deprivation; by closing his eyes to so much, he denied himself intimate contact with the shapes and textures of the world, cut himself off from the possibility of experiencing aesthetic pleasure. The world he looked at was a practical place [...] Each thing was understood only in terms of its function, judged by how much it cost, never an intrinsic object with its own

> special properties. In some way, I imagine it must have made the world seem a dull place to him. Uniform, colourless, without depth. If you see the world only in terms of money, you are finally not seeing the world at all. [TIS:57]

Similarly, if your life is entirely governed by habit and routine, then, because you no longer need to observe your surroundings carefully, you become utterly desensitized to them. The depth of his father's habits, and the blindness this entailed, are made clear in one of Auster's earlier anecdotes. His father moved to a new house. One day, through habit, he returned after work to the old house and, without noticing anything different, went into the bedroom, lay on the bed, and went to sleep. The woman who owned the house then returned and was profoundly startled to discover a strange man asleep on the bed. 'Even today,' writes Auster, 'it still makes me laugh. And yet, for all that, I cannot help regarding it as a pathetic story. It is one thing for a man to drive to his old house by mistake, but it is quite another, I think, for him not to notice that anything has changed inside it' [TIS:8].

The attitude which stands opposed to this state of 'permanent sensory deprivation' which embraces 'the shapes and textures of the world' and which disavows a world-picture that is 'uniform, colourless, and without depth', is the aesthetic attitude.[13] This is the state where we try to see something not as a means or an instance but as an end in itself. When we succeed, we see at last the quiddity of a thing, observe its thatness and suchness (to employ two Aristotelianisms), and contemplate it, disinterestedly, for its own sake. At the end of 'Livings I and III', the visions of both narrators rise to the aesthetic level, and with it come their first intimations of freedom and creativity.

Although the businessman and the don pay little attention to their companions, they are intensely alive to the details of their surroundings. The businessman does notice the pictures on the wall, the way the smoke hangs under the light, the big sky, the estuary, and the light in the Customs House. Again, in part III, the don pays attention to the way the candle flames 'grow thin, then broaden', and the details of the roofs, bells and fields outside. Clearly, both narrators become absorbed in looking at things for their own sakes. But there is an important shift in the quality of both narrators' experience in the last stanza of each section.

The diction of 'Livings I' is wonderfully slack, quotidian and well rubbed[14] ('dips and feeds', 'motor spares', 'who's taking the knock', 'stuff nobody minds', 'ex-Army sheets'), and the first two stanzas contain no images – in the sense of metaphors and similes – at all. Consequently, the first image comes as something of a shock:

> Later, the square is empty: a big sky
> Drains down the estuary like the bed
> Of a gold river [...]

The appearance of an image suggests a distinction of mind that we had not previously suspected. The image itself is also rather remarkable: it brings a touch of oriental splendour, a hint of Turner's palette, to the drab landscape of the east coast. Given that the narrator's imagination can provide such an image, we can well understand why he feels so dissatisfied with his companions.

Kant thought such figures of speech significant, because they freeze and capture a moment of what he termed the 'free play' of concepts. In such a thought-process, the mind pleasurably surrenders itself to the most remote and ludic associations of an object, and these associations simultaneously colour and imbue the object perceived. The series of likenesses is entertained or imagined rather than asserted (the businessman does not believe, for example, that the sky is literally the bed of a gold river), and a written figure of speech captures a moment of this psychological process. Kant observes that this free play is characteristic of aesthetic perception [CJ:192–3], and – because it reveals the depths of the unconscious mind – the related process of free association has long been of interest to psychoanalysis.

There is a parallel moment in 'Livings III':

> The fields around are cold and muddy,
> The cobbled streets close by are still,
> A sizar shivers at his study,
> The kitchen cat has made a kill;
> The bells discuss the hour's gradations,
> Dusty shelves hold prayers and proofs:
> Above, Chaldean constellations
> Sparkle over crowded roofs.

The first four lines are transitional. The narrator clears his mind in the cold and the darkness, and for the first time his perceptual imagination ranges beyond the college, imagining scenes that represent the greatest possible contrast to High Table. The chilling sound of the cat's attack, with its hint of the uncanny and supernatural, quickens his senses and further vivifies his imagination. His attention is now total: cold, poised and exact.

Twenty lines of the poem have passed without an image, yet now we encounter three in the last four lines. They provide us – and possibly the don – with valuable insights into his feelings, beliefs and attitudes. The first example is: 'The bells discuss the hour's gradations [...]'. A more commonplace narrator would simply be irritated by the chimes and, possibly, their lack of coordination, but the don's imagination turns the chiming into a courteous dialogue between metaphysicians. In the next image, 'Chaldean constellations', his imagination manages to embrace two pairings: the old and the new science; and the remotest regions of space and time as they were then known. 'Constellations' suggests astronomy and the most distant regions of space. 'Chaldean' suggests astrology and one of the civilizations which stands at the greatest historical distance from him. As, in the seventeenth century, the world was generally supposed to be a little less than 6,000 years old, and mankind a week or so younger, this means thinking back to the very dawn of the universe. The last image, 'crowded roofs', like 'the bells discuss', brings us close to Larkin's ideal of people without company; solitude without loneliness. And the air of great friendliness is enhanced by the verb given to the constellations. In spite of their awesome size and distance, they have a miniature Christmassy gleam: they 'sparkle'. He likes being alone; there is pleasure in the darkness.

When inside, both narrators find their aesthetic feelings frustrated. Their experiences are oddly Joycean. Both remind us of that artist manqué, Gabriel Conroy in 'The Dead', about to sit down to a noisy supper with people at once unlike him and overfamiliar: he longs for solitude, the river, the open places, and the cold outside [D:218–19].

In 'Livings II', the hints of aesthetic experience in 'Livings I and III' are extrapolated into full-blown creative ecstasy: a paean to the power of raw nature; a rapturous celebration of solitude; a rhapsody – sometimes at the very limits of sense – to darkness, magic (the divining cards) and wild air. The use of imagery is so prevalent as to suggest a descent into a more primitive animistic universe, and the keeper by his light seems to embody every emblem of the poet-magus: alone in his tower;[15] the guardian of both a mirror and a lamp;[16] at life's wild heart; his eye in a fine frenzy rolling from heaven to earth, from earth to heaven; even looking through high windows.[17]

Although calmer than Larkin's description, this moment of aesthetic ecstasy – alone by the sea, amidst wind and clouds and shellfish – is reminiscent of Stephen Dedalus's experience in the penultimate chapter of *A Portrait of the Artist as a Young Man* [POA:185]. This, of course, is the moment when Stephen's artistic vocation is revealed to him, and, as in Larkin, freedom brings the possibility of danger. It is a calling which not only requires Stephen triumphantly to create life from life, but, just as importantly, to fall into error and to fail [POA:186].

Joyce read widely in aesthetics, and in the final chapter of *A Portrait of the Artist* outlined an aesthetic theory which draws largely on St Thomas Aquinas and Kant. As Larkin had read and absorbed *A Portrait of the Artist* ([POA:269; SL:308, 511]), it is not wholly surprising that there should be affinities between Larkin's implicit understanding of aesthetics, and the aesthetic theory developed by Kant.[18]

In his *Critique of the Power of Judgment*, Kant argues that aesthetics has two goals. The first is beauty. For Kant, natural beauty stands on a higher level than works of art [CJ:179], and he gives as an example the beauty of a sunset: 'the recollection of everything agreeable in a beautiful summer day, drawn to a close, which a bright evening brings to mind [...] which arouses a multitude of sensations and supplementary representations for which no expression is found' [CJ:194]. I need hardly point out that part I of 'Livings' ends with the businessman contemplating the beauty of a sunset.

The second end of aesthetics for Kant is the sublime – the mingling of beauty and awe. This he divides into two kinds, the first of which he calls the dynamical sublime [CJ:143–8]. In this experience, we contemplate awesome power aware that it could easily bring about our own destruction. Kant attempts to explain our pleasure in it by saying that, although we realize these forces could destroy our body, we simultaneously realize that there are faculties in us which these forces cannot destroy, namely our powers of practical reason and freedom of the will. Our enjoyment of the dynamical sublime therefore is a complex mixture of pleasure and displeasure, and requires us to feel on the one hand puny and mortal, and on the other grand and immortal. He gives the following examples of events and objects whose contemplation is likely to provoke this experience: 'Bold, overhanging, as it were threatening cliffs, thunder clouds towering up into the heavens, bringing with them flashes of lightning and crashes of thunder, [...] hurricanes with the devastation they leave behind, the boundless ocean set into a rage [...]' [CJ:144]. Wind, rocks, towering clouds, the rage of the boundless ocean, are, of course, exactly what Larkin's lighthouse keeper experiences.

The second division of the sublime, Kant refers to as the mathematical sublime [CJ:134–40]. This arises when we contemplate something vast and try and take it in as a whole. Again, the enjoyment of such a spectacle is a mixture of pleasure and displeasure. On the one hand, there is the pleasure that our reason can grasp the idea of vastness, even infinity; and on the other, the displeasure that our imagination and perceptual systems are quite incapable of apprehending these things as wholes. As examples, Kant considers contemplating the Pyramids, and St Peter's in Rome [CJ:135–6]; but it is contemplation of the heavens that produces the most overwhelming experience: 'The immeasurable multitude of [the] Milky Way systems called nebulae, which presumably constitute such a system among themselves in turn, [and] does not allow us to expect any limits here' [CJ:140]. At the end of 'Livings III', Larkin's don contemplates the Chaldean constellations sparkling over his head, and his mind is elevated by the experience of mathematical sublimity.

Kant felt he had given a complete taxonomy of aesthetic ends. If he is correct, then Larkin – unconsciously, no doubt – has given a complete picture of the same aesthetic ends as well. He has also shown three different ways of *responding* to these aesthetic aspirations: becoming aware of a larger, natural world beyond one's own; actively deciding to change one's way of life in accordance with its promptings; living a life in communion with nature. These considerations go some way towards explaining why Larkin felt unable to extend 'Livings' beyond its three existent parts: as a work of art it was already finished and complete.

For Kant, the beautiful and the sublime are intimately if darkly connected with human freedom. The behaviour of human beings is not wholly determined, not wholly governed by scientific laws, because we have free will; and we have free will because we possess concepts and rational powers. These capacities allow us to judge our own behaviour by the same standards we apply to others; and to judge in this way is to judge morally. For Kant, to act morally is to act freely.

Aesthetic judgement prefigures and prepares the way for this kind of freedom. First, when you judge aesthetically, as when you judge morally, you overlook and transcend your own practical purposes [CJ:90–1]. Second, just as in moral judgement your actions implicitly legislate for all other rational beings, so your aesthetic judgements implicitly claim that all others *ought* to agree with them, even though you do not expect that they *will* agree [CJ:180]. Third, the aesthetic judgement, like the moral judgement, is a judgement about form and design, not about content [CJ:178]. Fourth, to value and take pleasure in the existence of natural objects is a sign of a good and receptive soul [CJ:180].[19]

The two kinds of sublimity have further connections with human freedom. The awe we feel in the face of the mathematical sublime is akin to the respect we feel for the moral law within, and observing the moral law is the way human beings escape from the determinate world of scientific causal law [CJ:143–8]. Similarly, as I noted above, the forces involved in the dynamical sublime can destroy the human body insofar as it can be explained by science, but they cannot touch freedom of the will or practical reasoning [CJ:131–43].[20]

At a less abstract level, the aesthetic realm hints at freedom for both Joyce and Larkin. For Joyce, the notion of the aesthetic is closely conjoined with the ideas of flight and escape from a culture which is oppressed, squalid and riddled with priests [POA:37]. For Larkin, the aesthetic offers a way of looking which outwits the force of routine, practicality and habit, and therefore holds out the possibility of change.

It offers this possibility for the following reasons. On the one hand, aesthetic contemplation seems to offer an escape from ourselves. When we look at something aesthetically, we try to suspend all thought of our normal practical projects and their resulting categories. We cease to think of who we are or where we are, and try to contemplate an object as pure knowing subjects. This gives the illusion that it is merely a contingent fact that we have this history and this embodiment, and that other embodiments and other lives are open to us.[21] Even though the possibility of being another person is an illusion, the very thought of another life is liberating and may well lead to practical change.

On the other hand, aesthetic contemplation puts us in closer contact with our real selves and desires. Although I try to suspend all thought of my history and practical projects, my real character still determines my aesthetic preferences, and my real preoccupations still determine the Kantian free play of concepts which surround them. Thus, I learn more about my real self – that which lies below the level of the conscious will – when I try to forget myself and my projects, because this is the condition in which my true feelings manifest themselves.

Consequently, aesthetic contemplation can offer two powerful incentives for change: it suggests the possibility of other lives; and it puts us in contact with our real, not our apparent, feelings.

VI

The aesthetic impulses felt by all three speakers flourish under the same conditions as Larkin's. To demonstrate this, I want to begin by looking at his odd and sometimes paradoxical attitude to property.

Unusually for a man of his status, age, income and financial sense, Larkin did not own any property until he was fifty-two. Nearly all his poetry until this point had been written in a succession of halls of residence and rented rooms and flats, often owned or connected with the institutions that employed him. The vast majority of his mature poetry had been written in his top-floor flat in Pearson Park owned by Hull University. This suited him admirably. As Andrew Motion writes:

> In the eighteen years he had lived there, his flat had been both a haven from the world and a source of many of the images which haunted his poems. Its high windows, its view of the tree-muffled park, and its romantic isolation had allowed him to feel that his life and his writing were intertwined. Furthermore, it had proclaimed him not simply as a determined bachelor but also as a kind of grown-up student, someone unencumbered by possessions, paying rent not a mortgage, free (in theory) to leave when he wanted. It was a place filled with the idea of youth, which he feared he would lose forever if he moved. [M:439]

In 1974, however, as part of a series of economy measures, the university decided to sell the house. Larkin was thrown into a panic, but eventually decided to buy 105 Newland Park.

The prospect did not cheer him. Owning a house seemed like participating in life rather than observing it; it diminished choice, it carried responsibilities, it smelt of age and death: 'The whole thing depresses me rather. Abbey National bum. Neighbours bum. Rates bum. Retirement bum. Pension bum. Emergency bum. Cause for concern bum. After a long illness bravely borne bum. In his day thought to be representative of bum. BBBuuuuuuuummmmmm ...' [SL:502].

He had trouble keeping up his two hours of writing in the evening towards the end of his time in Pearson Park, but 105 Newland Park put an end to it altogether. He would get home depressed, start to drink, cook himself something minimal, watch television, and fall asleep. Waking up later, feeling stale and hung-over, he would haul himself off to bed. Awaking early and anxious, he would then get up and write letters at six in the morning. To potential visitors, he described himself as 'not really meetable', and he asked his solicitor to draw up his will [M:442].

Larkin described the move as a 'dreadful experience' [RW:57] and several friends and acquaintances thought he was making too much of it. But it may really be the case that Larkin's poems needed the small, rented flat to sustain his writing regime, and that bourgeois house-ownership struck at the root of his creativity. His poetry certainly dried up. He gives a heavy hint as to the cause in 1982: 'Anything I say about writing poems is bound to be retrospective, because in fact I've written very little since moving into this house, or since *High Windows*, or since 1974, whichever way you like to put it' [RW:58]. And the reason is confirmed by Maeve Brennan: 'One reason he gave for his diminishing output was that he did not find the new house he had exchanged in 1974 for Pearson Park conducive to writing' [PLIK:64].

Friends were puzzled by Larkin's choice of house. They described the area as 'stiflingly bourgeois', and the house itself as 'remarkably ugly' [M:440]. With four bedrooms, it was clearly too big for him, the internal layout was unsuitable, and it had a large garden that required constant attention. It is not as if Larkin was unaware of most of these facts: 'I can't say it's the kind of dwelling that is eloquent of the nobility of the human spirit', he told Judy Egerton in February 1974 [SL:502]. And in June, just before he moved, he described it to Barbara Pym as 'an ugly [...] house [...] in a bourgeois area [... with] a vast garden *at the back*: at the side it's as near to its neighbours as a Council estate, washing and children' [SL:509].

Larkin was an efficient administrator; he had found two houses for his mother; he was sensitive to architecture; and he knew that having the correct kind of workplace was essential. It is thus something of a mystery why he decided to buy such a house, given that there are Victorian and Georgian houses and flats, of the right size and without gardens, in Hull and the surrounding area. He said that there was a shortage of suitable houses at the time [RW:57] but one suspects that he exaggerated this, just as he was later to exaggerate his difficulties with the garden, the doors, the central heating, and so forth.

My suspicion is that Larkin deliberately chose a house with which he could not identify. At some fundamental level, he knew that his poetry depended on not being at one with his surroundings, and therefore he chose a large, modern, ugly, stiflingly bourgeois house with a large garden that was too close to the neighbours. Perhaps he hoped that the house's sheer lack of poetry and atmosphere would overcome the misery of owning it. Perhaps his soul would hold itself creatively aloof from such dreary surroundings, in a way it would not remain detached from something more atmospheric and congenial. If so, the experiment failed horribly. As we would expect of someone so sensitive to his environment, the uncongeniality of the house simply made ownership worse: a depressing bourgeois house turned him into a depressed bourgeois, his writing dried up, his drinking grew worse, and he prepared himself for death.

We can see Larkin's attitude to creativity and its environment embodied in 'Livings'. In a letter, he said he hoped readers would hear the ecclesiastical sense of 'living' in the title [SL:453]. It is not immediately clear why he wanted to highlight this sense, since only the ordained fellows and the advowsons in their gift are directly concerned with it. I imagine he made the remark because this sense not only suggests work and being alive, but also a certain relationship with property. A living, in the ecclesiastical sense, typically consists of a parish, a stipend, a church and a vicarage in which to live. The place where the vicar lives is connected with his work, and no doubt a good deal of parish business and pastoral care go on within its walls. He does not own either of the buildings, they simply come with the position, and he may only hold the position for a short time.

All the speakers in 'Livings' have a similar relationship with their current dwellings. None of them is staying in a normal house or flat, and we do not know that any of them owns such a place; all of them are currently living in rented or granted rooms connected with their work. Because of his job, the businessman is staying in a hotel and using it as a place to make and affirm local contacts. The lighthouse keeper is currently living in his workplace; the don probably lives and works in college rooms. Even though all their rooms are rented or granted, there is still a powerful suggestion of stability and no sense of the random or itinerant. The businessman keeps to a precise timetable ('Every third month I book myself in [...] for three days'); the keeper is presumably on a rota; and the don lives in college all the time.

This is exactly the relationship with property that Larkin's muse required: he should not own the place he lives in, it should be connected with his work, it should be small, and its rental should be regular, predictable and reliable. This is the circumstance in which poems came, and this is the circumstance in which the narrators of 'Livings' find themselves when they have their visions of aesthetic freedom.

VII

Troubles with ownership recurred in Larkin's relationships with women. 'My relations with women are governed by a shrinking sensitivity, a morbid sense of sin, a furtive lechery. Women don't just sit still and back you up. They want children: they like scenes: they want a chance of parading all the emotional haberdashery they are stocked with. Above all they like feeling they "own" you or that you "own" them – a thing I hate' [SL:190].

Larkin saw the absence of women as a necessary condition for his art, because he regarded his muse as a woman who would be jealous of any relationship with another woman.[22] In 'Deep Analysis', for example, his muse speaks: 'I am a woman lying on a leaf; / [...] my flesh is golden, / Comely at all points [...]' [CP:4]; and in 'Waiting for Breakfast', the returning muse is greeted with a kiss, although he realizes she is jealous of his current relationship. The final lines make clear that his art requires him to relinquish his hopes for a normal adult life with someone else; 'you' is the muse, 'her' the girlfriend:

> Will you refuse to come till I have sent
> Her terribly away, importantly live
> Part invalid, part baby, part saint? [CP:20]

Stephen Dedalus also conceives of his muse as a young woman – a slender girl in the water with seaweed on her skin – and he, like Larkin's lighthouse keeper, cannot refrain from apostrophizing what he sees [POA:185–6].

In less symbolic terms, I suspect the absence of women allowed Larkin access to his own feminine, sensitive side. It was this aspect of his character that liked to imagine itself as a schoolgirl, or a sentimental spinster [SL:199], or P. A. Larkin (Mrs) [SL:707], and was the root and core of his inspiration; indeed, he sometimes invoked a scabrous, boorish, masculine persona to disguise and protect it. To further preserve his inspiration, Larkin refused to marry or let any woman live with him, and if a relationship threatened to became serious, he would deliberately start another affair and play the needs of one woman off against another. When Monica Jones fell seriously ill and he felt duty bound to let her live with him, his writing block deepened.

All the scenes in 'Livings' conform to his aesthetic requirement. As I pointed out in section II, the powerful female presences in the sources of both 'Livings I and II' are carefully excised. In the completed poem there is no sign of any relationship with a woman, no woman is present, and no woman is even mentioned. Where there is company it is male: the lighthouse keeper is shown as solitary (he keeps his own company), but the businessman has his acquaintances in the bar, and the don has his companions at High Table. Only male absences are noted (the dead father in I, and the absent Master in III) and the only reference to the female at all is in III where the misogynist dons raise the topic of 'Names for *pudendum mulieris* [...]'. Perhaps this is one of those moments beloved of Derrida, when the thing to be suppressed and pushed beyond the margins of the text suddenly re-emerges, in its most startling form, at the very centre.

VIII

There is an air of ineffable significance about 'Livings' which I hope my commentary has done nothing to dispel. But I also hope it is now possible to see that the poem does have a meaning; it is unified; it is complete; and it taps into some of Larkin's deepest preoccupations. No poet could be more present in his poem.

Notes

1. Because I do not believe the parts of 'Livings' have a meaning outside their place in the sequence, I use 'poem' to refer to 'Livings' as a whole, and 'parts' or 'sections' to refer to its numbered subdivisions.
2. The setting of this poem could be fictional; but if it is real it appears to be Lancaster. So far as I have been able to discover, this is the only town in England with the correct names and topography. You walk down Meeting House Lane from the station to Market Square. Now, the nearest hotel (The Sun Hotel and Bar) does not overlook the square (it is just round the corner), but at least one old pub (The John O'Gaunt) is on the square, and this could have offered accommodation in Larkin's day.
3. I prefer Petch's 'small businessman' [APL:103] to Motion's 'grain merchant' [M:415], or Booth's 'commercial traveller' [NC:191]. 'Grain merchant' sounds too agrarian and establishment, and hardly covers someone who sells dips as well as feed; 'commercial traveller' does not suggest the owner of a business – which this man clearly is.
4. I suspect the setting for this poem is fictional, but it would be interesting to discover if there was any place in England which had the correct layout and allowed the blanks to be filled with the appropriate single syllables. Puzzlingly, the blanks represented by solid lines in *Collected Poems* (whose publication Larkin did not oversee) are represented by a series of dashes in the original *High Windows* (which he did) [HW:13]. In the latter, the blank before 'Hotel' has six dashes, while the other two have only four. Was this simply to make the line length pleasing to the eye, or could the number of dashes hint at the number of letters in the missing syllable? These things can sometimes be important. The fact that Elgar used five dots (rather than the usual three) to indicate the missing name in the dedication of his violin concerto ('AQUI ESTA ENCERRADA EL ALMA DE .....' ['Herein is enshrined the soul of .....']) is generally thought to be significant.
5. I discuss this point and passage in 'On Being Brunette: Larkin's Schoolgirl Fictions' [CQ:Winter/2001:42–58].
6. The reference to 'liners', which by the seventies were fairly rare, may indicate that Larkin was thinking of an earlier decade – although the mention of the radio rules out a time before the 1930s.
7. The relevance of Lord Methuen's treaty to dating the setting of 'Livings III' was pointed out to me by an anonymous publisher's reader.
8. The similarities between 'Livings III' and 'Soliloquy of the Spanish Cloister' were first drawn to my attention by Michael Hulse.
9. Larkin was much surprised when this common factor was pointed out to him. Barbara Everett was the first to notice it [SL:653].
10. Lighthouse keepers worked in groups of three. It is not clear if Larkin was aware of this.
11. I am not implying this is the only reading of the poem or that my suggested interpretation is wholly original: something similar is implied by Motion [M:416] and James [EN:6/1974:68].
12. As so often in Larkin, it is not wholly clear whether the narrators in parts I and III imagine the scenes described in the last stanzas, see them through a window, or see them while outside.

13. I discuss the aesthetic attitude in detail in 'The Definition of "Art"' [PALB:148–62].
14. I take this expression from Clive James [EN:6/1974:68].
15. The suggestion that the keeper is reminiscent of Yeats's Platonist in his tower has been made by Tom Paulin [NC:173] and James Booth [NC:193] amongst others.
16. I couldn't quite resist the point about the mirror and the lamp, but I ought to confess that some lighthouses use lenses rather than mirrors to intensify the light.
17. The theories of art alluded to are: Yeats, Abrams, Joyce, Shakespeare and Larkin. Al Alvarez takes Larkin's poetic tendencies to task in his essay 'The New Poetry, or Beyond the Gentility Principle' [TNP:17–28], reprinted in [RB:195–204]. Perhaps nothing shows Alvarez's aesthetic distance from Larkin better than his own comparison between writers and lighthouse keepers: 'The writer at his desk is more like a lighthouse keeper than an explorer, bored and isolated and pining for distraction' [RB:112].
18. For a discussion of Joyce's aesthetics and its relations to Aquinas and Kant, see Kevin Barry's introduction to Joyce's occasional writings [OCPW: xxiv–xxvii]. There are many other causal routes which lead from Larkin back to Kant's aesthetics (most of them via Schopenhauer) but one, because of its links with essay II in this volume, is worth describing here. The origin of the phrase '*L'art pour l'art*' is first found in the diary of Benjamin Constant in 1804, and he heard it in his turn from Henry Crabb Robinson who was listening to Schelling's lectures on Kant's aesthetics. It is highly likely that Constant communicated the idea to Victor Cousin (a lover and companion of Louise Colet) and he included it in his lectures on aesthetics – which contained a good deal about Kant – delivered at the Sorbonne from 1818 onwards. This is almost certainly the source from which Gautier derived the phrase, and Flaubert also refers to Cousin's ideas directly. In September 1846, the novelist recommends Cousin's views to Louise as a corrective to her own 'impure' conception of art: 'Tell the Philosopher [Cousin] to explain to you the idea of Pure Beauty as he expounds it in his course of 1819, and as I conceive it. We'll speak about it next time' [FL:I:75]. Needless to say, '*L'art pour l'art*' is a gross oversimplification of Kant's view. For an introduction to a complex topic see [EA:I:118–21,448–50].
19. I have found the following works helpful for understanding the way Kant connects aesthetic and moral judgement: Andrew Ward, *Kant: The Three Critiques* [KTC:199–202], and Paul Guyer, 'Feeling and Freedom: Kant on Aesthetics and Morality' [KEF:27–47].
20. The Kantian system is extensive and complex, and the *Critique of the Power of Judgment* is notoriously obscure. I'm afraid my discussion of Kant is therefore slightly telegraphic and, in places, simplified. Paul Guyer's introduction to his edition of the *Critique* is helpful, comprehensive and clear [CJ:xiii–lii].
21. I hope these thoughts supplement and clarify my earlier remarks about the sky and heavenly bodies. For most of us, the sky and the heavenly bodies can play no role in our practical projects and are therefore looked at almost entirely as aesthetic objects. When we look in this way, we forget our bodies,

our surroundings, our plans and thoughts, and feel ourselves to be pure subjects who could be inserted into other bodies or other lives.

22. The section on women and Larkin's creativity is brief because I have already explored the issue at length in 'Unreal Girls: Lesbian Fantasy in Early Larkin' [NLO:79–96] and 'On Being Brunette: Larkin's Schoolgirl Fictions' [CQ: Winter/2001:42–58].

IV
Larkin and the Creepy

Superstition is rooted in a much deeper and more sensitive level of the psyche than scepticism.

Goethe

Some element of the supernatural is so constant in poetry that we have come to look upon it as part of the natural fabric of the art.

Virginia Woolf

This essay considers the significance of the supernatural in Larkin's life and work, and, in particular, examines the influence of M. R. James on both. Part one (sections I–XII) is largely concerned with the subject matter of Larkin's poetry, but part two (sections XIII–XXI) tries to show that Larkin's responsiveness to the eerie and ghostly – suffused and adjusted by James's influence – not only affected his choice of subjects, but imbued his deepest feelings about poetry itself.[1]

I don't want to claim that Larkin believed in the supernatural in any straightforward sense; he almost certainly didn't. But I do want to show that he found the uncanny interesting and creatively potent; and that by using the language of the supernatural he could sometimes convey certain poetic states of mind more easily. In other words, his invocations of the supernatural are: '*seemings* [...] used for artistic purposes'[2] [FR:176].

I

James was admired by two superstitious men who had an important influence on Larkin. A. E. Housman, the most exacting of critics, said he considered the 'country song' invented by James about Betton Wood ('That which walks in Betton Wood / Knows why it walks or why it cries') to be 'good poetry' [CR:332]. And in 1913, he sent Thomas Hardy copies of James's *Ghost-Stories of an Antiquary* and *More Ghost Stories of an Antiquary*, recommending in particular 'Oh, Whistle, and I'll Come to You, My Lad' and 'Count Magnus' from the first of these volumes. In his letter of thanks, Hardy reported that: '[two] or three of them have been read aloud in this house [Max Gate], and I was agreeably sensible of their eeriness, even though the precaution was taken of keeping them at a safe distance from bed-time. There is much invention shown in their construction, especially in those you mention' [CR:XX].

On John Betjeman, another major figure in Larkin's creative life, James was the formative influence. While at the Dragon School (then called Lynam's) in Oxford in 1920, the fourteen-year-old Betjeman heard James's stories retold by the headmaster – 'Skipper' Lynam – and they struck the future poet as 'the best stories I ever heard, and they gave me an interest in old churches, and country houses, and Scandinavia that not even the mighty Hans Andersen has eclipsed' [BS:7]. Later, Betjeman would write stories in James's style [YB:348]; read all the ghost stories many times to his family [BL:I:367]; say he preferred M. R. to Henry James [BL:II:491]; and acknowledge that the former's responsiveness to architecture was an important development in the history of English literature [TWT:154]. Above all, the Jamesian atmosphere penetrated deep into the younger man's poetic sensibility, and any reader of 'Portrait of a Deaf Man', 'Lord Cozens Hardy' or 'I. M. Walter Ramsden' can hear the haunting accent of his master's voice.

II

Larkin's own admiration for James is shown in a letter to Amis in October 1985: 'Some time ago there was a competition in the Guardian [...] to identify the first lines of books published by Penguin. I was especially struck by one which ran "The boy was there again this evening, and the dogs were not barking." It seemed a beautifully creepy, M. R. James, Lefanu kind of sentence that made you feel "I *must* read on." (Bloody few of the others – e.g. *Anna Karenina, Madame Bovary* – achieved this.)' [SL:752]. Later, he was amazed to discover that the sentence came from a novel by Iris Murdoch, a writer he generally found unreadable.[3]

His knowledge of the ghost stories extended back to at least the early 1940s. Nick Russel, one of the poet's contemporaries at St John's Oxford, remembered Larkin as being an excellent mime artist. Some of his more elaborate performances – 'the shoe fetishist', for example – were entirely light-hearted; others showed a different side to his character:

> [There] was one occasion I remember when a rather frightening, almost sinister, persona surfaced and seemed momentarily at least to have taken possession of the performer.
>
> This must have occurred late in 1941, when the blackout had become a way of life. I used to imagine that not since Archbishop Laud, who built it, had the wide vessel of the Canterbury quad been so filled with creeping murmur and the poring dark. With more than 80 undergraduates in residence, the college authorities tried vainly to turn us into efficient fire-watchers, obliging us to keep late and lonely vigil in the porter's lodge, and even allowing us, encumbered with stirrup pumps and sand buckets, to roam the college roof-tops at night in search of imaginary incendiaries.
>
> On this particular evening, marked only by a scatter of moonlight, a number of us had gathered in the Canterbury quad and were looking up towards the darkened windows of the Laudian library, a decidedly creepy place, where we liked to suppose we might be lucky enough to meet the spectral but headless body of the archbishop gliding between the bookstacks. Suddenly there came a weird cry from one of the colonnades, and a stooped crouching figure with staring orbs and dressed in what seemed to be flapping robes emerged. The light was so poor, it was difficult at first to make out the creature, but it soon began to make little darting movements towards us, moaning and keening like some M. R. James character.
>
> The sensation of terror mingled with delightful anticipation lasted only a bewildering half-minute before we could identify the culprit. Philip – of course. Philip! But the true touch of genius – indeed of horror – came from the fact that he was wearing a gas mask, which almost concealed his now beaming face. [PLT:85–6]

Russel is right to invoke James's name, and any reader of his stories will immediately recognize the particular tale that influenced the stoopings, dartings and flapping robes of Larkin's performance. In 'Oh, Whistle', Professor Parkins discovers an ancient whistle in the foundations of a ruined preceptory on a beach. On trying it out, he finds he has summoned up a peculiarly upsetting vision which prevents him from sleeping:

> A long stretch of shore – shingle edged by sand and intersected at short intervals with black groynes running down to the water [...] The

> light was obscure, conveying an impression of gathering storm, late winter evening, and slight cold rain. On this bleak stage at first no actor was visible. Then, in the distance, a bobbing black object appeared; a moment more, and it was a man running, jumping, clambering over the groynes, and every few seconds looking eagerly back [...]
>
> So far no cause whatever for the fear of the runner had been shown; but now there began to be seen, far up the shore, a little flicker of something light-coloured moving to and fro with great swiftness and irregularity. Rapidly growing larger, it, too, declared itself as a figure in pale fluttering draperies, ill-defined. There was something about its motion which made Parkins very unwilling to see it at close quarters. It would stop, raise its arms, bow itself toward the sand, then run stooping across the beach to the water-edge and back again; and then, rising upright, once more continue its course forward at a speed that was startling and terrifying. [...] [CM:90–1]

There are two further similarities between James's vision and Larkin's performance that are not evident from the quoted section of the tale. First, both fictional creatures have grotesque and unnatural faces created from the most ordinary materials: Larkin wears a gas mask; James's creature turns out to have 'an intensely horrible face of *crumpled linen*' [CM:99]. Second, in both cases there is something strange about the eyes: Larkin's mask gives the illusion of 'staring orbs'; James's creature is blind [CM:99].

III

James's figure is associated with the wind ('Goodness! what force the wind can get up to in a few minutes! What a tremendous gust!' [CM:89]), and in late 1945 and early 1946, Larkin wrote a cluster of poems which emphasize several sinister themes from the story – wind, blackness, night, rain, the living and the dead [CP:308,310–11]. One of these describes wind on a beach ('sing there upon the beach / Till all's beyond death's reach' [CP:308]); another takes up the idea of whistling for the wind:

> Who whistled for the wind, that it should break
> Gently, on this air?
> On what ground was it gathered, where
> For the carrying, for its own sake,
> Is night so gifted?

Mind never met
Image of death like this, and yet
(All winds crying for that unbroken field,
Day having lifted)
Black flowers burst out wherever the night has knelt. [CP:311]

A character in 'Oh, Whistle' explains that belief in whistling for the wind is current 'all over Denmark and Norway, as well as the Yorkshire coast' [CM:93]. It can certainly be found prior to 1900 in English literature. The myth is invoked by Scott ('What gales are sold on Lapland's shore! / How whistle rash bids tempest roar!' [PWS:233]); by Longfellow ('I was whistling to St Antonio / [...] And instead of a breeze he sent a gale' [LP:516]); and Kingsley ('Oh whistle for the wind / [...] My boat it lags behind' [CK:239]). In these sources, the wind is only whistled for by sailors at sea, it can be something they need, and it is only to be feared for its strength.

The publication of James's story in 1904 – by far the best-known work in which whistling for the wind plays a major role – gives a new inflection to the myth. The wind in the story is ominous; it is not feared for its power; it is not needed; and, above all, it is not raised by a sailor at sea. Larkin's clutch of poems shares none of the features which are distinctive of the myth's original form; but it does share three, and very probably four, of the features of the myth in James's tale. We can thus be fairly confident that Larkin is directly influenced by James's story.

IV

Russel recognized the source of Larkin's sinister charade, and as this suggests, James was widely read in Larkin's Oxford circle. In 1948, for example, Amis wrote to Larkin: 'All I have done this week apart from taking my Degrees [...] has been to do some reading in the collected ghost stories of M. R. James (I have got an idea for one of these and shall write it up soon) [...]' [LKA:162]. While Larkin himself, recalling the career of Bruce Montgomery, wrote: 'Leaving Oxford in 1943, he spent the rest of the war teaching at Shrewsbury school, where his pupils received a thorough grounding in detective fiction and M. R. James as well as more usual subjects' [FR:123]. One of Montgomery's ex-pupils makes no mention of detective fiction, but does recall that '[Montgomery's] favourite English lesson was to read aloud the ghost stories of Montague James' [BMEC:38].

James remained a potent creative influence in this group for over twenty years. When the critic Dale Salwak suggested to Amis that Montgomery's *Holy Disorders* (1945) influenced his own *The Green Man* (1969), the novelist responded with some irritation: 'You are wrong to suppose that I was influenced by HOLY DISORDERS at any time. Any resemblances are accounted for by the fact that both [Montgomery] and I greatly admired the ghost stories of M. R. James'[4] [LKA:1089].

Holy Disorders and *The Moving Toyshop* are Montgomery's most Jamesian works – the former even includes a self-contained ghost story written in a deliberate pastiche of James's manner [HDO:120–4] – and both benefited from Larkin's collaboration.[5] Shrewsbury School, where the two novels were written between 1943 and 1945, was close to Larkin's current place of work in Wellington, and the two friends met regularly for a number of years. *Holy Disorders* offers 'sincere thanks' to 'Mr Philip Larkin for reading this book in manuscript and making a number of valuable suggestions' [SL:199], and Larkin was even more heavily involved in *The Moving Toyshop*. The book is dedicated to him, and Larkin would later write: 'I [...] unwittingly provided the genesis of the [novel], by reporting that when I left his lodgings to catch the midnight train there was always one particular shop with its awning left down, flapping eerily in the empty street. Bruce was fascinated' [FR:123]. A letter to Winifred Arnott shows that he provided more than inspiration: 'The part of MT I wrote was not necessarily the best bit, in fact quite definitely *not* the best – that long rambling, shaming discussion of poetry. Bruce then rewrote it after me. But don't you think that all in all it's a charmingly-lighthearted book?' [SL:199].

V

Throughout his life, Larkin was a great haunter of empty churches and graveyards, and during the 1940s and 1950s, he wrote a number of works concerned with macabre superstition and folklore.[6] 'Ante Meridian', the 'autobiography' he wrote as Brunette Coleman, speaks of five scouts who will fall to their deaths over the cliff; of how her father's oilskins once belonged to a parishioner who had been tried for manslaughter in Truro; of how her father proclaims psalms into the teeth of a gale; and of how, if nine maidens ever gather at the local inn, something terrible would happen that would involve, 'the sun becoming black as a sackcloth of hair, and the moon as blood' [TWG:236].

Some of the early poems share the same superstitious outlook but are more explicitly ghostly. The Audenesque 'Ghosts', from 1940, is more interested in the ghosts of the living than the dead, although it gives an effective description of eerie chill: '[...] Cold as this tree I touch' [SL:10]. But 'The dead are lost [...]', from August 1945, comes closer to giving such a chill:

> The dead are lost, unravelled; but if a voice
> Could shake them back, reshape each sunless bone
> To cage a mind, and offer them a choice
> Of painful walking on the earth again,
> Or, once more, death – how their sad eagerness
> Would beat against this life! [SL:108]

Death is the theme which James and Larkin most obviously share. It is a contingent matter that a poet, like Larkin, is obsessed by death, but a ghost story is necessarily obsessed by death. Such stories involve the influence of the dead, and as James had little time for ghosts that are not malevolent, his protagonists often end up dead as well. In addition, it is not enough that the reader should find ghosts in a setting; landscapes and buildings must be suffused and coloured by them, so that the whole environment comes to speak of their uncanny presence.

The image of someone pursued to death, although without hurry, by sinister figures, can be found in a story like James's 'Count Magnus'. Here the protagonist is haunted by visions of 'a man in a long black cloak' and 'a short figure with dark cloak and hood' [CM:79] who eventually and inevitably track him down and kill him. James's presences and demons also have the power, before they kill, to sicken and depress. In 'Casting the Runes', 'Mr Dunning confessed to himself that he did not look forward with his usual cheerfulness to a solitary evening. It seemed to him that something ill-defined and impalpable had stepped in between him and his fellow man' [CM:168]. And having heard the cry in Betton Wood, the narrator of 'A Neighbour's Landmark' has a few Larkinesque reflections visited on him: 'images came to me of [...] forgotten graves [...] and of flying Time and all it has taken out of my life' [HD:111].

Larkin was preoccupied by the relentless progress of death, and it only required the smallest adjustment to turn one of James's deadly pursuers into death itself. We can find such a narrative in his 'Unfinished Poem' from 1951. In the opening stanzas, the narrator climbs to an attic and feels hopelessly depressed ('That was a way to live – newspapers for sheets, / A candle and spirit stove [...]'). He then tells us why:

> For (as you will guess) it was death I had in mind,
> Who covets our breath, who seeks and will always find;
> To keep out of his thought was my whole care,
> Yet down among sunlit courts, yes, he was there,
>
> Taking his rents; yes, I had only to look
> To see the shape of his head and the shine of his book,
> And the creep of the world under his sparrow-trap sky,
> To know how little slips his immortal memory. [CP:60]

Death climbs the stairs and lurks outside the narrator's door: 'But one night I heard the feet. // [...] There was no defence. / I sprawled to my knees. Now they came straight at my door' [CP:60–1]. Thus reminding us of the scene in 'The Treasure of Abbot Thomas': 'There was someone or something on the watch outside my door the whole night' [CM:119], and a similar incident in 'A Warning to the Curious' [HD:145].

VI

Signs of James's continuing influence can be found in one of Larkin's letters to his mistress, Patsy Strang, in November 1953 [SL:216]. This contains an early draft of a poem which was eventually published in *The Less Deceived* as 'Whatever Happened?', but in the letter it is called 'The Story of an Occurrence and a Disoccurrence'. This title seems cumbersome and unmotivated until we realize that it is an echo and inversion of a title from one of James's late ghost stories, 'The Story of a Disappearance and an Appearance', and that the poem, of course, has connections with the story.

'The Story of an Occurrence and a Disoccurrence' is about people lining a ship's rail who are recalling an incident which has happened on shore. Initially, the occurrence is recalled with great clarity ('Remembering each detail / We toss for half the night'), but gradually the experience fades ('We [...] find next day / All's kodak-distant'), and it is only later that the mind thinks it has determined the incident's significance ('"Perspective brings significance," we say') [SL:216]. In the letter to Strang, Larkin makes clear that this incident could have been sexual as well as violent, and that the poem is about 'the way in which the mind gets to work on any violent involuntary experience & transforms it out of all knowledge' [SL:216].

'The Story of an Occurrence and a Disoccurrence' ends with the lines: 'Curses, the darkness, fighting – what recourse / Have these tales now? Except to nightmares, of course' [SL:216]. The sense is a little obscure, and in the final version Larkin sharpened it to: 'Curses? The dark? Struggling? Where's the source / Of these yarns now (except in nightmares, of course)?' [CP:74]. However, 'The Story of a Disappearance and an Appearance' has close links with both versions and the letter which contained the first: it is a tale (or yarn), full of curses, darkness, fights (or struggles), involuntary events, confusion, and guilt revealed in nightmares.

James's story, which is set in December 1837, is about a country rector's murder by two men who run a travelling Punch and Judy show. After the most minimal introduction, it is told in a sequence of four unsigned letters (although the first ends with two initials) from the rector's nephew to a married brother. Written in a pastiche of early Victorian style, these letters report the progress of the investigation and the nephew's attempt to make sense of a baffling death. But he is not the only one who has to work hard. The letter form and the minimal amount of background information provided ensure that the reader also has constantly to be on his toes. To penetrate the obscurity, one first tries this hypothesis, then that; takes one clue to be highly significant, then another; rereads the story to ensure nothing important has been missed; and then begins the whole process again ... The oblique and fragmentary nature of the narrative has always made it one of James's most admired stories amongst writers. Consequently, at two levels, it is an excellent example of what Larkin felt is shown in his poem: 'how the mind gets to work on any violent involuntary experience & transforms it out of all knowledge'.

However, Larkin may well have come to feel that the story alluded to in the title, and the reasons for the allusion, were a little recherché, and decided to replace the Jamesian original with 'Whatever Happened?' – a question that would make an equally good title for the story.[7]

VII

The imprint of James can also be found earlier in the same letter to Strang. All Hallows was a significant date for James: he mentions it in several stories [e.g. HD:169], and he signs off the preface to *Ghost-Stories of an Antiquary* with '*Allhallows' Even*, 1904' [CM:254]. All Hallows was also important to Larkin, and he was at his most superstitious during the rituals and religious days around the beginning of November. Maeve Brennan gives such an excellent account of these days' significances, and Larkin's responses to them, that I quote her at length:

> At the end of the month came Hallow'en when Philip customarily made mulled wine, the warm, heady smell of which pervaded his flat and half intoxicated me before I even tasted it. We drank it by candlelight under the caustic grimaces of little models of witches on broomsticks he had suspended from the ceiling, and threw apple peel over our shoulders but it never formed our initials as superstition ruled. The only time I saw children carrying pumpkin lanterns was when I was with Philip. The romantic significance of the encounter added to the magic aura of the occasion. After Hallow'en came Guy Fawkes Night, when we sometimes strolled across the Park to watch the public bonfire and fireworks display but more often the 'high windows' of his sitting room provided a cosier vantage point.
>
> In between these dates fell the religious festival of All Saints and All Souls which I observed and Philip therefore acknowledged, usually with some reminder of Frances Cornford's sestet commemorating All Souls' Night:
>
> My love came back to me
> Under the November tree
> Shelterless and dim.
> He put his hand upon my shoulder,
> He did not think me strange or older,
> Nor I, him.
>
> The feast of All Souls, 2 November, following that of All Saints, is a day set aside by the Church when the faithful are asked to pray for the souls of the dead still in Purgatory. Out of this tradition grew the superstition that a dead lover would appear to a still faithful partner on All Souls' Night. Already a favourite poem of Philip's, it acquired a special significance for us both when, in 1974, after a parting of sixteen months, we resumed our affair on this day. He included the poem in the *Oxford Book of Twentieth-Century English Verse*. [PLIK:46–7]

Larkin also responded to the rather fiercer, more social rituals he attended every year with Monica Jones: 'For New Year I went up to

Northumberland,' he wrote to Barbara Pym, '& was in the square at Allendale, at midnight, where they have a huge fire, & a band, and toss tubs of pitch on to it (the fire), & sing *old lang syne*. Very thrilling' [SL:391].

Given the importance both James and Larkin assigned to these autumn and winter rituals, it is of some interest that Larkin heads the letter containing 'The Story of an Occurrence and a Disoccurrence', '1st November 1953, *All Hallows*'. But it is in the style and content of the letter that the significant link is to be found.

One of the great pleasures of James's stories is the haunting power of his descriptions of landscapes and buildings, which, for obvious reasons, tend to be melancholy and set towards evening. Three paragraphs – from 'Lost Hearts', 'Canon Alberic's Scrapbook' and 'Oh, Whistle' – will give their flavour:

> An evening light shone on the building, making the window-panes glow like so many fires. Away from the Hall in front stretched a flat park studded with oaks and fringed with firs, which stood out against the sky. The clock in the church-tower, buried in trees on the edge of the park, only its golden weathercock catching the light, was striking six, and the sound came beating down the wind. It was altogether a pleasant impression, though tinged with the sort of melancholy appropriate to an evening in early autumn [...]. [CM:14]

> It was near five o'clock; the short day was drawing in, and the church began to fill with shadows, while the curious noises – the muffled footfalls and distant talking voices that had been perceptible all day – seemed, no doubt because of the fading light and the consequently quickened sense of hearing, to become more frequent and insistent. [CM:3]

> Bleak and solemn was the view on which he took a last look before starting homeward. A faint yellow light in the west showed the links, on which a few figures moving towards the club-house were still visible, the squat martello tower, the lights of Aldsey village, the pale ribbon of sand intersected at intervals by black wooden groynes, the dim and murmuring sea. [CM:86]

The same eerie Romantic melancholy seems to pervade the opening of Larkin's *All Hallows* letter. It is written from Flat 13, 30 Elmwood

Avenue, Belfast, but he invents a time and landscape more appropriate to his mood:

> There's a slight increase in solitude after the post goes on Sunday. I felt it today strongly: as if I were in a remote spot where the postman is the incident of the day, and when he shakes the reins and turns down the road you turn back and things for a moment seem particularly still, the bare trees and the wisps of fine cloud like sifted dark grey sand: you busy yourself with lighting the lamp ... This is piling it on a bit, perhaps, but between 4 p.m. & dusk was a very still & lonely time here today [...]. [SL:215]

His mood suggests somewhere rural ('a remote spot') at some time in the past ('[the postman] shakes the reins [...] you busy yourself with lighting the lamp'). As James is alluded to in the next paragraph, and as the place, period, mood and time of day are all characteristic of James, I think we can feel confident that it is the atmosphere of James's work which permeates Larkin's imagination.

There may be further influence on the poetry of this period. Several of the poems Larkin wrote throughout his life have explicit Victorian or Edwardian settings: 'Deceptions', 'MCMXIV', 'How Distant' and 'Dublinesque', for instance. But he also gives an aura of the same period to poems which are not primarily intended to be historical evocations. This disposition of mind may have been formed by reading Barnes, Hardy or some similar figure, but since several of these poems were written at a time when Larkin was very aware of the ghost stories, it is natural to assume that James was exerting his influence too. In 'Going', for instance, we find the same time of day, rural spot, and mention of lamp-lighting that we find in the letter:

> There is an evening coming in
> Across the fields, one never seen before,
> That lights no lamps. [...] [1946] [CP:3]

The themes of dying and evening allow this poem – originally called 'Dying Day' – to be seen as part of the James-inspired night/death/ wind sequence written at the end of 1945 and the beginning of 1946. In fact, 'Going' – the earliest poem Larkin was prepared to publish in a mature collection – was probably written in February 1946, immediately after 'Who whistled for the wind [...]?' which was completed on

15 December 1945 [CP:3, 311]. It is significant that Larkin's first canonical poem seems to be tinged by James's influence.

Both 'Going' and the imagined scene in the letter may not be set too far back in the past; perhaps no further back than just before the Second World War. But in 'Days', a second poem about death, written only months before the letter, an earlier period is portrayed:

> Where can we live but days?
>
> Ah, solving that question
> Brings the priest and the doctor
> In their long coats
> Running over the fields. [3 August 1953] [CP:67]

Unlike the scene in the letter and 'Going', we do not know at what time of day this action occurs, but we do know the year is long before 1939. It is true that sending for a priest just before death was recently more common in Ireland than England, but the fact that neither the priest nor the doctor has transport – and the roads seem so inadequate – suggests some date before the First World War.

Why should death make Larkin think of lighting lamps, fields, and priests and doctors in long coats running over them? The period details might suggest James, and there are several scenes in his stories where men run through the countryside [e.g. CM:162], but I think it likely that this particular image came to Larkin not from James directly, but from James refracted through Montgomery. Shortly after the Jamesian ghost story in *Holy Disorders*, the hero surprises a priest performing a Black Mass. The priest fires a shot, and the hero gives chase: 'The Celebrant had a good start. Like some fantastic crow, with his black robes flapping in the wind, he was running across the wet fields into the gathering dusk' [HDO:127]. These sentences manage to combine the rural dusk from 'Going', with the priest in a long garment running across the fields from 'Days'.

VIII

Given the theme of 'Church Going', begun six months after the *All Hallows* letter, one might have expected the decline in Christian belief, and nostalgia for church ritual and community, to be explicitly discussed. In fact, they are barely mentioned.[8] Instead the whole of the fourth stanza and the end of the third are given over to an account of superstition. Whereas Larkin evidently thinks Christianity is a spent force, he clearly feels that superstition still has some power, and will continue to have it for some time:

> Shall we avoid [churches] as unlucky places?
>
> Or, after dark, will dubious women come
> To make their children touch a particular stone;
> Pick simples for a cancer; or on some
> Advised night see walking a dead one?
> Power of some sort or other will go on
> In games, in riddles, seemingly at random;
> But superstition, like belief, must die,
> And what remains when disbelief has gone?
> Grass, weedy pavement, brambles, buttress, sky, [...] [CP:97–8]

He considers two further potential visitors – an antiquarian and a Christmas-addict – and then asks:

> Or will [the last visitor] be my representative,
>
> Bored, uninformed, knowing the ghostly silt
> Dispersed, yet tending to this cross of ground
> Through suburb scrub [...]? [CP:98]

The meaning of the strange phrase 'ghostly silt' is unclear, but it probably refers, by way of 'Holy Ghost', either to God or an atmosphere of Christian belief. The reference is remarkably belittling. First, because the off-putting 'silt' suggests some kind of clogging deposit; second, because the reduction of 'Holy Ghost' first to 'ghost' and then to 'ghostly' suggests that Larkin is pointing up a parallel with the 'dubious women' who actually watch for ghosts in stanza four: '[...] will dubious women come / [...] [and] on some / Advised night see walking a dead one?' [CP:97]. Christianity and superstition, he seems to suggest, are much of a muchness, but at least superstition has no illusions of grandeur.

It might reasonably be thought that the central influence on 'Church Going' is Betjeman rather than James. Certainly, their influence can be difficult to disentangle, especially as Betjeman said he owed his interest in churches and country houses to the older man. However, when Betjeman writes about churches, he displays a deep love and nostalgia for Anglicanism and Anglican ritual, and his eerie poems ('Lord Cozens

Hardy', 'I. M. Walter Ramsden', etc.) do not have ecclesiastical settings (beyond mentioning sanctified graves). James, on the other hand, frequently sets his stories in churches, chapels or cathedrals ('Canon Alberic's Scrap-book', 'The Stalls of Barchester Cathedral', 'An Episode of Cathedral History', etc.) and Christianity generally plays little role in tales that chronicle the gradual revelation of pagan terrors. As 'Church Going' discusses paganism in an ecclesiastical setting, while showing little love or interest in Christianity, I am inclined to see the direct and pervasive influence of James's stories, which Larkin had been alluding to and imitating five months before the poem was begun.

There are also some specific echoes of James's tales in the poem. It is not difficult to see how superstitious ghost-watchers might be suggested by a collection of ghost stories, but how might this portrait of the Christmas-addict be influenced by James's work?

> [A] Christmas-addict, counting on a whiff
> Of gown-and-bands and organ-pipes and myrrh? [CP:98]

The details here are significant because Larkin had been exposed to most of these objects through the recently recalled 'Story of a Disappearance and an Appearance'. In this tale, gown-and-bands, Christmas, and organ pipes all play an important role: the missing uncle, the narrator says, is one of the few clerics still to wear gown-and-bands, and the dark figure in the dream is recognized by them alone; the whole story takes place over the Christmas period; and organ pipes are alluded to when the organ fails twice during the disturbances in the Christmas service.

The other candidate Larkin proposes as the last true church visitor is:

> [...] [One] of the crew
> That tap and jot and know what rood-lofts were?
> Some ruin-bibber, randy for antique [...]?

Again, Larkin had come across many such church antiquarians in *Ghost-Stories of an Antiquary* and *More Ghost Stories of an Antiquary*. The tales' protagonists often show a passion for ecclesiastical architecture: Dennistoun, in 'Canon Alberic's Scrap-book', for example, 'proposed to himself to fill a notebook and to use several dozens of plates in the process of describing and photographing every corner of the wonderful church that dominates the little hill of Comminges' [CM:1]. And prose like this is not uncommon:

> The organ is in the triforium, and what is seen of the case is Gothic. The reredos and its surroundings are like every other. [...] Careful engravings of a hundred years ago show a very different state of things. [...] There is a baldacchino of wood over the altar, with urns upon its corners. Farther east is a solid altar screen, classical in design, of wood, with a pediment, in which is a triangle surrounded by rays, enclosing certain Hebrew letters in gold. Cherubs contemplate these. [CM:183]

Larkin may also have had James at the back of his mind when he notes that the ruin-bibber is 'randy for antique'. The phrase clearly implies that the enthusiast has sublimated his sexual desires into antiquarian pursuits, and James is a particularly clear case of such displacement. James had published his autobiography in 1926; many obituaries appeared when he died in 1936; there was much Oxbridge gossip about him; and a large number of diaries and memories mentioning James's life and work were published before Larkin began 'Church Going' in 1954. Consequently, he may well have known that James was always falling in love with his male pupils, but had no sexual relationship in his life; spent long cycling holidays exploring old buildings; visited 141 out of the 143 existent French cathedrals; wrote a book on abbeys, and was exactly the kind of person who tapped and jotted and knew what rood-lofts were [see CM:vii–xvii].

IX

James and Larkin were in some ways similar kinds of men. Both were lifelong bachelors; both had Oxbridge Firsts; both held senior administrative posts; both were professionally involved with books (Larkin was a librarian, James a bibliographer who wrote a descriptive catalogue of all the manuscripts held by Cambridge colleges); both were expert mimics; both were inclined to timidity; both held opinions that many of their contemporaries felt were regrettably reactionary; both lived rather uneventful retired lives in a limited number of academic institutions; both were suspicious of abstract thought; both are best known for literary work which was not a part of their professional career.

They also shared deep feelings for autumn. Even late in life, Larkin loved kicking piles of leaves, and throughout his life it was the season in which he felt most at home. It is mentioned, for example, in 'Afternoons' ('Summer is fading: The leaves fall in ones and twos [...]' [CP:121]), and 'Broadcast' ('I lose / All but the outline of the still and withering // Leaves on half-emptied trees [...]' [CP:140]), and there is a long poem, 'Autumn' – written immediately after 'Whatever Happened?' – which he considered a failure and chose not to publish [CP:75]. Autumn, he explains, has lower expectations than spring and summer: '[I] am easiest when the leaves are gone; / Too often summer days appear / Emblems of perfect happiness I can't confront [...]' [CP:68].

Autumn and winter, like dusk and night-time, are also the most congenial times for writers of ghost stories: the light is bad, there are fewer people about, the natural world appears to be dying, and we enter the season of All Hallows, All Saints, All Souls and Guy Fawkes. James makes full use of these resonances. 'Lost Hearts' begins in September, 'The Tractate Middoth' begins '[towards] the end of an autumn afternoon' [CM:140], 'Mr Humphreys and his Inheritance' is set 'on a date late in August or early September', and so on [CM:216].

Larkin, as one of my earlier sections hints, was also fascinated by the wind. One naturally thinks of the exhilaration of 'Wedding-Wind' ('The wind blew all my wedding-day, / And my wedding night was the night of the high wind' [CP:11]), and in letters, he is always keen to report its moods: 'The wind's blowing hard tonight as it did last night and during the days, but it's entirely without malice, like a dog jumping up around you in fun (or what he thinks is fun), whereas in autumn the same kind of wind is intent on doing damage, quite a different spirit. I expect the seas are rough [...]' [SL:193].

Folklore makes extensive use of the wind, partly because it seems to have so many qualities of the spirit: of mysterious origin and destination, apparently immortal and self-moving, invisible and without size or mass yet capable of affecting people and physical objects. James draws on some of these ghostly features. Apart from its central role in 'Oh, Whistle', the wind appears in 'The Stalls of Barchester Cathedral' ('Lest he be fetcht away / Whether by night or day, / But chiefly when the wind blows high / In a night of February' [CM:195]). And the first part of 'The Residence at Whitminster' concludes with an immense storm which prevents the rescue of Viscount Saul: 'All night the gale buffeted the high windows of the church, and howled over the upland and roared through the woodland' [HD:9].

I suspect that some of this joint outlook can be ascribed to the powerful influence of Irish writing. James sometimes mentions Irish folklore directly (in 'The Ash Tree' [CM:47] and 'The Residence at Whitminster'

[HD:3], for example) but in all his stories he was deeply influenced by the Irish writer Sheridan Lefanu. James thought him much the best writer of supernatural tales: he rediscovered many of Lefanu's tales buried anonymously in old periodicals; wrote several essays about him; and published an anthology of Lefanu's shorter tales with an introduction, which is still in print. From the evidence of the letter quoted near the beginning of this essay, Larkin also read and admired Lefanu, but he had other routes into Irish literature as well – his early adoration of Yeats and his years in Belfast being the most important.

X

There are several differences between *The Whitsun Weddings* and *High Windows* but two are particularly striking. In the later collection, many of the poems are set at twilight or night; and human activities and rituals are described against a slightly ominous background of natural change and decay. One setting encountered several times is the lamp-lit building which stands amidst the empty dark. In the earlier book, this is only obviously found in 'Broadcast' – but as this is a love poem, its preoccupations are very remote from those of *High Windows*. In the later collection, however, the lit building can be found in 'Livings I', 'Livings II' and 'Livings III', 'Friday Night in the Royal Station Hotel', 'The Card-Players', 'Vers de Société', and there are metaphorical hints of the same situation in 'The Old Fools' ('Perhaps being old is having lighted rooms / Inside your head [...]' [CP:196]), and 'The Building', where the 'lucent comb' of the hospital tries forlornly to contravene the 'coming dark' [CP:193].

Such a setting is a natural home for eerie thoughts, and it is thus not surprising that we find a touch of the primitive and superstitious in this collection. In 'The Card-Players', for instance, Larkin conjures up a seventeenth-century Dutch genre painting, a scene of bestial, elemental cosiness, where a group of grotesques carouse away a night of rain and storm. There are clearly elements here – the fire and drunken night-time crowd – of the celebrations Larkin relished in Allendale, and he makes his Dutch scene even more primitive by describing what is evidently an inn as '[this] lamplit cave' [CP:177]. A hint of *memento mori* is introduced by the reference to old Prijck's 'skull face', and Jan's gob at the grate, which misses and hits 'the queen of hearts' [CP:177]. Spitting is associated with luck, and hitting the queen of hearts (the name also used in the Low Countries for the particularly unfortunate Elizabeth, Queen of Bohemia) can only hint that, for all his current contentment, very ill luck will attend him – and possibly the others too.

The superstitious poems and practices Larkin enjoyed with Maeve Brennan were a mixture of the Christian and the straightforwardly pagan, and we find the same combination in *High Windows*. Besides 'The Card-Players', the pagan is explicitly represented by the lighthouse keeper's 'divining-cards' in 'Livings II', but 'The Explosion', the last poem in the collection, ends with a Christianized vision of the dead miners walking towards their wives:

> *The dead go on before us, they*
> *Are sitting in God's house in comfort,*
> *We shall see them face to face –*
>
> Plain as lettering in the chapels
> It was said, and for a second
> Wives saw men of the explosion
>
> Larger than in life they managed –
> Gold as on a coin, or walking
> Somehow from the sun towards them [...] [CP:175]

Paying attention to the creepy element in another lit-building poem, 'Friday Night in the Royal Station Hotel', can adumbrate some of its interpretative problems. The transition between the first and last sections, and the fragmentary second section itself, are deeply mysterious:

> [...] A porter reads
> An unsold evening paper. Hours pass,
> And all the salesmen have gone back to Leeds,
> Leaving full ashtrays in the Conference Room.
>
> [...] How
> Isolated, like a fort, it is –
> ....
> [...] *Now*
> *Night comes on. Waves fold behind villages.* [CP:163]

No one has given a good explanation of why the hotel is like a fort, or why the poem ends with a vision of night coming on and waves folding behind villages, although I think Barbara Everett is on the right track when she suggests that Larkin's poem 'reaches back to some Dark

Age of the imagination, where isolation is a fortress' and that 'his verse has never lost certain ghostly memories of a larger literary universe' [MW:138]. She draws attention to affinities with St-John Perse and T. S. Eliot, but the memories of M. R. James's dark and primitive visions are even more telling. In 'Oh, Whistle', for example, a solitary man in a virtually deserted hotel, in a waterside town, has a vision of a beach towards night, with waves breaking in front of a village, and this is exactly what is described in the second section of Larkin's poem. Even the image of the fort may have been suggested by James's story, since 'a squat martello tower' [CM:86] stands on the edge of the darkening beach. A tale which possessed his imagination as an undergraduate and young poet may still be exerting its influence here.

Larkin was utterly preoccupied by the fragility of life and the omnipresence of surrounding death. It is thus natural to see his lamp-lit buildings as symbols of human consciousness, and the poring dark as an emblem of the mortality to which it must eventually succumb – as in the Venerable Bede's famous parable of the sparrow and the mead hall.[9]

XI

The creepy element in *High Windows* is particularly prominent in 'Livings'. Its three parts were written in the autumn and winter of 1971, the time of year which includes the period from Halloween to Guy Fawkes, and 'Livings III', with its portrait of Cambridge college life in the late seventeenth century, has close connections with at least three of James's tales. He frequently uses Oxbridge settings. The hero of 'Canon Alberic' is a Cambridge academic; the action of 'The Mezzotint' takes place in a set of don's rooms in an Oxford college; 'Oh, Whistle' begins with a long discussion amongst dons at the high table of a Cambridge college. The late seventeenth century was also one of James's abiding interests. He was an avid reader of the State Trials, particularly any trial over which Judge Jeffreys presided, and he used them as the basis for several stories: 'A Neighbour's Landmark', 'The Rose Garden', and especially 'Martin's Close', which is, in large measure, a pastiche of one of Jeffrey's trials.

Only in 1990 did it become widely known that James had written a story which combined his love of Oxbridge and the late seventeenth or early eighteenth century. Found amongst his papers, and previously unpublished, 'The Fenstanton Witch' begins with a talk amongst the Fellows of a Cambridge college from this period. The conversation is so uncannily like the one described at the opening of 'Livings III' that we feel we could be listening to the same people on another night. The scene opens with the fellows of King's College dining without the Master (at King's called the 'Provost') because he has strolled back to his Lodge after a service in chapel. Perhaps nocturnal vapours do not please – the rheumy River Cam flows through the grounds of King's. The Fellows then move to a table in their parlour and begin to drink; and James even raises for us the issue about the history of port-drinking discussed in the previous essay:

> [The Fellows] were sitting at a large table, clothless, with some decanters of wine (I don't know whether it was port or claret: much depends upon the date of Lord Methuen's treaty with Portugal), and something like a conversation has broken out.
>
> ....
>
> [Then had] a short discussion of the Witch of Endor, then the conversation drifted to Dr Hody's versions of the Bible, then by a not uncommon fate to Dr Bentley's late enormities, and thence back to the old question of College livings and probable vacancies. [HD:215–16]

Larkin could not have known this story, and any similarity can only be put down to a common outlook, the direct influence of James's other stories, and the indirect influence of James through Betjeman, Montgomery, Amis and others. However, a joint but separate discovery of the same scene suggests a remarkable commonalty of interests and imaginative preoccupations.

The hint of the creepy contained in the discussion about witches is also to be found when: 'A sizar shivers at his study / The kitchen cat has made a kill'. The sinister aura of cats plays an important part in several of James's stories. In 'The Stalls of Barchester Cathedral', for example, Archdeacon Haines keeps a diary of the supernatural disturbances that afflict him: '[A] cat – a large one by the feel of it – slipped between my feet, but again, of course, I saw nothing. It *may* have been the kitchen cat, but I do not think it was' [CM:189]. 'There *is* no kitchen cat' [CM:191]. Eventually, he dies from an injury caused by a fall: 'but, in addition to this, there were injuries inflicted upon the eyes, nose and mouth, as if by the agency of some savage animal, which, dreadful to relate, rendered those features unrecognizable' [CM:193].

It is not clear in the poem whether the sizar hears the cat or its victim or both. But Larkin was particularly responsive to the sound of cats and this too has an echo in James. In a letter to Sutton in March 1948, Larkin writes:

> It's a warm night & numerous cats are giving their unearthly song outside, like wraith-children crying. Between the black walls it has a deep resonance. And I seem to have been hearing birds very frequently also – beautiful ingenious twists of sound, aren't they, their notes I mean. [SL:146]

James knew about cats' unearthly cries. In 'Number 13', a cat is thought to be a reason for the horrible sound coming from the room next door: 'It was a high thin voice that they heard, and it seemed dry, as if from long disuse. [...] It was a really horrible sound [...]' [CM:62]. And as 'The Ash Tree' builds to its climax, a cat falls into the hollow tree: 'It is known to most of us that a cat can cry; but few of us have heard, I hope, such a yell as came out of the trunk of the great ash. Two or three screams there were, the witnesses are not sure which [...]' [CM:49].

Larkin likens the cry of cats to the cries of wraith children. Crying wraith children are not common in literature, and the reference is surely a reminiscence of the wraith children which emerge towards the end of James's 'Lost Hearts':

> Still as the night was, the mysterious population of the distant moonlit woods was not yet lulled to rest. From time to time strange cries as of lost and despairing wanderers sounded from across the mere. They might be the notes of owls or water-birds, yet they did not quite resemble either sound. Were not they coming nearer? Now they sounded from the nearer side of the water, and in a few moments they seemed to be floating about among the shrubberies. Then they ceased; but just as Stephen was thinking of shutting the window [...] he caught sight of two figures standing on the gravelled terrace that ran along the garden side of the Hall – the figures of a boy and a girl [...]. [CM:21]

At the end of 'Livings III' the mystic and supernatural is deliberately invoked. 'Above', run the last two lines, 'Chaldean constellations / Sparkle over crowded roofs'. 'Chaldean' literally means 'an inhabitant of ancient Chaldea or Babylonia', but it has come to mean 'a person skilled in occult matters, an astrologer'. Babylon, and the occult and the astrological, play prominent roles in James's work. The demon in

'Canon Alberic' is likened to 'the night monsters living in the ruins of Babylon [by Isaiah]' [CM:12]. Mr Abney, the sorcerer in 'Lost Hearts', is wrapped up in 'the Mysteries, the Orphic poems, the worship of Mithras', and other ancient occult matters [CM:15]. In addition, the two Cambridge students in 'The Fenstanton Witch' use astrology as part of their ceremony to acquire three locks of hair and the winding sheet from the dead witch: 'They [...] drew two large circles and they marked out with some pains the symbols of the planets and a few Hebrew letters [...]' [HD:219].

There are further routes back into James's work. Like 'The Fenstanton Witch', 'Livings III' is a work which begins with a discussion over port (?) and ends by moving outside to survey the cold and muddy fields around Cambridge. Like Lady Sadlier in 'The Uncommon Prayer-Book' [HD:93] the dons have an interest in regicide. But the most significant debt to James lies in the dons' riddle: 'Why is Judas like Jack Ketch?' Ketch's name occurs in 'The Story of a Disappearance and an Appearance', at the moment in the real Punch and Judy show before the show-box is turned over:

> We went on. Punch dealt faithfully with Judy, and in fact with all comers; and then came the moment when the gallows was erected, and the great scene with Mr. Ketch was to be enacted. [...] I expected [the figure in a white night-cap] to emerge into [...] view, but instead of that there slowly rose for a few seconds an uncovered face, with an expression of terror upon it, of which I have never imagined the like. It seemed as if the man, whoever he was, was being forcibly lifted, with his arms somehow pinioned or held back, towards the little gibbet on the stage. I could see the night-capped head behind him. Then there was a cry and a crash. The whole show-box fell over backwards [...]. [HD:67]

There seems to be no connection between Judas and the real Mr Ketch, but by 1699, the name 'Jack Ketch' was being used as a generic name for anyone who held the office of hangman, and by 1820 'Jack Ketch' was the name of the hangman in the Punch and Judy show [ODNB:31:445–6]. This is the character that Punch dupes into putting his own head in the noose. The connection between Judas and Jack Ketch is now clear – both die by their own rope. Accordingly, Larkin in 'Livings III' is not referring to the real Jack Ketch, he is referring to Jack Ketch as he appears in early nineteenth-century Punch and Judy shows; in fact, to the very scene which James describes and subverts in 'The

Story of a Disappearance and an Appearance'. We might also note that this story is a twentieth-century pastiche of early Victorian style, and the same is true of 'Livings III'.[10]

XII

In what way does 'Livings I', set in 1929, bear the imprint of the ghost stories? The narrator, we assume, is a bachelor past his first youth, and we find him in a hotel whose surroundings are reminiscent of the East Anglian and south Lincolnshire coast. Both the narrator and his setting recall James's work. The standard protagonist in the ghost stories is a retiring, middle-aged, undemonstrative bachelor usually engaged on some bookish pursuit – church history, picture collecting, writing a guidebook, bidding in auctions, cataloguing manuscripts. He characteristically travels by train or by bicycle, and often the stories are set when he is off home ground: staying with friends, moving to a newly inherited property, or – most frequently of all – staying in an inn or hotel. Several stories are set abroad, but most take place in England; and the east coast – the melancholy, flat landscape of Crabbe, Tennyson and Larkin himself – is the background to several of his most famous works. 'Oh, Whistle', for example, is largely set in a town that James calls 'Burnstow' which he based on Felixstowe on the Suffolk coast. (The same town plays a more minor role in 'The Tractate Middoth'.) 'A Warning to the Curious' is set in 'Seaburgh', based on the town where James spent some of his childhood, Aldeburgh, on the coast of the same county. James favours small hotels, which, like that in 'Livings I', typically have a 'boots' [HD:150] and a 'smoke-room' [HD:87].

'Livings I' was partially inspired by a holiday in King's Lynn, and thus it does not seem wholly surprising, as Larkin travelled through Lincolnshire and arrived at the East Anglian coast, that he should be reminded of two stories which derive so much of their atmosphere from their settings. Perhaps he was also reminded of a certain historical period. Unusually, the plot of 'A Warning to the Curious' requires it to have the fairly contemporary setting a few years after the First World War, but the events described must take place before the story was first published in August 1925. Could a story about a bachelor staying in a hotel on the East Anglian coast in the 1920s have helped inspire a poem with a similar setting? Intriguingly, when the BBC filmed 'A Warning' in 1972, the director – Lawrence Gordon Clark – enhanced the sense of foreboding by explicitly moving the story to 1929.

XIII

There are close traditional links between the supernatural and the written word; the two topics imbue and interpenetrate one another. Written language, we like to think, is a disembodied voice through which the dead can speak to us; and Milton once famously described a good book as 'the precious life-blood of a master-spirit [...] a life beyond life' [A:6]. The links between fiction and the supernatural are closer yet: Plato, writing of artistic representation, describes it as a 'phantom' or 'phantasm' of the real; he goes on to say that poetry's extraordinary emotional effect makes it a kind of 'witchcraft' [R:598b–c]; and the role of the muses in classical accounts of inspiration is familiar enough – indeed, the word 'inspiration' still signals its supernatural origin.[11]

For Larkin, the notion of a muse was not a formal or empty piece of classicizing. In a long review of Betjeman's *Collected Poems*, he makes clear that the kind of poetry Betjeman writes, and the kind of poetry he himself writes, is the variety where the question of inspiration, even of supernatural origin, can still intelligibly be raised:

> [Betjeman] has been carried through by propensities and techniques common to all but his immediate predecessors: a belief that poetry is an emotional business, rather than an intellectual or moral one, a belief in metre and rhythm as a means of enhancing emotion, a belief that a poem's meaning should be communicated directly and not by symbol. These were characteristics of poetry in the days when it was deemed a kind of supernatural possession. (How much today requires hypotheses of divine inspiration?) [FR:193]

The idea is developed at slightly greater length in the discussion of poetry which Larkin wrote for Montgomery's *The Moving Toyshop*. Montgomery, as Larkin tells us, revised this section, but since the passage has a sureness and profundity that outdistances anything else in the novel, I think we can be confident that Larkin's ideas still guide and animate it: 'The poetic emotion's impersonal: The Greeks were quite right when they called it inspiration [...] all that matters is that you've got a good receiving set for the poetic waves. Poetry's a visitation, coming and going at its own sweet will' [MT:127–8].

Two poems from about the same period supply more information about Larkin's conception of the muse. 'Deep Analysis', from 1946, shows that it is young, female, beautiful and sexualized; indeed, the act of inspiring is symbolized by kissing:

> I am a woman lying on a leaf;
> Leaf is silver, my flesh is golden,
> Comely at all points, but I became your grief
> When you would not listen.
>
> Through your one youth, whatever you pursued
> So singly, that I would be,
> Desiring to kiss your arms and your straight side
> - Why would you not let me? [CP:4]

The reason he would not let her, appears to be that he was always trying to win her, trying to grasp her, when all he needed to do was become wisely passive and make no effort at all: 'Why would you never relax, except for sleep, [...]', she continues, 'And / Why was all / Your body sharpened against me, vigilant, / Watchful [...]?' [CP:4].

In 'Waiting for breakfast [...]', from the next year, Larkin continues to portray the muse as a sexualized young woman who cannot be bidden but comes and goes at her own sweet will. But this time he introduces the idea that she can be jealous of his normal human girlfriend:

> Are you [the muse] jealous of her?
> Will you refuse to come till I have sent
> Her terribly away, importantly live
> Part invalid, part baby, and part saint? [CP:20]

More significantly, he shows that the muse approaches and manifests herself by imbuing his ordinary surroundings and objects with poetic meaning. He begins the poem by thinking that this is another ordinary day, but suddenly the scene takes on an unlooked for significance, and he realizes with an upsurge of joy that inspiration has returned:

> I thought: Featureless morning, featureless night.
>
> Misjudgment: for the stones slept, and the mist
> Wandered absolvingly past all it touched,
> Yet hung like a stayed breath; the lights burnt on,
> Pin-points of undisturbed excitement; beyond the glass

The colourless vial of day painlessly spilled
My world back after a year, my lost lost world
Like a cropping deer strayed near my path again,
Bewaring the mind's least clutch. Turning, I kissed her, [...] [CP:20]

An occasion when the ordinary unexpectedly takes on aesthetic significance is what Joyce refers to as an epiphany, and, like Larkin, he characterizes the experience almost entirely in spiritual and supernatural terms. In *Stephen Hero*, the protagonist says an epiphany occurs when the soul of an ordinary object becomes radiant, and we seem to be experiencing the unexpected manifestation of a spirit [SH:211–13], and Joyce repeatedly uses terms like 'calling up' and 'enchantment' when he tries to convey what the state feels like [SH:211–13; POA:229–31]. In one sense, what we see in an epiphanic moment is entirely familiar; in another, it seems novel, heightened, enhanced, as if we had never seen it before. As Larkin says through Montgomery: 'It's a curious passive sensation. Some people say it's as if you've noticed something for the first time' [MT:127–8]. However, Larkin adds one further thought which is not found in Joyce: 'But I think it's more as if the thing in question noticed *you* for the first time. You feel as if the rose or whatever it were is shining at you. Invariably after the first moment the phrase occurs to you to describe it [...]' [MT:127–8].

XIV

For Larkin, there is an internal connection between the onset of what he calls 'the poetic emotion', and the sense of the eerie and creepy: both anticipate the approach of a spirit.

Let me return for a moment to the *All Hallows* letter which he sent to Strang. This begins with the description of the lonely dusk quoted in section VI ('I felt [the increase of solitude] strongly today: as if I were in some remote spot [...]'). He then goes on to describe a short illness, and how he now spends most of his evenings at home, 'writing poems that seem brilliant when I go to bed, but are mediocre on rising'. In the next paragraph, he compliments Strang on a French poem she has just written, and makes some rare remarks about his own creativity: 'In one way I think you are wise to be alone. I find that with the absence of other people one becomes more sensitive to things that make for poetry. Once the kitchen door is slammed the mice come out to play, very hesitantly, but they do come [...].'[12] He then types out 'The Story of an Occurrence and a Disoccurrence' on the back of the sheet [SL:215–16].

I have already argued that the poem and the description of the dusk are imbued with the atmosphere of James's stories. This is the atmosphere where the mice of creativity, very hesitantly, come out to play: he is writing poems (although these are subject to his usual self-deprecation) and the letter itself contains a very beautiful description of the dusk. The same is true of the 1948 letter to Sutton where, under the influence of James, he likens the night-time cry of cats to wraith children. This passage is followed by another very striking image: 'And I seem to have been hearing birds very frequently also – beautiful ingenious twists of sound, aren't they, their notes I mean' [SL:146]. Both the description of birdsong and the description of the falling dusk were quoted by the *Letters'* first reviewers as examples of just how beautifully Larkin could write [JC:5]. Creativity of the highest quality seems to be inspired by this mood, and makes one feel there is perhaps more meaning in the phrases 'hauntingly beautiful' and 'beautifully creepy' than one first supposes.

How are heightened aesthetic awareness and a sense of the eerie and creepy related to one another? One point of contact is evident in the *All Hallows* letter: both are most naturally experienced when you are by yourself; specifically, when there is a great sense of loneliness. A second similarity lies in a heightened sense of awareness and vigilance: every sense becomes quickened, every sound or movement becomes imbued with meaning and significance, and a place which is familiar suddenly becomes strange.

The third affinity is that, when the eerie, creepy mood descends, we find ourselves thinking in a more primitive, animistic fashion: the coat behind a door is momentarily taken for a man, the gloomy woods seem to be watching us, the rustle and creaks of old buildings become soft footfalls. At such times, the personifications and anthropomorphic metaphors of poetry do not seem like mere literary decorations, they seem to register and respond to something that really exists in the world. This is why poetry seems so at home in pre-Enlightenment, pre-mechanistic ages, and why the Romantics made such a determined effort to re-establish belief in the supernatural. Sometimes this takes the form of discursive criticism. Keats, for example, in *Lamia*, complains that science attempts to conquer by means of 'rule and line' and that this has emptied 'the haunted air and gnomed mine' [K:163]. More often it takes the form of choosing supernatural subject-matters: the Gothic novel, the *Ancient Mariner*, *Christabel*, and *Lamia* itself.

From the very first, Larkin thought of himself as a Romantic poet. Writing to Amis in 1942, he remarks: 'Do you know anything about

Dryden? I don't know about you but I'm definitely a romantic in art, if that means anything. This means I expect colour, idealism & mysticism, to a certain extent. Now Dryden hasn't got any of these qualities [...]' [SL:44]. Given this outlook, it is completely foreseeable that Larkin would fall under James's spell. The idea that animism and poetic thought lie together in the unconscious explains why thinking about the supernatural might induce a mood conducive to poetry, and also why James's work seems so poetic, so haunting. If James does not have idealism, he has colour and dark-hued mysticism in abundance, and these are the qualities which suffuse the passages to Sutton and Strang.

Even towards the end of his career, Larkin remained committed to Romanticism. 'Livings II' is his portrait of the poet – the ecstatic, solitary creator – and here the superstitious and astrological hints of 'Livings III' are extrapolated into a full-blown animistic vision of the universe. The lighthouse keeper is at one with the surging sea, the wild wind, the shellfish, the rocks, the radio, the darkness. Everything in the poem is described as if it were alive or raised to a higher level of consciousness: the sea 'slavers', rocks 'writhe', shellfish 'husband their tenacity', the radio 'rubs its legs'. The keeper hymns them in religious ecstasy: 'Running suds, rejoice!' 'Creatures, I cherish you!' and then sets out his divining cards. He is at the wild heart of an ecstatic living universe, and the other two narrators have only the dimmest intimations of it.

What the 'approach of the muse' means at a more literal level is that the world seems animated by our deepest and most primitive thought processes. The way we understand the world and the way we understand the human seem to be one: and the world suddenly takes on significances and valences that it lacks when seen in the common light of day.

XV

Larkin was most subject to the creative mood when staying in places he did not own (the approach of the muse in 'Waiting for breakfast [...]' occurs in a hotel); and all three narrators in 'Livings' have their intimations of aesthetic experience when staying in rented or granted accommodation. As I pointed out above, these are also the circumstances in which James's protagonists are subjected to their terrifying experiences: they are usually staying in a friend's house, in a hotel, in a college. A strange place seems to heighten our sense of loneliness and the uncanny; and here it is worth recalling that the German for 'uncanny' is *unheimlich* which literally means 'not being at home'.

Larkin's muse is sexualized, and a hint of the erotic encourages her approach. Awareness of the creepy may have been something Larkin experienced most strongly when alone, but his mood is undoubtedly heightened by consciousness of an absent woman. The *All Hallows* letter is written to an absent Patsy Strang; and the only other time he uses a similar heading is when, on 31 October 1982, he writes 'All-Hallows' Eve' on a letter to an equally absent Judy Egerton [SL:680].[13] The eerie and creative moods are linked by a sharpening of perception and a sense of the world made new and strange, and we can establish a link between these moods and erotic attraction by noticing that Larkin associates the same qualities with the transforming power of love. In his late love poem, 'When first we faced, and touching showed', for example, he asks, 'Only what meeting made us feel, / So new, and gentle-sharp, and strange?' [CP:205].

However, in 'Livings', with one important exception, the absence of women is emphasized. None of the narrators is a woman; none of the narrators seems to have a relationship with a woman; no woman keeps the narrators company; the absences noted (the dead father, the Master) are all male; and in the first two sections, Larkin carefully removed all the female elements found in his sources. James's stories have a similar outlook on gender. The twenty-five full-length stories in the collected edition all have male protagonists, and most are bachelors. When women play a central role, they are long-dead witches and simpletons, but usually women fill the peripheral roles of nagging middle-aged wives, aunts or comic servants. All are non-sexual, and James was adamant that sex and sexual relationships should play no role in ghost stories. Discussing some modern American stories, he writes: 'They drag sex in too, which is a fatal mistake; sex is tiresome enough in the novels; in a ghost story, or as the backbone of a ghost story, I have no patience with it' [HD:259].

There would thus seem to be parallels with Larkin's need for the absence of women, but none with the sexual feelings that seem to have inspired him most keenly. But it is an error to suppose that sexuality is absent from James's work or that it does not play a crucial role in his stories. This is because, as Richard Holmes has pointed out, it is a suppressed disgust at female intimacy and the female genitalia which underlies and animates his best stories [MRJO:161–71]. James has a strange horror of wet mouths, hair, holes, and embraces; and several of these are associated with beds and sheets. There is Mr Dunning, for example, looking for a match under his pillow:

> [He] put his hand into the well-known nook under the pillow; only it did not get so far. What he touched was, according to his account, a mouth, with teeth, and with hair about it, and he declares, not the mouth of a human being. [CM:169]

Or the guilty Archdeacon Haines trying to sleep:

> I am much troubled in sleep. No definite image presented itself, but I was pursued by the very vivid impression that wet lips were whispering into my ear with great rapidity and emphasis for some time together. [CM:191]

Or most of all, there is Mr Somerton's story in 'The Treasure of Abbot Thomas'. He is down a well at night, trying to remove the treasure from the wall, but wary of the 'guardian' the abbot had written about:

> "Well, I felt to the right, and my fingers touched something curved that felt – yes – more or less like leather; dampish it was, and evidently part of a heavy, full thing. [...] I went on pulling out the great bag, in complete darkness. It hung for an instant on the edge of the hole, then slipped forward on to my chest, and *put its arms round my neck*. [...] I was conscious of a most horrible smell of mold, and of a cold kind of face pressed against my own [...]" [CM:117]

James said he had no inclination to write any fiction apart from ghost stories, and this suggests that his and Larkin's creativity is associated with the physical absence but psychic presence of the female. In James, this is because the suppressed and sexualized female, grotesquely transformed into a malevolent spirit, revenges itself on his protagonists. In Larkin, this is because he felt sexual longing most keenly when women were absent, and it was sexual longing which induced the 'new, and gentle-sharp, and strange' feeling that helped inspire aesthetic creation. It was on such occasions that a female spirit – his muse – could appear without inspiring either envy or conflict.

Larkin, however, allows himself a truly Jamesian moment in his most Jamesian poem, 'Livings III'. Here, amidst misogynist dons, the shivering sizar, the wail of cats, Chaldean constellations, and seventeenth-century Cambridge, he makes his only reference to the female in the whole of the 'Livings' triptych – 'names for *pudendum mulieris*' [CP:188]. This, we note, is a reference to the female genitalia, lightly disguised under James's beloved Latin.

XVI

It is the strange in the sense of 'the puzzling' that seems to have captured Larkin's attention in two of the creepy passages that most intrigued him. In Murdoch's sentence, 'The boy was there again this evening, and the dogs were not barking', we naturally wonder why the dogs were not barking, and why the last clause is introduced with an 'and' and not a 'but'. Is the boy so familiar that he no longer excites the dogs' interest? But in that case, why is his presence worth commenting on, and why can he only be described as 'the boy'? Is he a ghost so the dogs are not aware of his presence? But this would be odd given that animals are generally thought to be more sensitive to spectral presences than humans. And so on. Similarly, in Cornford's 'All Souls' Night', we wonder why the lover does not think the narrator strange or older. Is it because he has watched from the afterlife? And why does she not find him strange or older either? Is it because she remembers him just as he was, and he has remained at the same age in the next world? Both works are little more than fragments, and yet they are pregnant with wonderful and baffling possibilities. Not only our senses but our thoughts are quickened.

We can also make a guess as to why Larkin was so impressed by these incidents: both reminded him of the approach of his muse. First, there is nothing weird or terrifying about the figures he selects; both are, in a sense, utterly ordinary. Second, they are figures who have been seen before; they are both *recognized*. Third, although they are recognized, they are also defamiliarized, heightened, ringed by the strange. Fourth, like the muse, they are silent, reticent visitations apparently coming and going 'at their own sweet will'. Fifth, like Larkin's muse, we not only recognize *them*, but they can potentially recognize *us*. We can thus see them as his emblems of the poetic.

XVII

The ordinary plays a major role in James. Giving some hints on how to write a ghost story, he said: 'Let us be introduced to the characters in a placid way; let us see them going about their ordinary business, undisturbed by forebodings, pleased with their surroundings; and into this calm environment let the ominous thing put out its head, unobtrusively at first, and then more insistently, until it holds the stage' [HD:248]. In these opinions he was at one with Henry James. '"The supernatural [...] requires a powerful imagination in order to be as exciting as the natural. [A] good ghost story [...] must be connected at a hundred points with the common objects of life," and loses half its force if it is detached from its "prosaic, commonplace, daylight associations"' [HJG:50].

M. R. James's practice is more risky than his doctrines require. Not only are his introductions and transitions about the ordinary, but the writing is frequently – and one feels deliberately – fussy, slack, stale and facetious. The introduction to 'Oh, Whistle', one of his greatest stories, is a good example: '"I suppose you will be getting away pretty soon, now Full term is over, Professor," said a person not in the story to the Professor of Ontography, soon after they sat down next to each other at a feast in the hospitable hall of St James's College' [CM:81]. The dull near-joke in the first half of the sentence and the obviously made-up names and titles do not bode well, and the heart slightly sinks on reading a paragraph, at the end of three pages of conversation, which says explicitly what the dialogue has previously tried to show. In interludes of the story, matters do not improve: '"I don't know about superstition," said the Colonel, [...] "But it's your drive" (or whatever it might have been: the golfing reader will have to imagine appropriate digressions at the proper intervals)' [CM:93]. M. R. James did not have his namesake's worries about lack of seriousness and authorial intrusions.

And yet this facetiousness is counterpointed against excellent, and excellently serious, writing in the supernatural sections. For example, when Parkins tries the whistle he has found:

> He blew tentatively and stopped suddenly, startled and yet pleased at the note he had elicited. It had a quality of infinite distance in it, and, soft as it was, he somehow felt it must be audible for miles round. It was a sound, too, that seemed to have the power (which many scents possess) of forming pictures in the brain. He saw quite clearly for a moment a vision of a wide, dark expanse at night, with a fresh wind blowing, and in the midst a lonely figure – how employed he could not tell. [CM:89]

Somehow one feels that the supernatural parts gain from being set against the slack, off-hand writing of the introductions. I suspect this is partly because the background throws the foreground into perspicuous relief, and partly because it heightens the believability of the stories: 'If someone so dusty, so unimaginative, so fussy can report this,' we feel, 'then it *must* be true.'

Sometimes the supernatural qualities which Joyce found in an epiphany – the way that a soul or spirit can suddenly 'show forth' and manifest itself through ordinary objects – can be found concentrated on one element in a poem – the symbol. Such a symbol, says Stephen in *A Portrait of the Artist*, calls up a kind of still and abstract enchantment, as though light were emanating from some other world [POA:229–31]. This kind of symbolism, indeed, is one important aspect of the Romantic outlook which M. H. Abrams characterized as 'natural supernaturalism' [NS].

We can find such symbols in late Larkin, and like James, he draws attention to them by setting them in the context of the slack and the ordinary; in fact, the more striking the symbol, the more deliberately stale, flat and slangy the surrounding tends to be. 'High Windows', for example, begins 'When I see a couple of kids / And guess he's fucking her and she's / Taking pills or wearing a diaphragm [...]' and ends:

> [...] And immediately
>
> Rather than words comes the thought of high windows:
> The sun-comprehending glass,
> And beyond it, the deep blue air, that shows
> Nothing, and is nowhere, and is endless. [CP:165]

Robert Lowell, while saying this was his favourite poem in the collection, commented: '[All] the poetry is in the last lines, [although] these would count for little without the others' [M:430].

The late poems are full of such sudden transitions: from 'Groping back to bed after a piss' to 'One shivers slightly looking up there. / The hardness and brightness and the plain / Far-reaching singleness of that wide stare' [CP:169]; or 'My wife and I have asked a crowd of craps' to '[...] hearing the noise of wind, / And looking up to see the moon thinned / To an air-sharpened blade [...]' [CP:181]. We find a similar transition in 'Friday Night in the Royal Station Hotel'. On the one hand, there is the ordinary ('A porter reads / An unsold evening paper'); on the other, there is a daring plunge into symbolism and obscurity: 'How / Isolated, like a fort, it is – / [...] *Night comes on. Waves fold behind villages*' [CP:163]. In these passages, the uncanny is deliberately invoked, and the natural world seems to let through a strange and other-worldly light.

XVIII

Coleridge once said that Wordsworth tried 'to give the charm of novelty to things of everyday, and to excite a feeling analogous to the supernatural, by awakening the mind's attention from the lethargy of custom' [PLT:104–5].[14] But the appropriateness of the analogy with the supernatural goes beyond merely awakening the mind from the lethargy of custom. Often the poet intuits a half-spoken meaning in what he sees and feels, and frequently this will be an implied human presence or association. One thinks of Hardy meditating on an old suit, a broken sunshade, a worn stair.

'Friday Night in the Royal Station Hotel' is an excellent but more complex example. It is remarkably eerie. All those chairs facing one another, unsold papers and full ashtrays imply the palpable presence of the absent, and there is a tense although apparently meaningless sense of expectation. The bafflement we feel is exactly captured by Virginia Woolf's description of Henry James's ghosts: 'They have their origins within us. They are present whenever the significance overflows our powers of expressing it; whenever the ordinary appears ringed by the strange' [VWCE:291]. The uncanniness Larkin finds latent in a deserted hotel, with its bright shoeless corridors, has affinities with the greatest of all horror films about ghosts and possession – *The Shining*[15] – and it is not remarkable that 'Oh, Whistle' should have come into his mind at this point.

Frequently, the meaning the poet discerns in his perceived subject matter will be a historical significance, and he will try to make manifest his almost tangible sense of absent forebears. No poetry conveys a more potent sense of the past than 'Deceptions', 'MCMXIV' and 'Livings I & III'. And in 'Church Going' we can see Larkin work through various motives before he discovers that his reason for visiting churches lies in a sense of the past: the feeling that this place is 'proper to grow wise in, / If only that so many dead lie round' [CP:98]. It is this palpable sense of history that Henry James himself saw as the modern way of seeing ghosts. Recalling a visit to Haddon Hall in Derbyshire one evening in 1872, he wrote:

> The twilight deepened, the ragged battlements and the low, broad oriels glanced duskily from the foliage, the rooks wheeled and clamored in the glowing sky; and if there had been a ghost on the premises, I certainly ought to have seen it. In fact, I did see it, as we see ghosts nowadays. I felt the incommunicable spirit of the scene with almost painful intensity. The old life, the old manners, the old figures seemed present again. [HJG:105]

As I mentioned in section IX, both Larkin and James were excellent mimics, and this talent makes an important contribution to the historical atmosphere of their work. In 'Livings', historical parody transcends itself and becomes art. 'Livings III' makes loving use of period vocabulary and detail: 'Nocturnal vapours do not please', 'Which advowson looks the fairest', 'rheumy fevers', 'a sizar shivers at his study', and so on. Such details are equally carefully observed although less obvious in 'Livings I': the blanks that stand for names, 'the boots', 'a single where I hang my hat', the dreary menu, 'soup to stewed pears', 'the smoke room', and the 'ex-Army sheets'. It is these features which help give such a powerful sense of 'the old life, the old manners, the old figures' and make them seem present again.

M. R. James's use of historical parody is even more extensive and expert. Almost every story supplies an instance, but the report on the death of Sir Matthew Fell in 'The Ash Tree' is admirably effortless and low key:

> There was not any the least Trace of an Entrance having been forc'd to the Chamber: but the Casement stood open, as my poor Friend would always have it in this Season. He had his Evening Drink of small Ale in a silver vessel of about a pint measure, and to-night had not drunk it out. [CM:41]

Indeed, one of James's greatest qualities is that he seems to allow his stories to develop from such documents, and his ghosts seem reifications of his intense and overwhelming sense of the past.

XIX

The idea that in poetry we recognize a spirit (and are sometimes recognized by it) may explain why so many feel that we respond to poetry in the same way we respond to the supernatural – with a shudder. Attempting to characterize his response to true poetry, A. E. Housman invokes a remark by Eliphaz the Termanite: 'A spirit passed before my face; the hair of my flesh stood up'. And in a passage Larkin alludes to with approval [AWJ:175], Housman proceeds to describe this and three other physical symptoms in greater detail:

> Experience has taught me, when I am shaving of a morning, to keep watch over my thoughts, because, if a line of poetry strays into my memory, skin bristles, so that the razor ceases to act. This particular symptom is accompanied by a shiver down the spine; there is another which consists in a constriction of the throat and a precipitation of water in the eyes; and there is a third which I can only describe by using a phrase from one of Keats' last letters, where

> he says of Fanny Brawne, 'everything which reminds me of her goes through me like a spear'. The seat of this sensation is the pit of the stomach. [NNP:50]

Sylvia Plath reports similar symptoms. Recalling her first response, as a child, to Matthew Arnold's 'The Forsaken Merman', she writes: 'I saw gooseflesh on my skin. I did not know what made it. I was not cold. Had a ghost passed over? No, it was poetry. A spark flew off Arnold and shook me, like a chill. I wanted to cry; I felt very odd. I had fallen into a new way of being happy' [JP:118]. And Larkin himself draws the same parallel when writing to Monica Jones: '*Not a line of her writing have I, not a thread of her hair, If it's ever Spring again, Spring again*: At these my spine contracts & a shiver runs over my ribs' [LM:11]; 'I shan't believe I am insensitive to poetry as long as Hardy can make me tingle all over like a man menaced by a *revenant*' [LM:219].

If the alchemy of poetry can make the familiar world seem visionary, precise and strange; if it can make the most powerful emotions of the long dead seem like living presences; if it can pierce us so unerringly that it harrows and interrogates; and if, at the same time, it can convey an overwhelming sense of mutual recognition, then it is no wonder that responsive souls should want to characterize their experience in terms of the supernatural.

XX

Both poems and ghost stories are risky undertakings: if real poems and real ghost stories can both be detected by a shudder, and the effect is very rare, then both run a substantial risk of not creating their intended and obvious effect.

Writing verse or writing a novel is a task you can set yourself, and although the outcome may be bad verse or a bad novel you can see these productions form part of a continuum with good verse and good novels. But no one can set himself the task of writing poetry, and the difference between poetry and verse seems a difference in kind not degree. Larkin certainly felt poetry could not be written to order (this was one reason why he rejected the Laureateship), and the difference between his genuinely inspired works and those which were commissioned ('Going, Going', for instance) is obvious to any attuned reader.

In the same way, most ghost stories fail, and those which arouse a genuine chill are few and far between. This is evident when reading through M. R. James's complete stories. The early works and one or two late productions (like 'A Warning to the Curious') are masterful, but as he grew older his inspiration diminished, and some of his final stories are painfully threadbare and facetious.

It is therefore understandable that both Larkin and James felt their works depended on something outside of themselves – a visitant – that was beyond their control. By the mid-seventies, Larkin sensed that poetry had given him up [FR:112], and James, responding to the American librarian Bella da Costa Greene, who had requested a new story, wrote: 'I'm afraid the vein of ghost stories has run rather dry. If it opens again, you shall know' [GS:5].

XXI

Larkin first became known to the reading public for his scepticism, portrayal of welfare-state England, and disavowal of Romanticism, obscurity and myth. These are all real aspects of his personality, but their place in his psyche is only understood when we see how they control and overlay his deeper feelings for Romanticism, ritual and the supernatural. He would have appreciated both Housman's point in the following passage, and the notably Jamesian image with which he illustrates it:

> [Words in] poetry [...] find their way to something in man which is obscure and latent, something older than the present organization of his nature, like the patches of fen which still linger here and there in the drained lands of Cambridgeshire. [NNP:49]

Notes

1. There are four or fives places in Larkin's life and work where James's influence is obvious and unequivocal, but his influence strikes me as much more important than these few places alone would suggest. As I hope sections I and IV demonstrate, James was hugely popular around the early mid-century (his *Collected Ghost Stories* first appeared in 1931) and was very much part of the literary air Larkin breathed. I feel I can often sense James's ghostly presence in Larkin's work, particularly in *High Windows* when the nights draw in, although I cannot always offer clear and brief parallel passages to prove the point. Consequently, I have had to resort more often than usual to lengthy quotation and paraphrase in an attempt to prompt the reader into acknowledging a similarity of structure or atmosphere. In my view, this is necessary because James is such a *deep* influence: he no longer sits on the surface of Larkin's mind in the form of remembered quotations and incidents, his influence has been completely absorbed and assimilated into Larkin's creative personality: it is no longer something he sees, it is something which colours his whole manner of seeing.
2. The phrase, although quoted by Larkin, is actually by Thomas Hardy.
3. As Larkin wrote to Kingsley Amis: '... [The sentence] turned out to be the opening of *The Sacred and Profane Love Machine*, by none other than I[ris] M[urdoch], wch I took the trouble to borrow from my library. I got nearly to the bottom of p.3. SHE IS UNREADABLE *why do people read her*? They *can't*' [SL:752].
4. It might reasonably be wondered why there are not more references to James in Larkin's letters. But as this section shows, Larkin's two most James-obsessed friends were Amis and Montgomery, and there are problems with the letters Larkin sent to both of them. Amis admitted that, after two marriages and many moves, he'd simply lost many of the letters – particularly early letters – which Larkin sent to him [SL:xii]; and Larkin's letters to Montgomery were deposited in the Bodleian Library, Oxford, by Montgomery's widow, who forbade all inspection until 2035 [SL:xii]. Consequently, more discussions of James by Larkin may eventually emerge.
5. Apart from parallels between James's works and the two Montgomery novels I mention in the text, the following are striking. In *Holy Disorders*, James is quoted on p. 60; 'Count Magnus' is referred to on p. 67, and a detail from 'The Ash-tree' on p. 98. In *The Moving Toyshop*, 'Lost Hearts' is alluded to on p. 9, and one character's alarm at feeling the wet arms of a woman's corpse around his neck is reminiscent of the horror felt by Mr Somerton in 'The Treasure of Abbot Thomas'.
6. I would connect Larkin's admiration for James with his feeling for the Victorian painter, John Atkinson Grimshaw (1836–93), who specialized in beautifully detailed paintings of moonlit roads at night, the lights of great houses seen through dank winter trees, and similar subjects. Larkin wrote in 1972: 'The Ferens Art Gallery has got its Atkinson Grimshaw – *bought in 1950 for £10* ARRGHGH. It's lovely: so delicate. Different from the one in the Ferrers Gallery catalogue, though v. similar' [SL:467]. A picture by Grimshaw seems compulsory on all modern editions of James, and it seems that those which do not use one have consciously resisted the temptation. Grimshaw's

Moonlight Walk appears on the cover of the Wordsworth Classics' *Collected Ghost Stories*, while *Where the Pale Moonbeams Linger* graces the latest Oxford World's Classics edition.

7. Paraphrasing the plot of 'The Story of a Disappearance and an Appearance', and discussing the difficulties of interpreting it would require too much space in the main text and clog the forward movement of my argument. I shall thus confine both matters to this note.

   The story is told in a series of letters dated 1837. They are written by an anonymous nephew who goes in search of his uncle, a country rector, who has disappeared just before Christmas. Initially nothing is found, but the nephew falls in with a salesman who tells him of a wonderful Punch and Judy show he has seen in a nearby town. That night, the nephew has a dream about a disturbingly violent Punch and Judy show which ends with Punch being chased and caught by a figure in black with a bag over his head. The nephew wakes the next morning to find the landlord of the pub arguing with a serving girl, and the Christmas service he attends is subject to some odd disturbances. In the afternoon, a real Punch and Judy show sets up in the market square, but the showmen's dog runs off howling, and from the high vantage point in his room, the nephew can see that a real man, terrified and with his arms pinned to his side, is being lifted towards the on-stage gallows by someone in a white cap. The showbox collapses and a figure, or possibly two figures, run off. The crowd gives chase, the man they are pursuing breaks his neck falling into a quarry, and the body of the uncle is discovered in the same place – the tip of the white bag over his head was showing above ground. When the crowd returns, the body of the second showman is found dead under his showbox.

   The general outline is clear. The two Punch and Judy men have killed the uncle. The narrator receives an intimation of this through a dream; and the disruptions of the Christmas service are prefigurations of the deaths and funerals to come. The same supernatural forces which explain these events scare away the showmen's dog. And the man being lifted towards the gallows is one of the Punch and Judy men being given a supernatural foretaste of what will happen to him. Perhaps it is the ghostly uncle who accounts for the numerical confusion over how many men are running away; he may be pursuing one of his murderers to his death in a place where the crowd will later discover the uncle's own corpse.

   Beyond the general outline, everything else is far from clear. I am completely unsure why the showmen murdered the uncle (although he was something of a martinet). I am also unclear whether the landlord of the hotel is involved with the uncle's murder (there is a good deal of text devoted to the argument between them), or whether the row with the serving girl is part of the story or only comic development of a minor character. In addition, the disappearance is clear enough, but which is the appearance – the uncle's arrival in the dream, or during the show, or after the show, or in the ground, or perhaps all of these?

8. 'Church Going' is largely a poem about Christian *objects* which have fallen out of use, although rituals that were once part of Christianity are mentioned towards the close of the poem.

9. 'The present life of man on earth, O king, as compared with the whole length of time which is unknowable to us, seems to me to be like this: as if, when you are sitting at dinner with your chiefs and ministers in wintertime, [...] one of the sparrows from outside flew very quickly through the hall; as if it came in one door and soon went out through another. In that actual time it is indoors it is not touched by the winter's storm; but yet the tiny period of time is over in a moment, and having come out of the winter it soon returns to the winter and slips out of your sight. Man's life appears to be more or less like this; and of what may follow it, or what preceded it, we are absolutely ignorant' (The Venerable Bede, *Ecclesiastical History of the English People*, Bk. II, Ch. 13 [BTQ:400]). Was this scene at the back of Barbara Everett's mind when she said that Larkin's poem made her think of the Dark Ages?
10. This consideration gives another reason for thinking 'Livings III' attempts to show early nineteenth-century college life. However, it still does not settle the question of the era that poem tries to portray. The first records of Ketch being hanged in a Punch and Judy show are from 1820, but this event may have been portrayed very much earlier; Pepys, after all, mentions Punch and Judy shows in his diaries. It is also unclear how much Larkin knew about the history of Punch and Judy shows – I suspect very little.

    My case for saying the style of 'Livings III' is probably early nineteenth-century is given in section III of the previous essay.
11. Several thoughts in this paragraph were inspired by the opening of Timothy Lustig's *Henry James and the Ghostly* (Cambridge: Cambridge University Press, 1994).
12. Larkin sometimes likens the muse to shy animals: here it is like hesitant mice, in 'Waiting for breakfast [...]' like a 'cropping deer' [CP:20].
13. Is this idea refuted by the fact that in 'Waiting for breakfast [...]' the approach of the muse occurs when he is in a room with his girlfriend? I don't think so. First, Larkin has *detached* his attention from the girl (who is brushing her hair), and looks – initially aimlessly – out of the window. Thus paying less attention to a woman who is present may have the same effect as consciousness of a woman who is absent. Second, his immediate thought, once the muse has approached, is to send his girlfriend 'terribly away' [CP:20].
14. The passage from Coleridge is quoted, and applied to Larkin, in R. L. Brett's essay 'Larkin in Hull'. Here is the whole passage which includes a report of Larkin's response. 'I once wrote in a review-article that his poetry matched Coleridge's description of Wordsworth's endeavour "to give the charm of novelty to things of everyday, and to excite a feeling analogous to the supernatural, by awakening the mind's attention from the lethargy of custom". On seeing this he wrote to me, "Thank you for your kind words about myself. I am so glad you made the point about enhancing the everyday. It is my contention that this is the real test of the imagination – anybody can create an effect with properties such as madness, violence or horror, just as one can flavour a dish more easily with pepper than whatever it tastes of naturally"' [PLT:104–5].
15. When we recall Larkin's rose, *The Shining*'s title may strike us as significant.

Aubade

I work all day, and get half-drunk at night.
Waking at four to soundless dark, I stare.
In time the curtain-edges will grow light.
Till then I see what's really always there:
Unresting death, a whole day nearer now,
Making all thought impossible but how
And where and when I shall myself die.
Arid interrogation: yet the dread
Of dying, and being dead,
Flashes afresh to hold and horrify.

The mind blanks at the glare. Not in remorse
- The good not done, the love not given, time
Torn off unused – nor wretchedly because
An only life can take so long to climb
Clear of its wrong beginnings, and may never;
But at the total emptiness for ever,
The sure extinction that we travel to
And shall be lost in always. Not to be here,
Not to be anywhere,
And soon; nothing more terrible, nothing more true.

This is a special way of being afraid
No trick dispels. Religion used to try,
That vast moth-eaten musical brocade
Created to pretend we never die,
And specious stuff that says *No rational being*
Can fear a thing it will not feel, not seeing
That this is what we fear – no sight, no sound,
No touch or taste or smell, nothing to think with,
Nothing to love or link with,
The anaesthetic from which none come round.

And so it stays just on the edge of vision,
A small unfocused blur, a standing chill
That slows each impulse down to indecision.
Most things may never happen: this one will,
And realisation of it rages out
In furnace-fear when we are caught without
People or drink. Courage is no good:
It means not scaring others. Being brave
Lets no one off the grave.
Death is no different whined at than withstood.

Slowly light strengthens, and the room takes shape.
It stands plain as a wardrobe, what we know,
Have always known, know that we can't escape,
Yet can't accept. One side will have to go.
Meanwhile telephones crouch, getting ready to ring
In locked-up offices, and all the uncaring
Intricate rented world begins to rouse.
The sky is white as clay, with no sun.
Work has to be done.
Postmen like doctors go from house to house.

Philip Larkin, 29 November 1977

V
'Aubade': Death and the Thought of Death

What's history to me? Mine is the first and only world
Wittgenstein

When the commonplace 'We must all die' transforms itself suddenly into the acute consciousness 'I must die – and soon', then death grapples us and his fingers are cruel
George Eliot

Larkin invariably uses French words and French titles ironically. For him, French is the language of style, sophistication, sensuality, urbanity, passion and worldliness: it is the language of *la politesse* [CP:179], *sens d'occasion* and *savoir vivre* [SL:629] – all qualities he felt he and his world conspicuously lacked. Appropriately therefore, in the only poems with French titles from the forties – 'Femmes Damnées' [CP:270] and 'Ballade des Dames du Temps Jadis' [TWG:247–8] – Larkin takes two rather elevated French poems and affectionately reduces them to something more quotidian. Baudelaire's lesbians – Hippolyte and Delphine – become Rosemary and Rachel, and they are set amongst builders' estates and cabbage patches rather than 'languishing lamps' and scented cushions. Villon's majestic elegy for great women in history – Thaïs, Heloïse, Joan of Arc – and his refrain of 'But where are the snows of yester-year?', becomes a lament for now dispersed school friends – Valerie, Julia, Elspeth – with a last line that rings the changes on 'So many summer terms away'.

There are no French titles in the fifties and sixties, possibly because Larkin took the official Movement line on foreign cultures. However, in the seventies he wrote two, and we can here note a subtle change of approach. In the forties he takes particular poems by particular poets as his models, and is largely interested in deflating their contents. (Even his one poem with a German title, 'Traumerai' [CP:12], mocks the quiet rapture of Schumann's famous piano piece,[1] a work found in many pre-war piano stools.) In the seventies, his titles allude to *forms* or general *kinds* of poetry, although, to a certain extent, the nature of the form or kind determines the nature of the content. Perhaps he was still enough of a Movement poet to feel that poems whose enjoyment depended on a knowledge of specific foreign models could only be arty and affected.

The irony has also grown more complex. Consider 'Vers de Société' [CP:181], the first of these seventies poems. In a way, the poem is vers de société (the versification's light and accomplished); in another way it isn't (it glories in crudities quite unsuited to the drawing room). On the other hand it isn't light in either sense – smooth or coarse – since it contains some of Larkin's most memorable images and soul-searchings. But the complexities do not end there. 'Vers de Société' could also mean verse *about* society. And this seems true; until we reflect that it's more about solitariness.

I

Before approaching the ironies in 'Aubade', we need to know what Larkin thought the word's straightforward meaning was. This is by no means easy to determine as the word has never quite taken root in English: many competent native speakers have never heard it, and those that do know it frequently admit to an uncertain grasp of its meaning. Most informed speakers would probably say that 'aubade' is a French word referring to a kind of open-air dawn serenade, and that it has something to do with the troubadours.

There is some truth in this. The word's first recorded use in English was in 1678 when one Phillips – presumably a musician or music publisher – advertised: '*Aubades* (French) songs, or instrumentall music, sung, or playd under any ones Chamber window in the morning' [OED]. Despite its age, the word does not appear in Johnson's dictionary of 1756, and modern dictionaries, even those produced by the same publisher, diverge in their definitions. The OED has: *A musical announcement of dawn, a sunrise song or open-air concert.* The *New Shorter Oxford English Dictionary* has: *A piece of music or a poem written to be heard at or appropriate to dawn.* The first is unsatisfactory because it omits all reference to poetry; the second because it omits all reference to the open air and the occasion of performance. A more satisfactory (if rather more cumbersome) definition than either might be: *A piece of music, song or poem either about or to be performed at dawn. Usually, it is played in the open air outside a house, often in honour of the woman inside it. The word can also refer to the occasion of performance as well as the piece or poem performed.* The etymological sections of all dictionaries agree, however, that the word derives from an old troubadour lyric song called the *alba*, and that later forms of this lyric, in Old French rather than Old Provençal, began to be referred to as 'aubades' at the beginning of the fifteenth century.

Give or take a few details, it's natural to assume that this was Larkin's understanding of the term, and he certainly knew several aubades that conform to the definition sketched above. From its first appearance in 1900, until it was replaced in 1972, the standard poetry anthology in schools and universities was Sir Aurthur Quiller-Couch's *The Oxford Book of English Verse 1250–1900*. It was a book Larkin knew well. This contains two poems entitled 'Aubade': Shakespeare's 'Hark! Hark! The Lark' from *Cymbeline*, and Sir William Davenant's 'The lark now leaves his watery nest'. Both songs are sung to a young woman in bed by a young man outside her window. These works were written prior to the OED's first citation of the word; and in both men's collected works they are merely called songs. The title 'Aubade' would therefore seem to be an editorial initiative, but there is no reason for thinking Larkin knew this.

Louis MacNeice, whom Larkin much admired, wrote two aubades in the thirties: 'Aubade for Infants' [SPM:85], and one titled simply 'Aubade' [MCP:86] which is one of his best-known poems. These are about the beginning of life rather than the beginning of day, and they are slightly ominous, threatening works. They belong to the category of ironic or subverted aubades: the one warns of the harsh adult world, the other of tedium and war. If Larkin thought of the aubades of Shakespeare and Davenant – as well as MacNeice's inversions – as paradigmatic aubades, then he would think of an aubade as an erotic and joyful dawn song.

II

However, several commentators have assumed that Larkin's understanding of 'aubade' was *not* that outlined above. Andrew Swarbrick writes that Larkin's 'Aubade' alludes to 'the traditional dawn which *separates* lovers' [my italics; OOR:151]. Lawrence Lerner is more specific: 'The *aubade* or *alba* was a well-known and popular lyric genre in the Middle Ages, [...] Larkin's poem makes no explicit reference to this tradition, but the title invites us to notice the contrast: this speaker is not with his beloved but alone, he grieves when dawn comes not because the joys of love and companionship are over, but because he is terrified of death' [LE:38]. They think that Larkin does not use 'aubade' in its standard modern sense (insofar as there is one), but that he uses the word to refer back to the troubadours' *alba*.

The *alba* is not a lover's dawn serenade to a woman in bed.[2] Of the nineteen surviving *albas*, six are religious and describe how the dawn brings an enhanced awareness of sin. The others are erotic, and generally involve a knight in bed with a lady whose jealous husband is away. The couple have enjoyed a night of illicit sexual passion but know the dawn means the end of their bliss. When they are woken by the birds or the cry of the castle watchman the lady denies that dawn has arrived. When the lover affirms it has, both of them curse the rising sun. The knight departs, leaving the lady prostrated by misery and longing. The lyric is always dramatized: sometimes the knight speaks, sometimes the lady, sometimes the watchman, although straightforward dialogue is avoided.[3]

It is quite likely that Larkin knew about this. He had studied medieval and Renaissance literature at Oxford, where he had been lectured by Neville Coghill and C. S. Lewis. Even if the *alba* was not an object of study, it is quite possible that one of them mentioned that it was a profound influence on the morning after the wedding in *Romeo and Juliet* or the dawn scene in Chaucer's *Troilus and Cresyede*. Larkin had studied both works, and frequently remarked how bored he was with the latter [SL:38]. In July 1942, he read Lewis's *The Allegory of Love* [SL:37], a book which makes extravagant claims for the troubadours' importance ('Compared with the [effect of the troubadours on literature] the Renaissance is merely a ripple on the surface [...]' [AOL:4]) and Lewis explicitly mentions the *alba* in his discussion of the morning scene in *Troilus* [AOL:196].

Even better evidence for Larkin's familiarity with the *alba* comes from his knowledge of modern aubades, because several of these were conscious attempts to revive the *alba* tradition.[4] Larkin knew William Empson's 'Aubade' because he selected it for his anthology, the *Oxford Book of Twentieth-Century English Verse*, published in 1973; in fact, it is the only poem with that title in the book. He soon came to know it better than he wanted. Shortly after publication, Christopher Ricks pointed out that the anthology missed out the second half of the poem. Larkin found this deeply upsetting, and one can easily imagine the vexed and anxious checking the news must have caused: a letter to Anthony Thwaite [SL:477–8] expresses his mortification, and there is a long correspondence with OUP as to how the matter could best be put right.[5]

Empson's poem describes being woken early in the morning by an earthquake, and his indecision about whether to leave Japan and his Japanese girlfriend now war is imminent. In a note on the poem he later wrote: 'an aubade is traditionally the song warning lovers to separate before dawn' [WECP:316]. His aubade not only has this story, but it is the only modern aubade with a refrain (in fact it has two which alternate), something also shared by its medieval ancestor. Ricks wrote to Larkin about Empson's poem in March 1973. A little over a year later, in April 1974, Larkin began work on his own poem, and the title 'Aubade' first appears in the manuscripts on 1 June 1974.[6]

Another aubade he would have known is by Stevie Smith, one of his favourite poets. If Empson drew his inspiration from the *alba* tradition then Smith's is a conscious reconstruction. Hers is the only modern poem which contains – except for the refrain – every feature of the troubadour lyric: the mode of dramatization is identical, the content is the same, and the language is studiedly antique. In the first stanza the woman denies the dawn has arrived. She says: ''Tis not the day lights yonder sky / It is too soon / I hear the cock's discordant cry, / He doodles to the moon'. The man then replies: 'Alas my love it is the day, / [...] Farewell, my love, adieu, it is the dawn' [CPSS:46]. The revivification of the *alba* tradition has proved so influential that, in our own day, the *Oxford Companion to English Literature* now defines 'Aubade' as: '[A] dawn song, usually describing the regret of two lovers at their imminent separation' [OCEL:50].

If you do not know about the *alba* tradition then it is easy to read these two poems as ironic or subverted aubades; works designed to undercut the innocence of the joyful dawn song. If you do know the tradition, then one sees that 'aubade' is used in a perfectly straightforward descriptive sense, and that no mockery of any kind is intended. When Larkin wrote his 'Aubade', therefore, he could well have had these two models in mind rather than an aubade in its more usual modern sense. If this were so, then an aubade for Larkin would be a poignant, dramatized poem about lovers who curse the dawn and have to separate.

III

When Larkin called his poem 'Aubade' was he making reference to the *alba* tradition or was he using the term to mean a morning serenade? Contrary to Swarbrick and Lerner's opinion, the latter seems the more likely alternative. Larkin may have known about the *alba*, but he was very aware of, and wrote for, the ordinary reader who could not be assumed to know about it. It could be replied that the same consideration ought to apply to Empson and Smith, but they seem very different kinds of poets. Empson is deeply obscure and academic – his work positively demands exegesis – while a good deal of Smith's charm depends on being quirky and oblique. In addition, assuming an aubade is an erotic dawn song from a lover outside to the beloved inside makes the ironies of Larkin's own 'Aubade' less muted and equivocal. If the *alba* interpretation is correct, then the only major irony in Larkin's title would be the one Lerner identifies – the narrator has no lover to part from. Most of the other features of the *alba* – the dread and pain of dawn, for example – would just be straightforwardly true. As the erotic serenade interpretation gives the title much more poignancy and point, I think it is safe to assume that Larkin's 'Aubade' is a subverted aubade in the tradition of MacNeice.

In this context, it is worth pointing out that 'Aubade' became a regular title for pieces of music after the 1860s. French composers in this period were eager to escape the influence of Wagner and German Romanticism generally, and turned for inspiration to the more finely etched archaic forms of their native land – a trend which culminated in works like Ravel's *Le Tombeau de Couperin*. As part of this endeavour, they returned to the word 'aubade' and made a concerted attempt to remove the military and ironic accretions the word had acquired in the nineteenth century: Bizet's *Aubade* for piano, and Lalo's *Aubade* for strings and five wind instruments, are well-known early examples.[7] These musical aubades are invariably small-scale, fresh, joyful pieces that carry no taint of loss or departure. 'Aubade' became an internationally popular title for pieces of music – particularly for wind instruments – in the early to middle twentieth century, and Larkin, who knew more about classical music than he often pretended, could well have come across a few examples.[8]

IV

Having clarified Larkin's intention, we can see that the ironies Larkin finds in 'Aubade' are less multivalent than those in 'Vers de Société', but the word's larger stock of historical associations makes them richer. Had he chosen to entitle the poem 'Morning Song' (like Sylvia Plath) or 'Dawn Song' there would be no Gallic gloss to roughen. It would also sever our link with the troubadours. With them comes the hint of the warm south and Provençal mirth; nobility and refinement; courtly love and the devotion to an exalted woman; chivalry and the celebration of heroes and crusades; the clarity and gravity of the pre-Raphaelite world; a life of wandering and artistic freedom; a life devoted to the refining of music and lyric; a young, richly costumed, amorous performer; a life set amongst castles, winding staircases, woods, the glint of dark wine in goblets, rich tapestries, feasts, and most speaking looks. In fact, it is quite likely that no troubadour ever sang a joyful dawn song outside his lover's window. The *alba* is not joyful or sung from outside, and troubadours tended to leave performance to *jongleurs*. But the myth is firmly rooted in our imaginations, and continues to be nourished by children's history books and pre-war costume dramas. This is the mental landscape in which a poem's title is intended to resonate; not in that of esoteric, hard-won, historical facts.

Larkin systematically subverts all these associations. His 'Aubade' is not a song, and is the kind of poem which could not be sung; nor is it set outside but in a stuffy bedroom ('hot as a bakery' as he later described it [CP:215]). The poem is set in the north; the outskirts of Hull. The weather is cold; there is no sun; the sky is white as clay. It does not celebrate the life of freedom but endures the routines of administration. There is nothing rich or antique about the life portrayed; it is savourlessly bland and contemporary. Its narrator is ageing, hung-over and staled. It does not greet the dawn but dreads it. As an aubade is a dawn greeting, usually from a man outside to a woman within, Larkin's ironic implication may be that he is alone, and that all thoughts of love and romance are simply bitter memories. Alternatively, we could recall that in 'Essential Beauty', Larkin portrays death as a woman: 'that unfocused she / No match lit up [...]' [CP:144]. The irony in 'Aubade' may be that a man inside a house offers horrified acknowledgement of the woman who approaches. Finally, we must not forget that, after the Empson debacle, the title 'Aubade' would have been a cause of discomfort and anxiety to Larkin. Far from being innocent and fresh, it was already sicklied o'er with the pale cast of irritation and embarrassment.

A further striking inversion in Larkin's 'Aubade' is its sensory blankness. The traditional aubade, as Larkin knew it, celebrates awakening nature, and the sharpness and precision of the senses. For example, Davenant's: 'The lark now leaves his wat'ry nest / And climbing shakes his dewy wings' [OBEV:308], or Shakespeare's, 'Hark! Hark! The lark at heaven's gate sings, / And Phoebus 'gins arise, / His steeds to water at those springs / On chaliced flowers that lies' [OBEV:184]. Even in later aubades that want to ironize and subvert this aspect, there is an awareness that this quality needs to be emphasized in order for the forthcoming misfortune to be heightened. MacNeice's 'Aubade' begins with the striking sensory immediacy of: 'Having bitten on life like a sharp apple / Or, playing it like a fish, been happy, // Having felt with fingers that the sky is blue / What have we after that to look forward to?' [MCP:86], before throwing this into contrast by saying all that lies ahead is boredom and conflict.

Larkin's does not begin with the first stirrings of life, but with soundless dark; he is alone with his thoughts. The lack of sight, sound and movement already make him seem partially anaesthetized; they act as a portent and analogue for the oblivion to come. Even when some light does appear, the fear of death is so overwhelming and paralyzing that it has bleached all life and colour from the sensory world: no sounds, textures, tastes or smells are noticed; no colours are mentioned but 'dark' and 'white'. In the entire poem, the only objects he certainly perceives are the curtain edges in the first stanza, and the strengthening light and the room's shape in the last. The wardrobe in the last stanza may just be part of a simile, the telephones and offices are merely things he knows about, and it's not even clear whether the sky, postmen and non-sun are seen or only posited. He fears death because it will eliminate his senses; and yet the fear of death has virtually done this already. Similarly, he wants the coming day, but he is quite incapable of enjoying it because the fear of death has so shrunken and reduced it that it now serves only as a sign that death is one day closer.

V

Trevor Tolley describes the language of 'Aubade' as 'resolutely declarative, unwavering in its intent' [MPG:135], and Larkin's last workbook shows this tone was hard won. There are three early intimations of the poem. The first sign is a short squib jotted down at the end of 1972:

Spare Time

In the old days
I used to come home
And settle to write
In the famous evenings.

Now I hit the jug
And go out like a light.

Waking, go to bed
With a hangover. [13.11.72]

The second sign is contained in a letter written to Judy Egerton on 11 January 1974. Here we find him returning to the topic of his routine: 'As I say it's late, & I am rather worn out: my life at present resembles that of the French plongeurs in *Down & Out in Paris and London* – work all day, drink at night to forget it' [SL:498].

The third sign is a short imagistic fragment noted down eight days later on 19 January 1974. This sketch – reminiscent of a de Chirico landscape – takes up at least four major symbols from Larkin's previous collections:

Daily the deaths like a scatter of unemphatic waves
Breaks in the personal columns.

I turn and look at my life
There is little to see
Except the blue sky and sand-coloured sand
And here and there white buildings.

I think of love.

Larkin's first formal attempt at 'Aubade' can be found about three months later on 11 April 1974. On the one hand, he uses the idea of death and looking back over his life from the wave-fragment; on the other, he takes phrases and the description of his routine from the squib and the letter:

I work all day and hit the jug at night.
Waking at five, I stare into the dark,
And watch the curtain edges to grow light.
The hours of thought, when daily I remark
Life is three-quarters done. If I look back
Some twenty years it's nothing. Yet with luck
That's all that's left. Not good years either.

Matters did not progress smoothly. In May he writes to Robert Conquest, almost certainly referring to 'Aubade': 'An hour spent at a poem without adding a single (sodding) word [...] One never gets any better at this lark. Perhaps I shouldn't be sipping an expensive bottle of cheap port [...]' [SL:505]. Over the next two months, he made at least fourteen attempts to get this stanza right, and eventually gave it up on 7 June.

One of the main difficulties was that he would not abandon facetious phrases from the squib which destabilize the tone. Consider this, his last attempt at the first verse before setting it aside for three years:

> I work all day and hit the jug at night.
> Waking at five, I stare into the dark.
> In time the curtain edges will grow light.
> Till then I have leisure to remark
> That more than half of life has elapsed by now
> (two thirds, three-quarters), and I lie wondering how
> And where and at what season I shall die.
> Routine/Ancient preoccupation, yet the dread
> Of dying and being dead
> Flashes afresh to hold and horrify. [1.6.74][9]

The diction, and consequently the tone, is uncertain and incongruous. 'Hit the jug' is slightly dated, semi-humorous taproom slang. It is the kind of masculine jocosity which Larkin likes to use in his short comic pieces but proves too weakly slangy for this context. It also mixes poorly with 'at what season I shall die' (which has a slightly eighteenth-century ring) and 'I have leisure to remark [...]' (which suggests a pose of languid connoisseurship). The staleness of the narrator's circumstance demands flat, quotidian speech, but it was difficult to do this and at the same time to attain the right kind of poetic weight. Achieving this was a matter which extended far beyond revising the diction alone; it also meant rethinking the way he approached structure, imagery, subject matter, metre and narration. It was because resolving these difficulties meant abandoning several stylistic habits of long standing that the poem proved so troublesome to write. In consequence, the finished 'Aubade' is a substantially different kind of poem from the other long serious pieces in the Larkin canon, and it is worth giving detailed consideration as to why this is so.

VI

In his longer poems, Larkin frequently likes to hint at the character of the narrator and send him up a little. He wears cycle-clips, he eats awful pies, he disdains to notice what is happening in the shade, he had parents who listened to the same seaside quack. But in 'Aubade', fear, inaction, the dark, and the universality of the foreseen end, strip the narrator of personality. The only hints about his life and age that might distinguish him from anybody else are the remark that he gets half drunk at night, and the indication that death is coming 'soon' – although the latter term is so elastic that it could include more or less anyone. Larkin fears loss of his individuality in death, and yet the poem is already profoundly depersonalized. Just as the thought of losing sensation appears to deprive him of sensation, so fear of losing his personality appears to diminish his sense of self. Dread of death has begun to accomplish what death will finish, and the narrator already appears to exist in a panic-stricken limbo.

Early drafts of the poem show that it originally contained more details of his personal circumstances, in particular, his age. He spent some time calculating how much of his time was already over: '[...] I have leisure to remark / That more than half of life has elapsed by now / (Two-thirds, three-quarters) [...]', and 'If I look back / Some twenty years it's nothing. Yet with luck / That's all that's left. Not good years either.' But these details are quickly dispensed with. Larkin must have realized one advantage of a narrator whose personality has been erased: he becomes a kind of Everyman.

Just as the narrator does not present a figure to be sent up, so Larkin avoids humour and facetiousness generally. There are no quirky and amusing observations: no girls in hair-do's fetching their separates from the cleaners; uncles shouting smut; mustachioed women shaking in flowered frocks; pound-note men decamping. Once again terror, inaction and the dark prevent the achievement of any kind of observation or ironic distance.

The sudden changes of speech register found throughout *High Windows* are also absent. The reason is plain enough. In this poem, Larkin is obsessed with himself, and the presence of others is utterly minimal. He is also too terrified to take on another persona or mimic the tone and diction of another voice. *High Windows* contains many feats of ventriloquism: 'A decent chap, a real good sort' [CP:168]; 'Just let me put this bastard on the skids, / I'll get a couple of semesters leave / To work on Protest Theatre' [CP:170]; 'Next year we are to bring the soldiers home / For lack of money, and that is all right' [CP:171]. 'Aubade' contains no such parodies. Similarly, in this poem, Larkin does not tease us by veering between disparate vocabularies. We find no 'crowd of craps' alongside 'the moon thinned / to an air-sharpened blade' [CP:181]; no 'Groping back to bed after a piss', followed by 'clouds that blow loosely as cannon-smoke' [CP:169]. Moreover, in earlier work, Larkin occasionally likes to heighten awareness of himself by using the odd rare word ('prinked' [CP:52]; 'cicatrized' [CP:184]; 'blort' [CP:126]) but the diction of 'Aubade' is plain, self-denying and unfussy throughout.

High Widows contains many sudden shifts from statements to images that try to move beyond words: from thinking about contraceptive precautions to 'The sun-comprehending glass, / And beyond it, the deep blue air [...]' [CP:165]; from contemplating money, to 'looking down / From long french windows at a provincial town [...]' [CP:198]. Occasionally, as in 'Solar' [CP:159], one gets the pure unmediated image. The wave fragment would have fitted into such a pattern, but after several attempts to incorporate it into 'Aubade', Larkin gave up. This is because the latter is primarily a poem of abstract statement, and the occasional illustrative images indicate psychological exhaustion and damage.

The images are worth looking at in more detail. They fall into two groups. Those in the first are used to convey the reality of death and the fear of death. They are fleeting and immaterial, lacking in definition and outline. Into this category fall the flashes, glares, blurs and chills. Those in the second establish connections with more recognizable material objects, but they exist in remarkable proximity to the ideas they are supposed to illuminate. The narrator's mind does not have the energy to travel far, and the images have difficulty raising themselves above the level of the literal. Something of the same pathos is found in 'The Building' [CP:191–3], a work that goes through the motions of being a puzzle although it no longer has the heart to be one. Fear of death saps this poem too.

Describing death as 'the anaesthetic from which none come round' is barely a metaphor but rather a direct statement of the truth: a permanent anaesthetic would, from the point of view of consciousness, be equivalent to death. 'That vast moth-eaten, musical brocade' seems more like a synecdoche than a metaphor; after all, churches do contain music and moth-eaten brocade. In '[Death] stands plain as a wardrobe' the object compared with death is (probably) literally seen; all the imagination does is establish the connection. 'The sky is white as clay' is deliberately plain and drab; anything more exuberant and flashy would be wholly out of character with the established mood – washed-out, energyless. Finally, a simile is supposed to be a non-literal comparison, and yet postmen going from house to house could well genuinely look like doctors, in the same way that someone could look like his own brother. The vagueness and inertia of 'Aubade''s imagery is quite as telling – because it is subliminal – in its impact on the reader's emotional response as any of the poem's direct and gloomy statements.

Generally, Larkin's long, serious poems tend to begin hesitantly: he starts with detailed descriptions of a place and then gradually teases the thought from the reality around him. As the thought emerges, Larkin conveys a genuine sense of self-discovery, and frequently takes several wrong turnings.[10] Towards the end, the poems grow more reflective and abstract until they arrive at a transcendent image or philosophical conclusion.

'Aubade' is certainly not a voyage of self-discovery. Rather than the fear of eternal oblivion coalescing and clarifying from details of the material world, it is horribly clear to begin with. The idea presents itself in the middle of the first verse fully formed and unusually quickly: it has clearly been thought through countless times before. Although the main argument of stanzas two and three is *why* the narrator fears death, this cannot disguise the fact that the poem's main problematic is the natural *fact* of death and how to cope with it. Any alternative explanations offered for his feelings of horror are to prevent misunderstanding on the part of the reader; they do not allow *Larkin* to discover what he really feels; he knows quite well already.

At first glance 'Aubade' seems to be written the wrong way round. All the philosophical conclusions and reflections seem to occur at the beginning and in the middle, and all the detailed observations of the world occur at the end; only in the last stanza does the thought fray and dissipate back into objects. But this is not strictly accurate. The beginning of 'Aubade' does have a physical context, but, apart from the anticipated light around the curtain edges, it is characterized negatively: no sound and no light. Just as the journey in 'Dockery and Son' [CP:152] both symbolizes and prompts the thought of ageing, so the soundless dark symbolizes and prompts the thought of blank non-existence. (The same is true of the blanked mind at the beginning of stanza two: this mirrors its object and anticipates the state it will soon arrive at.) It is in the middle section that the poem broadens out into philosophical reflection. The poem begins with 'I', but at the beginning of the second verse Larkin speaks of '[the] mind' rather than 'my mind'. This prepares the way for the first person plural in line seven: 'The sure extinction that *we* travel to' (my italics) and the pronoun is retained until the end of the poem.[11] This broadening often occurs in Larkin's longer poems, but here the shift is unusually early and suggests how frequently this path has been travelled. It is true that most of the objects occur in the last stanza and with the coming of daylight, but this brings no comfort. On the contrary, any sense of tentative solidarity achieved in the middle verses appears to evaporate as each of us is squeezed back into the narrow channel of our own lives.

Most of the other long poems tend to be about day-trips: either the journeys themselves or the things seen when away. (Even 'Vers de Société' considers the *prospect* of going out, and implies that the narrator probably will.) 'Aubade' is quite other. One cannot get closer to home or more static than being in your bedroom in bed. Larkin shows that the thought of death is like death itself in Kingsley Amis's quip: 'Death has got something to be said for it: / There's no need to get out of bed for it; / Wherever you may be, / They bring it to you, free' [OBD:17].

Metrically, 'Aubade' is also slightly different from the other longer poems. The opening line of the poem is the only one of Larkin's major pieces to begin with a strict pentameter, and the opening verse as a whole is strikingly regular: in four lines the opening foot is formally inverted, but apart from this there are only five additional unstressed syllables.[12] I think there are two basic reasons for this. First, he makes the stale ordinary speech registration he selects for the poem memorable and weighty by setting it to a sombre, classical, undeflectable rhythm. This feature is enhanced by the fact that 'Aubade' lacks the enjambments between stanzas found in all his other major, one-section poems. Second, observations about places, people and events in the other long poems tend to break in on a poem's metre, producing a lively, choppy, slightly unpredictable line. The most rhythmic irregularity, for example, is found in 'Show Saturday' [CP:199–201], the poem most heavily freighted with observation. Soundless dark and inaction, on the other hand, are uniform, even and uneventful.

VII

In 'Aubade''s final version, no traces of the squib or the wave fragment are visible. The jocosities of the one, and the images of the other, finally proved to be incompatible with the poem's mood. Significantly, it is only the plain language of the letter that remains:

> I work all day, and get half-drunk at night.
> Waking at four to soundless dark, I stare.
> In time the curtain-edges will grow light.
> Till then I see what's really always there:
> Unresting death, a whole day nearer now,

Making all thought impossible but how
And where and when I shall myself die.
Arid interrogation: yet the dread
Of dying, and being dead,
Flashes afresh to hold and horrify.

The language of the opening line is now appropriately stale, flavourless, and without humour; these, we feel, are dull, grey words. Although, as I observed above, the line is a strict iambic pentameter, you can imagine it passing unnoticed between virtual strangers in a bar: 'Me? I work all day, and get half-drunk at night.' The diction is deliberately drab, but Larkin ensures memorability by being careful with his vowel sounds. By laying the stress on 'work', 'day', 'get', 'drunk' and 'night', he manages to emphasize every major vowel in the language – o, a, e, u, i.

This first line consists of ten monosyllables. Sometimes this device can convey trenchancy and vigour, but frequently it can be used to drain energy from a line altogether: one thinks of Pope's 'And ten low Words oft creep in one dull Line' [PAP:154], or Wordsworth's 'The things which I have seen I now can see no more' [WW:297]. Compared with Larkin's statement, however, these lines positively pulse with meaning: Pope's words, besides self-referential wit, have a certain beady purposiveness; and Wordsworth's convey a powerful sense of stunned introspection – like the character in Proust who looks into his hat as though it were twenty feet deep. Larkin's words never aspire to such evocative power. The unnecessary comma after 'day' makes the line flatter still. Syntax would only require this if the sentence were long, or if it changed its grammatical subject, but neither holds true in this context, and the comma serves only to break the back of an already flaccid utterance.

Lack of movement is striking in the next two lines: 'Waking at four to soundless dark, I stare. / In time the curtain-edges will grow light'. Like the first line, they too end in full stops. Larkin's thoughts, we feel, are cold and depressed. We remember his remark about 'the drink gone dead' [CP:215]; nothing grows or develops. It's only when the thought of death makes its inevitable entry that his thoughts begin to gather momentum and start to take on a disagreeable life of their own. The colon after 'always there' suggests more to come. Now there are only commas, and suddenly the sentence begins to run away with no punctuation at all: '[...] / Making all thought impossible but how / And where and when I shall myself die' with powerful rhythmic impetus being supplied by emphases on 'how', 'where' and 'when'.

At least three commas could have been used here, but Larkin wants to give the sense that one thought about death brings all the others rushing unstoppably in its train. We also notice the slight literary swell as the idea of death begins to take hold, his mind begins to function, and unwanted passions are engaged. The diction becomes more polysyllabic and Latinate – 'impossible', 'interrogation' – and words begin to alliterate: 'dread [...] dying [...] dead', 'Flash [...] afresh', 'hold [...] horrify'.

The diction takes on additional force when we notice, as Seamus Heaney notices [TRP:155–6], that several key words in the stanza glance backwards at and subvert their earlier employment in Larkin's poetry. The first stanza of 'Aubade' echoes the last stanza of 'The Trees.'

> Yet still the unresting castles thresh
> In fullgrown thickness every May.
> Last year is dead, they seem to say,
> Begin afresh, afresh, afresh. [CP:166]

In the later poem, what once brought solace now enhances despair. In 'The Trees', the adjective 'unresting' characterizes the soothing sway of ample trees; in 'Aubade' it is used to release the all too goal-directed enmity of unresting death. Similarly, 'afresh' which signals new hope and new life in 'The Trees' enhances the terror of dying and being dead in 'Aubade'. These self-allusions and self-reversals are not surprising, since there is a sense in which 'The Trees' is a dishonest or at least sentimental poem. The central verse acknowledges that trees cannot provide a message or example of immortality – 'Is it that they are born again / And we grow old / No, they die too'. But the last stanza forgets this and affirms what the trees *seem* to say – it is the years which die, we always begin anew – and no line in Larkin relies so heavily on its sheer *sound* as the last line of this poem. On the manuscript Larkin wrote 'Bloody awful tripe' [M:372]; 'Aubade' provides more conclusive criticism.

VIII

Part of the first stanza's weight and authority of utterance derives from the way sentences, and the natural pauses within sentences, are correlated with line length. This natural relationship is not found in the second stanza. Sentences spill across line-endings or end in mid-line;

parentheses run across line-breaks. The general effect is altogether more torturous; the restless turnings of a man facing the unfaceable:

> The mind blanks at the glare. Not in remorse
> - The good not done, the love not given, time
> Torn off unused – nor wretchedly because
> An only life can take so long to climb
> Clear of its wrong beginnings, and may never;
> But at the total emptiness for ever,
> The sure extinction that we travel to
> And shall be lost in always. Not to be here,
> Not to be anywhere,
> And soon; nothing more terrible, nothing more true.

Many readers have found 'Aubade' to be a cancellation, an annulment, of the Christian message; a further negation of the troubadour world from which aubades sprang. Of course, this is largely because religion is disparaged as a 'trick', something 'created to pretend we never die', but it also has to do with the whole sensory tone and atmosphere of the poem. Heaney notes the ironic significance of its first being published – in the *Times Literary Supplement* – on 23 December 1977, so that many people first read it on Christmas Eve or Christmas Day. He continues: 'It would be hard to think of a poem more opposed than this one to the life enhancing symbolism of the Christ child in the Christmas crib. It is as if the mid-winter gleam and promise of medieval carols had been obliterated completely by the dread and dolour of a medieval morality play like Everyman' [TRP:155].

The 'mid-winter gleam and promise of medieval carols' was an aspect of Christmas to which Larkin proved responsive. Explaining why he liked the 'Coventry Carol' in 1976, he remarked: 'This suggests to me Christmas, not the Christmas of Dingly Dell, more the Christmas of the illuminated manuscripts and the book of hours with the red and blue robes and the gold crowns and the gold haloes and the snow [...]' [FR:109]. Medieval carols suggest Christmas to Larkin, and Christmas suggests the rich colours of illuminated manuscripts: red robes, blue robes, gold crowns, gold haloes, white snow. How utterly these are obliterated by 'Aubade''s colourless, anaesthetized, blank.

We can see just how deeply 'Aubade''s negation penetrates Christianity if we consider the sentence: 'The mind blanks at the glare'. This is the second time that dread of 'the coming dark' [CP:193] is characterized in terms of light: it gives off a glare; earlier it 'flashes'. Perhaps this is less paradoxical than it seems: you can see total blackness either by looking at blackness or by looking at brilliant light too long. Larkin noticed this when he wrote: 'Light spreads darkly downwards' in 'Friday Night in the Royal Station Hotel' [CP:163]; Milton noticed it when he wrote of God: 'dark with excessive bright thy skirts appear' [PLO:III:380]. For Larkin, fear of death has the properties of light which blind, frighten and hurt, but not those which illuminate. It is this painful negation of light which extinguishes the midwinter gleam of medieval Christianity.

If we think of glare, dazzle, and a light-source which is painful to look at, we are likely to think of the sun. Usually this is a life force in Larkin's poetry, most notably in 'Solar': 'Single, stalkless flower / You pour unrecompensed' [CP:159]. When sunlight is moving and human, so that it congregates [CP:93] or throngs [CP:110], it is usually benign and joyous; but when it is fierce or direct it can be damaging and destructive: in 'Deceptions', for instance, we read that '[...] light, unanswerable and tall and wide, / Forbids the scars to heal' [CP:32]. Larkin acknowledges a connection between the destructive power of sunlight and death when he approvingly quotes La Rochefoucauld's famous remark: 'Death and the sun are not to be looked at steadily' in his review of Enright's *Oxford Book of Death*. Significantly, it is an aphorism which does not occur in the book [FR:333].

Light, particularly the light of the sun, and religion are closely associated in Larkin's mind. 'If he were called in / To construct a religion [...]' he says in 'Water', then the climax of its liturgy would be raising '[...] in the east / A glass of water / Where any-angled light / Would congregate endlessly' [CP:93]. Similarly, 'Solar', his hymn to the sun, summons Christian imagery to express his sense of the sun's bountifulness: 'Our needs hourly / Climb and return like angels' [CP:159].

This association of light and Christianity is, of course, traditional: we remember that God is clothed in light [Psalm 104.2], Christ is the light of the world [John: 3.18 and 8.12], and that those who discover God see the light [Eph.5.11–13].[13] Milton, at the beginning of Book III of *Paradise Lost*, says 'God is light' [PLO:III:3], something that the Bible does not say directly. But for Milton, and for other traditional Christians, God and death are utterly opposed; indeed, in Book II of *Paradise Lost*, Satan, Death and Sin form a kind of grotesque anti-trinity which stand in opposition to God the father, God the son and God the Holy Ghost [PLO:II:629–889]. For Larkin, unprepared to meet his unmaker, the 'coming dark' which flashes and glares, has taken the place of God. All is now hellish 'darkness visible' [PLO:I:63]; Milton's 'universe of death' [PLO:II:662] has become the universe.

Alternatively, we can think of Larkin's glaring dark as a ghastly parody of another conception of the Christian God. This is because, for some Christians, God himself is a kind of darkness: 'The Divine Darkness is unapproachable light, in which God is said to dwell' [HVCP:629], wrote Dionysius the Areopagite, a thought brought into the mainstream of English literature by Henry Vaughan:

> There is in God (some say),
> A deep, but dazzling darkness [...] [HVCP:290]

A further negation of Christianity can also be found in 'Aubade''s next lines: 'Not in remorse / - The good not done, the love not given [...]'. Lawrence Lerner argues that these thoughts echo, but take issue with, T. S. Eliot's morning agonizings in 'Little Gidding'. Here, Eliot faces the ghosts of his literary ancestors, and is forced to confront one of the central miseries of old age: the growing awareness that actions and motives once taken to be virtuous actually caused great pain and hurt to others [ECP:218; L:38]. For the Christian Eliot, regret rather than approaching death is probably the greatest problem of age.[14] For the agnostic Larkin, the implacable blankness of death utterly occludes the significance of regret and remorse.

Such solemnity of phrasing, however, is undercut in the next phrase: 'time / Torn off unused', a remark which is itself slightly puzzling. It could simply signify the waste of something which seems abundant: tissue paper, for example, might be torn off and not used. But this isn't helpful because it's hard to see why Larkin should use an example where the product is so *cheap*, and it's difficult to think of something which is both characteristically torn off and valuable. Much more likely is the idea that Larkin is thinking of a particular kind of calendar. Here each leaf represents a day, and you begin each morning by ripping off the old page. Usually, these are cheap, plain calendars found in offices, and this also fits with the bureaucratic world imagined at the end of the poem.

About 'nor wretchedly because / An only life can take so long to climb / Clear of its wrong beginnings, and may never', it's worth remarking that, as Larkin grew older, he seems to have become more conscious that there was something seriously amiss with his childhood and to blame it for his failures. In the early published poetry, his childhood is simply 'unspent' [CP:81], 'a forgotten boredom' [CP:33], 'opaque' [CP:184]. But in one of his last poems, he hopes his failing memory and lack of perspective will 'blank out whatever it is that is doing the damage' [CP:211], and by the time we arrive at his last significant poem he hints that his failure in love is 'Something to do with violence / A long way back [...]' [CP:215]. So far as I know, nobody has given a convincing interpretation of what Larkin means by this. Is he referring to his childhood? Is he talking about physical violence? By whom on whom? Why did this conviction grow as he aged? Perhaps he simply felt freer to articulate it. His mother died in 1977, and he may have felt less inhibited about making his feelings public.

The last line is metrically interesting. The last lines of stanzas one, three, four and five are more or less perfect ten syllable iambic pentameters. The phrase 'And soon' introduces a significant and unexpected irregularity. The line retains five stressed beats, but the syllable count would lead one to expect:

> [...] Not to be here,
> Not to be anywhere,
> [...] nothing more terrible, nothing more true.

The same pattern is hinted at by the symmetrical rhetorical structure:

> Not to be [...]
> Not to be [...]
> [N]othing more [...] nothing more [...]

The step-like lineation also makes us expect, as would make perfect grammatical sense, a full stop after 'Not to be anywhere.' For at least three reasons, therefore, the extra two syllables of 'And soon' come as a nasty and unexpected jolt. The phrase interposes itself; it shoulders all our expectations aside and supplies an ugly, brusque reminder that these things will not only happen but happen shortly.

For Larkin, the word 'true' has close affinities with death, as if nothing could be more real or truer. In 'Ambulances', as in 'Aubade', he emphasizes this by end-stopping a line with the word:

> [They] sense the solving emptiness
> That lies just under all we do,
> And for a second get it whole,
> So permanent and blank and true. [CP:132]

However, in 'Aubade' he is readier to confront his fears, and the poem represents two kinds of advance over 'Ambulances'. Firstly, 'Ambulances' is one of a number of poems about ageing and dying, all of which have death in view but none of which quite confronts the topic squarely. Thus we have poems about heads in women's wards, hospital visits, hospitals, ambulances, old people, helplessness and senility. But 'Aubade' is not about ageing or even dying; it is unequivocally about death itself, shorn of its usual preliminaries. Secondly, 'Ambulances' does not call death by its usual name, but refers to it as 'the solving emptiness'; indeed, part of the poem's unique tone is the undertaker's tact which death is dealt with. Cities at midday are noisy, ambulances are noisy, and yet the poem is full of verbs of silent discretion: the ambulances 'thread', they 'come to rest', 'recede', patients are 'borne away', traffic 'parts'.

In this indirectness at least, 'Ambulances' is of a piece with most of Larkin's earlier poems in *The Less Deceived* and *The Whitsun Weddings*. Here, death is not mentioned by name, but referred to by rather beautiful euphemisms. It is 'oblivion' [CP:42], 'a black- / Sailed unfamiliar' [CP:52]; it 'Brings, the priest and the doctor [...] Running over the fields' [CP:67]; it is found 'down Cemetery Road' [CP:148]; it is 'the only end of age' [CP:153] and 'the coming dark' [CP:193].

By the time of *High Widows*, Larkin is able to mention death more directly. In 'The Building' he says, 'All know they are going to die. / Not yet, perhaps not here, but in the end [...]' [CP:192] while in 'The Old Fools' we find: 'At death you break up [...]' [CP:196], but these only mention death in the third and second person, and it is part of a general misfortune. But 'Aubade' is the first occasion when 'death' and the first person encounter one another; where Larkin says, 'Yes, I'm going to die soon' and the ramifications of this fact are explored not glancingly, but for five gruelling stanzas.

IX

This is a special way of being afraid
No trick dispels. Religion used to try,
That vast moth-eaten musical brocade
Created to pretend we never die,
And specious stuff that says *No rational being*
Can fear a thing it will not feel, not seeing
That is what we fear – no sight, no sound,
No touch or taste or smell, nothing to think with,
Nothing to love or link with,
The anaesthetic from which none come round.

The image of a 'vast moth-eaten musical brocade' is strange. It is true, as I pointed out above, that churches frequently contain music and brocade, and 'moth-eaten brocade' is clear enough. Larkin often used elaborate clothes and materials as emblems of fuss and excess, as when he remarks that women are always finding excuses to show you their emotional haberdashery [SL:158], or that Art Tatum is like someone who has discovered that if one frill looks nice, then ninety-nine would be better still [AWJ:173]. But what exactly is a *musical* brocade? One way to answer this is to assume that Larkin is using a deliberately incoherent image to describe an incoherent thing, or possibly something that he cannot be bothered to think about coherently, like the 'brass and stuff up at the holy end' from 'Church Going' [CP:97–8].

Another, complementary answer is provided in *The Philip Larkin I Knew*. Here Maeve Brennan says that some years before 'Aubade' was written, she and Larkin had read Cardinal Newman's *The Dream of Gerontius* together, and that Larkin had subsequently asked to borrow Elgar's setting from her father's record collection. Shortly after Larkin's mother's death, when Brennan first heard 'Aubade', she suggested to him that the poem was an agnostic's response to Newman's poem. 'He did not dispute this view,' she says, 'but turned away, overcome by his recent bereavement and the thoughts of his own end' [PLIK:64]. The notion of a brocade, a rich and elaborate material, is clearly more fitted to (Newman and Elgar's) Catholicism than to any of the Protestant churches; 'moth-eaten' could well apply to the vanished Edwardian and Victorian eras; 'vast' captures the epic scale of Elgar's setting; and the adjective 'musical' is surely applied to religion because one of Larkin's most prolonged recent exposures to religious eschatology was through Elgar's music.[15]

The idea that Larkin was thinking of religion through the twin filters of Newman and Elgar is supported by a number of parallels between 'Aubade' and *The Dream of Gerontius*. In the latter, these occur at the beginning of the second part. Here, the soul of Gerontuis, like Larkin at the beginning of his poem, wakes from sleep, but in Gerontius's case it is the sleep which precedes eternal life and the emotional tenor is wholly different: 'I went to sleep: and now I am refresh'd, / A strange refreshment: for I feel in me / An inexpressive lightness [...]' [DGE:817]. The emotional reversal between Gerontius waking to Life-in-Death, and Larkin waking to Death-in-Life, ramifies later: Larkin dreads experiencing '[...] – no sight, no sound, / No touch or taste or smell [...]'. The middle of this list is foreshadowed by a similar list, in the same order, in Newman's poem, but whereas Larkin's senses are non-existent and consequently blank, Gerontius's are redeemed, perfected, and glutted by glorious music: 'And hark! I hear a singing; yet in sooth / I cannot of that music rightly say / Whether I hear, or touch, or taste the tones [...]' [DGE:819]. Finally, the Angel tells Gerontius two lines later, 'My work is done', whereas for Larkin, 'Work has to be done'. The thought that 'Aubade' is a partial unwriting of *The Dream of Gerontius* is hard to resist.

If religion is disparaged by a deliberately inflated, over-elaborate, unworkable image, then philosophical consolation is dispatched in a phrase: it is 'specious stuff'. '*No rational being / Can fear a thing it will not feel*' is probably a summary of a view held by the ancient Greek philosopher Epicurus (c.341–270 BC), who, in his *Letter to Menoeceus*, writes: 'So death, the most terrifying of ills, is nothing to us, since so long as we exist, death is not with us; but when death comes, then we do not exist. It does not then concern either the living or the dead, since for the former it is not, and the latter are no more' [BTQ:180]. The view is sometimes expressed as 'Where death is, I am not; and where I am, death is not', but probably receives its most memorable modern formulation in Wittgenstein's *Tractatus*: 'Death is not an event in life: we do not live to experience death' [T:6.4311]. Understandably enough, Larkin, contemplating the thought of never seeing or feeling again, finds the alleged solution to be merely a restatement of the problem. The dismissive phrase and images are the only points in the poem where there is a hint of levity, presumably because the topic is now hopeless human theorizing about death, or more accurately human wish-fulfilment fantasies, rather than the natural, grim actuality of death itself.

The eighth and ninth lines are some of the most contentious in the poem:

> [...] this is what we fear – no sight, no sound,
> No touch, or taste, or smell, nothing to think with,
> Nothing to love or link with,
> The anaesthetic from which none come round.

In his *Memoirs*, Kingsley Amis says that the rhyme '[...] with / [...] with' shows that Larkin's skill deserted him for a moment [KAM:62] William Pritchard, on the other hand, feels the doubled 'with' has a point: 'The specious stuff of religion and philosophy is dismissed, but there is nothing specious about the rhyming, especially the double one of 'think with' and 'link with' which touchingly links itself with the reader who both sees and hears a life-affirming connection made in the midst of death' [AL:4/1998:9].

Neither explanation really works. Amis's fails to carry conviction because Larkin was a most fastidious and observant poet, he was clearly very proud of this poem, and it was slowly polished over a period of three years. If the two lines were a blemish, he could easily have rewritten them. Pritchard's interpretation does not make clear why this kind of doubled rhyme reaches out to the reader more effectively than any other kind of rhyme. In addition, to hear 'a life-affirming connection made in the midst of death' seems far too cosy in the context of a poem which insists that death is the end of all connections.

The real reason for the doubled 'with' is surely that the rhyme scheme enacts and dramatizes the failure of linkage. There are two ways lines can fail to rhyme: either the final syllable of the word at the end of the second line has no sound in common with the final syllable of the word at the end of the first line; or the word at the end of the second line is the same as the word at the end of the first line. After all, if I ask you for a rhyme for 'lost' and you reply with either 'chipmunk' or 'lost' then I will think you are being uncooperative in both cases. In Larkin's lines, 'or link with' looks for the previous line to link with and discovers only 'to think with'; the hand reaching out fails to find another. Lines about failing to link fail to link. The idea of the doubled 'with' gives Larkin the paradoxical ability both to maintain and not maintain his rhyme-scheme, because the point at which a rhyme becomes perfect is exactly the point where it ceases to be a rhyme. The rhyme of the penultimate words in each line – 'link' and 'think' – proves a wholly misleading anticipation and encouragement; it sets us up for disappointment. The use of a doubled rhyme in 'Aubade' is no more accidental or dissonant with the poem's message than the doubled rhymes used in 'Homage to a Government' [CP:171]. Here, such rhymes are used throughout to indicate the brain-death and spiritless conformity of the speaker.

The grammatical mistake in the last line, however, *does* appear to be an oversight, as Larkin later admitted. Writing to C. B. Cox he asks: 'Tell me, as a professor of English, are you offended by "None come round"? Would you be happier with "None comes round"? As a natural illiterate, I never think of these things until it is too late. But it could be changed if the poem is ever collected' [SL:669].

X

At one stage in the workbook, Larkin tries to work the obituary idea from the wave fragment into stanza three: '[...] was it [religion] put / Aside when death was driven into age, / And shrunk to the obituary page?' [7.6.74]. Three years later, he decides to begin the fourth stanza with a more complete version of the fragment: 'Death breaks each morning like a tiny wave / In newspapers' [11.6.77].

If the remarks about his own age were too personal, then these remarks about obituaries were too public to survive into the poem's final version. Somehow the thought of reading about other people's deaths – as well as the comfy domestic regimes of reading newspapers and having them delivered – democratizes and thereby defuses the terror that confronts Larkin. This is because he confronts *his own* death, and no poet ever felt the difference between a misfortune happening to him, and a misfortune occurring to somebody else, more keenly. Looked at in the third person, and from the point of view of society, a plurality of deaths, like a plurality of births, is part of a natural process. But Larkin is not interested in a plurality of deaths; he is interested in one – his own – which is quite different from all the others. Not only does Larkin dismiss the possibility of immortality, he does not show any interest in what happens after his death at all. One striking absence in 'Aubade' is that, unlike many poems about death, no mention is made of funerals, mourning relatives, the gap in colleagues' lives, the evaluations of posterity. In a certain sense, as Wittgenstein implies in my first epigraph, the world comes to an end at my death, and this is the only sense of 'the world' in which Larkin was interested. Obituaries, being part of the social world and published *post mortem*, are wholly alien to 'Aubade''s grimly solipsistic focus.

In the poem, Larkin is hideously aware that his is an 'only life' and that nothing that happens before it, after it, or to others, is of any account. It is for this reason that he denies himself the comfort of the routines, rituals, ceremonies and traditions he so frequently contemplates elsewhere – county shows, Remembrance Days, annual seaside holidays, and so forth. This is especially noticeable in his treatment of Christianity. Although he was an agnostic, he was deeply attached to the Anglican Church, and derived much comfort from the history and continuities it represented. This is evident at the end of 'Church Going'. Here the narrator 'tends to this cross of ground' because 'it held unspilt / So long and equably what since is found / Only in separation – marriage, and birth, / And death, and thoughts of these'. And he discovers in himself 'a hunger [...] to be more serious' and gravitates to the ground 'If only that so many dead lie round' [CP: 98]. But Larkin's feelings for the building, the institution and its history, are only comforting because they are based on incoherence. He knows that many dead lie round and *notionally* assents to the idea that he will one day join them. In this way he can think of his death as part of a pattern sustained and sanctified by tradition. But when he awakes panic-stricken at four in the morning, he *really* assents to the fact of his own death, and in doing this realizes it is quite unlike any of the others.[16] His death will bring the world to an end; history and tradition have nothing to do with him. Christianity as institution is irrelevant; only Christianity as doctrine is of any account here – and he bitterly dismisses that as so many tawdry rags.

The other notable lacuna in 'Aubade' is nature – and not only the sun, trees and larks, characteristic of aubades. This is slightly surprising because *High Windows* differs from his two previous mature collections in the number of times that nature and its continuities are evoked. As Larkin aged, these cycles provided a source of solace and comfort: the apparent rebirth of trees, the passing of day into night, 'Celestial recurrences, / The day the flowers come, / And when the birds go' [CP:184]. But contemplation of their permanence and his impermanence would make his situation worse rather than better; and he realizes that nature is responsible for the dark that will shortly greet him. Consequently, he says nothing about nature in 'Aubade', and when his mind begins to turn towards the outside world, he focuses on its least meaningful and most ephemeral aspects. He does not think about churches, or seasons, or people's homes; instead he conjures up the 'uncaring / Intricate rented world' of locked offices and crouching telephones. This world is impersonal and impermanent; those who use it do not own it; it is sanctified by no religion, ritual or history; it is denatured and artificial; it is deliberately ephemeral, bland and flavourless. This is the world which conforms most precisely to his state of mind now; like him it is temporary, and no one who loses it could care for it.

In its final version, the fourth stanza runs:

> And so it stays just on the edge of vision,
> A small unfocused blur, a standing chill,
> That slows each impulse down to indecision.
> Most things will never happen: this one will,
> And realization of it rages out
> In furnace-fear when we are caught without
> People or drink. Courage is no good:
> It means not scaring others. Being brave
> Lets no one off the grave.
> Death is no different whined at than withstood.

It is as if, just for a moment, all the philosophical thought of the previous two stanzas – largely moral in the second, largely metaphysical in the third – has allowed him to distance his fear of death and get it under some control. He remembers that in everyday life death is omnipresent but on the *edge* of vision, and it is indistinct and cold rather than ragingly central. But the respite is short-lived because in his current state he lacks the distractions of normal life. At 'this one will' the fear of death floods back, and he is again plunged into the tortured imaginings of the opening verse. The similarity of state is mirrored by similarity of language. Here again the energy of dread is expressed by alliteration: 'realisation [...] rages', 'furnace-fear', 'being brave', 'death [...] different [...] whined at than withstood'. 'Aubade' contains rather more alliteration than Larkin's other long poems, no doubt because, in the absence of a story or sharply characterized setting, the language itself needs to work harder.

The stanza then moves on to consider the uselessness of courage, and Larkin's analysis is deeply questionable. In an early draft of the stanza, he is inclined to argue that it is an archaic military virtue that he simply doesn't have. The verse of the draft also illustrates the desperate uncertainty of tone and diction which characterizes the early drafts as a whole:

> Courage, that dated helmet-head
> Among the virtues: When you've found
> You haven't got it, what d'you do?
> Stay away from where it's needed –
> Love and war and wanting, all
> The rot that makes the world go round [...] [17.1.75]

In the final version, in line with its generally greater impersonality, he removes the reference to his personal lack of courage, and instead attempts to devalue the concept altogether; a move which has the effect of making his own lack less significant. He does this, not by developing the idea that it's dated, but by saying that all courage amounts to is not scaring others. If courage only has to do with outer expression, and not inward motivation, then it looks a very minor virtue.[17]

However, the analysis of courage only looks plausible because of the particular kind of danger Larkin is facing. If we consider some other examples then we can see that courage amounts to much more than this. A soldier who walks calmly off the battlefield without scaring anyone has not shown courage. There also seem to be circumstances where you *do* scare others by your emotional state but still show courage. For example, a man in a burning building may be beside himself with fear, and may convey this fear to those around him, but if he goes in deeper to rescue someone we would still say he'd shown courage – we might even be more impressed by his courage because he was evidently so scared. These cases make us see that courage involves acting appropriately and for the good, even though you have a full imaginative realization of the dangers you are facing.

The difficulty with trying to say what courage is when faced – as we all are – by the inevitability of death, is that it is not at all clear what the appropriate and beneficial action is. (Hence the initial convincingness of Larkin's analysis.) The only option is, not to lie gibbering in bed, but go about your normal business, live up to your station and its duties, care for those who depend on you, get on with your daily life. This, it seems to me is exactly what Larkin does in the last stanza; a stanza Motion correctly characterizes as 'stoic' [M: 468]. There, his behaviour demonstrates both that the analysis offered in the fourth stanza is false and trivializing, and that he actually does have the real courage which, in the early version of the stanza, he claimed to lack. Larkin *says* in the early draft that he doesn't have courage, and then in the later draft that courage is trivial or irrelevant; his behaviour in the last stanza *shows* he does have it and it isn't either trivial or irrelevant. I think Larkin does get up to draw the curtains, look at the sky, and watch the postmen. I also think that, when he arrives at the library, he will go about his work stoically, efficiently and courteously.

XI

The last stanza is masterly. If you try to read the poem and stop at the end of any of the other verses there is a palpable diminution of the poem's power. It is in this stanza that Larkin's consciousness begins to move beyond its private tormented thoughts and starts to spread out into the world again.[18] This ought to make it seem heartening; indeed, many have found the last verse more optimistic than the others. To me, it seems utterly desolate. This is largely because one sees how his struggle has bleakened waking; how it has saddened and stunned the coming day. His nocturnal terrors have not been left behind in the darkness: they imbue the early world, suffuse it, seep into its detail and texture, rendering every aspect void and savourless.

> Slowly light strengthens, and the room takes shape.
> It stands plain as a wardrobe, what we know,
> Have always known, know that we can't escape,

Yet can't accept. One side will have to go.
Meanwhile telephones crouch, getting ready to ring
In locked-up offices, and all the uncaring
Intricate rented world begins to rouse.
The sky is white as clay, with no sun.
Work has to be done.
Postmen like doctors go from house to house.

This, as Motion points out, is a verse full of *things* [M:468], but in line with the poem's lack of observation, and the depersonalization of the narrator, we should observe how unindividual these things are. The curtains in the first verse do not fall within five inches of the sill [CP:102], they are simply curtains, anybody's curtains; they tell us nothing. Similarly, fear has washed away all identity from the room: the wardrobe (if there is one), the locked office, the telephone are bleached-out and generic. On the one hand, this makes them unsettlingly numb and blank; on the other it makes them more universal. It requires an act of imagination to be with Larkin on his rail trips and his seaside holidays; but nearly every reader woke this morning to a room, curtains and a wardrobe. Here only memory is required.

Why do Larkin's thoughts turn to the world of work? One reason may be that the end of the poem negates and undercuts two kinds of poem that were at the forefront of Larkin's mind as he wrote: Christian meditations on death and aubades in general. Christian poems about the afterlife often end with visions of rest and peace. At the beginning of part two of *The Dream of Gerontius*, for example, Gerontius awakes to experience '[...] the deep rest, so soothing and so sweet' [DGE:817]. For Larkin, on the contrary, there is no rest, only the grim reality of toil and drudgery. However, work can have its cheering and enlivening aspects. Aubades frequently end with a vision of work, as the day comes to life and others stir. Davenant's last verse, for example, begins with merchants and ploughmen who are already about their business: 'The Merchant bowes unto the Seamens Star, / The Ploughman from the Sun his Season takes' [OBEV:308]. Davenant's characters appear to find joy and invigoration in work, whereas Larkin finds only a grim and painful duty.

Andrew Swarbrick detects a hint of cheer in Larkin's vision of work. He recommends that we think of the scenes Larkin sketches as aspects of 'that workaday world which sustains itself by individuals' mutual reliance' [OOR:152] but this sounds a little too communal and healthy-minded to be wholly persuasive. As he comes close to admitting, for his suggestion to carry conviction, two of the three adjectives in 'uncaring / Intricate rented world [...]' would need to be ignored:

> Tucked between two dismissive adjectives but prominent at the beginning of the line, 'Intricate' pays tribute to whatever resists, however temporarily, the encroachments of death. It is the intricacy of 'smells of different dinners' ('Ambulances'), of 'sports finals / stuck / In front doors' ('Show Saturday'), of 'Fathers, brothers, nicknames, laughter' ('The Explosion'). [OOR:152]

What gives Swarbrick's other examples of intricacy their positive affect is the warm social relationships – sports, meals, families, laughter – in which they are embedded. If we remove these, then we are left with bare intricacy, and intricacy *tout court* has nothing to recommend it – surely simplicity is better. If we then apply a few adjectives like 'uncaring' and 'rented', and place the word in a context of locked-up offices and crouching telephones, then it surely gestures away from sustaining communities towards the stressful, indifferent and impersonal. If Larkin had wanted to illustrate a world that 'sustains itself by individuals' mutual reliance' in these central lines of the stanza he could surely have chosen a better example, since, at best, the people in Larkin's scene are merely implied. He could have imagined people who are already up and at their trades (like the postmen he sees at the end of the stanza); he could have imagined his own workplace once the people had arrived; he could have imagined sitting in the bar with friends.

Late in life, Larkin made a number of remarks about work that could support Swarbrick's interpretation. To Roy Plomley, in 1976, he said: '[...] over the years I've come to think that I rather like work' [FR:103]; and in the same year he had written to Winifred Bradshaw: 'And of course *work*, paradoxically enough *is* a comfort. One wakes up wanting to cut one's throat; one goes to work, & in 15 minutes one wants to cut someone else's – complete cure!' [SL:551]. More intimate friends were aware, however, that his attitude was changing. 'As time passed,' writes Maeve Brennan, 'it became very noticeable that he was increasingly depressed and dependent on alcohol. I remember how shocked I was when he confessed to regularly drinking half a bottle or more of sherry before going to work, just to enable him to face the day' [PLIK:90]. 'When the poetic muse deserted him [he described 'Aubade' as 'the death-throes of a talent' SL:574] [...] personal sorrow took over and his soul became once more trapped in the dark recesses of his mind. By the mid-1970's, feeling that he had also given of his best professionally, even "the toad work" no longer afforded the challenge and fulfilment it had once done' [PLIK:135]. Work is no longer a comfort. It comes to mind only because he will shortly have to go to his office, and it's an indifferent, uncaring, impersonal place that offers no solace. It is also slightly aggressive; to be locked out is to be deprived of power, and the telephones crouch in readiness to attack rather than in submission.

In the last line, as in MacNeice and Davenant, Larkin turns his attention to the street: the postmen who go like doctors from house to house. His observation seems inconclusive. The sentence has none of the imposing resonance of the previous stanzas' final lines which complete or encapsulate what has been said, but it is all the more powerful for that. This is because the action of the poem is implied to continue long after the poem has finished. The postmen will continue their task after the poet's glance has left them, and one has a sense of death gradually spreading itself out through the city and into the countryside beyond. The final stanza's deadly chill seeps out through the membrane of the final line and into our lives.

Of course, for many critics, the image of the postmen is not a pessimistic image at all. According to Anthony Thwaite, it is a symbol of hope: 'the image', he says, 'is one of healing or renewal, of the diurnal comfort of letters through the post' [SL:xi]. Andrew Swarbrick endorses this reading: 'The final "Postmen like doctors" are emblems of that workaday world which sustains itself by mutual reliance [...]' [OOR:152]. Certainly, there are several pieces of evidence that can be offered in support of their view. Larkin was a great letter writer and hugely enjoyed receiving letters. Thwaite quotes the lines 'I know, none better, / The eyelessness of days without a letter' [SL:xi]. Swarbrick mentions an early optimistic version of the final line found in the relevant workbook: 'Postmen go / from house to house like doctors to persuade / Life to resume' [12.8.77; OOR:152].

On the other hand one can point out that, in Larkin, doctors and medical services are rarely shown as healers but usually anticipate and attend on death. 'Where can we live but days? // Ah, solving that question / Brings the priest and the doctor / In their long coats / Running across the fields' [CP:67]. Hospitals are places that you die in ('not yet, perhaps not here, but in the end' [CP:192]); and ambulances bring to mind that solving emptiness rather than a return to rude health. Like 'Aubade''s doctors, these ambulances spare no one: 'all streets in time are visited' [CP:132]. Medical services are as cheerfully quotidian and democratic as death.

Against Thwaite's endorsement of the optimistic reading, it can be pointed out that if even postmen – those emblems of optimism and renewal – can come to look like doctors, then this shows how far death has negated all hope. Swarbrick's citation of the cancelled version of the last line is not conclusive either. The very fact that Larkin cancelled it and replaced it by something altogether gloomier shows that he realized the earlier version was too facile: it didn't fit the poem; it wasn't what he wanted to say.

Although I have argued that the abstract thoughts of the earlier part of the poem dissipate into things in the final stanza – they fade into the common light of day – death still permeates the whole of this last verse. Consider the 'it' at the beginning of the second line: 'It stands plain as a wardrobe'. When we read this line, we naturally assume that the 'it' refers to one of the nouns in the previous line – either 'light' or 'room'. This assumption is strengthened by the fact that both the light and the room probably have some relationship with the wardrobe – one illuminates it, one contains it. Surprisingly, this is not what the word denotes. The 'it' at the beginning of the second line actually refers back to death, and the narrator's assumption that we will take this for granted, in spite of the sentence before and the new topic of the illuminated room, shows the depth of his preoccupation. The weight of his knowledge is emphasized by the concatenation of '[...] know / [...] known, know [...]'. The arrival of day does not disperse his fears; they still stand in front of him more clearly than what he actually sees. This makes the meaning of the slightly obscure 'One side will have to go', plain enough: we can't accept death but death will happen; it is we who will go.

We then have a sketch of the world of lifeless impersonal offices, before reaching the next image: 'The sky is white as clay'. One reason why the image might have come to mind is that clay is the very substance of our mortality; it is what we are made from; it is what we will return to. The mortality suggested by this clay is enhanced by its colour: clay is normally brown or grey; this particular clay has been bled white. This clay may suggest death in another way. It may be that the narrator anticipates looking at the interior of his own grave,[19] and the words 'with no sun' reinforce this idea. In many poems the idea of removal from sunlight indicates death. In the song from *Cymbeline*, Fidele's apparent death is memorialized by the line 'Fear no more the heat o' the sun' [NOBEV:141]; and one line in Browning's 'A Toccata of Galuppi's' runs, 'Death stepped tacitly and took them where they never see the sun' [NOBEV:667]. If this interpretation is correct then the line fits a frequently noted pattern in this poem: the thought of death prefigures what death itself will bring. Fittingly, the phrase '[...] with no sun' consists entirely of stressed syllables: spondees. All life has been taken from it. In one more line we arrive at the final image of the postmen, and we should understand it as the culmination of a number of images and rhythms about the idea of death which, although dissolved in things, is still omnipresent.

Rhythmically, the poem ends as it began: each of the four lines is end-stopped; each is a complete sentence. But here the emotional effect is different. At the opening the full stops reinforced the sense of staleness and inertia; here they indicate the gritted teeth of stoicism: work has to be done.

XII

There are, no doubt, many reasons why 'Aubade' was Larkin's last significant published poem, even though he lived for another seven years. Some of these are external reasons: reasons concerning his life and circumstances. His new house – to which he could never properly adjust – may have had something to do with it, as might growing responsibilities, drink, depression, illness, cohabitation, even success. Alternatively, there may be internal reasons for his lack of productivity: reasons to do with the development and shape of his oeuvre. One of these has already been hinted at. 'Aubade' is the poem where death is clearly and unequivocally confronted for the first time: death is not screened by the process of dying, or merely glanced at, or called by soft names. But why should this affect his creativity? It could be that the significance of this topic, and the conclusiveness of the poem, dwarfed all other subject-matters, making them seem trivial or peripheral. It could be that a repressed horror of death coloured and animated his poetry, in a way that the same horror confronted, dissected and analysed could not.

But the most significant clue is to be found in his review of Enright's *Oxford Book of Death*. This is largely a prose reprise of many things he had said in 'Aubade' although he adds a few twists and details, but there is one point which he does not, with good reason, make in the poem. He begins the second paragraph of the review by discussing the hopelessness of using religion as a palliative, and continues:

> But there is also literature, where death is still the only possible end to the story, except marriage. Unfortunately nothing is quite real in literature, not even death; either we are left feeling that in some indefinable way it is *all right*, or that the characters will get up unharmed and advance bowing to the footlights. This is not how death affects us in reality. [...] [FR:331] [The] intrusion of death into our lives is so

> ruthless, so irreversible, so rarely unaccompanied by pain, terror and remorse, that to 'anthologize' it, however calmly, quizzically and compassionately, seems at best irrelevant, at worst an error of taste. [...] [By] their nature anthologies do not look steadily, nor do they explain or console: they entertain. And death is not entertaining. The chapter on 'Care of the Dying' in any nursing manual makes this point more clearly. [FR:333]

Larkin never abandoned the principle that 'poetry, like all art, is inextricably bound up with giving pleasure, and if a poet loses his pleasure-seeking audience he has lost the only audience worth having [...] [No] pleasure [...] no poetry' [RW:81–2]. And yet now he discovers that a truthful treatment of death cannot give pleasure; the topic that has come to dwarf all others in his consciousness is therefore beyond the powers of literature to depict. For all its unflinching, wintery bleakness, 'Aubade' is still a poem, it is still literature, and that means it falsifies to entertain.[20] The unproductive years ahead would be reserved for brooding on 'Care of the Dying'. And death itself, of course.

Notes

1. Schumann, *Kinderszenen*, Op. 15, No. 7.
2. 'Serenade' – which derives from the troubadours' *serena* – literally means 'evening song', just as 'aubade' literally means 'dawn song'. I therefore apologize for the slightly oxymoronic flavour of 'dawn serenade', but it seems to be the easiest way to convey my intended meaning. 'Serenade' has been much more happily assimilated into the language than 'aubade'. The former does appear in Johnson's dictionary and its meaning has grown more inclusive over the years. 'Aubade' only refers to single pieces of music, but a serenade can either be a single movement or a suite of pieces. 'Serenade', of course, can also be a verb.
3. I have found the following books and articles particularly helpful in researching the history of the *alba* and the troubadours: Jonathan Saville, *The Medieval Erotic Alba: Structure as Meaning* [ME]; Peter Dronke, *The Medieval Lyric* [ML]; Robert P. Miller (ed.), *Chaucer: Sources and Backgrounds* [CSB]; Jeffrey Dean, 'The Alba', in *The New Grove Dictionary of Music and Musicians* [GDMM]; Percy Scholes, 'Minstrels, Troubadours, Trouveres, Minnesingers, Mastersingers', in his *The Oxford Companion to Music* [OCM].
4. Besides the aubades mentioned in the text, I have found poems with this title by the following authors: Frederick Bock, Madison Cawein, Marylin Chin, Nuala Ni Dhomhnaill (trans. from Irish by Michael Longley), Ibn Hani (trans. from the Arabic by A. J. Arberry), Richard Howard, Richard Keney, Thomas Merton, Vassar Miller, Karl Shapiro, Timothy Steele, Robert Wallace, Robert Penn Warren. There are also two anonymous aubades: 'O Lady, awake, the azure moon', and 'Stay, O sweet, and do not rise'. The latter is sometimes attributed to John Donne. Some of these works were written after Larkin's death, and it seems unlikely he knew the others. On the other hand, he may have known the aubades by Agnes Robinson, Edith Sitwell, Sir Osbert Sitwell and Sylvia Plath. The last of these is a juvenile poem collected in Hughes's 1981 edition which Larkin reviewed in 1982; Edith Sitwell's poem appears set to music in William Walton's *Façade II*.
5. The forty-three letters concerning the *Oxford Book of Twentieth-Century English Verse* are unpublished, and are deposited in the Brynmor Jones Library in Hull.
6. Larkin's drafts for 'Aubade' are found in his last workbook, Workbook No.8, deposited in file DPL 1/8 (formerly DPL/11) in the Larkin archive of the Brynmor Jones Library. I identify each entry by Larkin's own datings.
7. 'Aubade' is a much more familiar word in French than English. We can see this from its occurrence in French idioms, whereas there are no English expressions which make use of it. Thus 'donner une aubade à une jeune fille' means to have early morning sex with a girl; 'recevoir une aubade' means to be thoroughly told off; and 'aubade' is frequently used ironically to refer to the clatter of servants or other 'bruits hostiles'. Its connotations are also slightly different in French. The leading sense of the word is to refer to a dawn performance rather than the piece performed, and the latter is just as likely to be a fanfare or full-scale military band concert as a song. Berlioz's 1839 song *Aubade*, for example, a setting of Alfred de Musset's 'Le lever', is accompanied exclusively by two cornets and four horns. The *Trésor de la*

Langue Française defines an aubade as: 'Concert de voix ou d'instruments donne a l'aube en honneur de quelq'un, sous ses fenêtres ou a sa porte; air compose pour ce concert' [TLF]. The military and ironic connotations of the word are presumably the reason why there are so few French poems called 'Aubade' in the nineteenth century.

8. His interest in and knowledge of classical music are made clear in [PLIK:52–3].
9. The stanza Larkin uses in 'Aubade' is prefigured in his early poem about death, 'And the wave sings because it is moving' [CP:6–7] [See M:150]. 'The wave sings [...]' doesn't have a regular rhythm or rhyme scheme, but it too has a ten-line stanza with the ninth line shortened.

   It's quite difficult to say why Larkin chose this unusual stanza structure. He may have enjoyed the way the shortened ninth line precipitates one into the generally gloomy and sonorous final line. It's also worth pointing out that 'Aubade' inverts the stanza of Larkin's most affirmative long poem, 'The Whitsun Weddings'. This uses a ten-line iambic pentameter except for the *second* line which is truncated.

   Appropriately, the ABBA rhyme-scheme of the final four lines is reminiscent of Tennyson's *In Memoriam*. And Tennyson – whose collected works Larkin reviewed in 1969 [RW:182–7] – may have been at the back of Larkin's mind at several points in 'Aubade': for example, 'The casement slowly grows a glimmering square' from 'Tears, idle tears [...]' in *The Princess*.
10. The differences between 'Aubade''s certainty and Larkin's usual poetic hesitations are also noted by Trevor Tolley [MPG:135]. For some more detailed remarks about the structure of 'Dockery and Son' see M. W. Rowe, 'Poetry and Abstraction', especially pp.169–73 [PALB].
11. This point is made on pages 51–2 of Jack B. Bedell's 'The Metrics of Connection: Form and Tone in Philip Larkin's "Aubade"' [HJP:8,1,1997:47–58].
12. 'Vers de Société' also has a strictly iambic first line, but the tone and diction of that poem are rather different from Larkin's longer, serious, pieces: 'Church Going', 'Faith Healing', 'Dockery and Son', 'The Whitsun Weddings', 'To the Sea', and so on.
13. If Freud's speculation in *Moses and Monotheism* is true, then the Jews took their monotheism from the Egyptian cult of Aton, the sun god, and the Christians derived their conception of God from the Jews. A common emphasis on light is therefore not surprising.
14. There are two reasons why a conventional Christian like Eliot might think death less important than sin. First, for a sinless man, or a man purged of sin, death is blissful eternal life; if death is unpleasant, this is a direct result of one's own sinfulness. Second, death only came into the world because of man's sinfulness. [See Romans 5.12, and Milton PLO:II: 629–889.] I am grateful to Harry Orr for drawing the passage in Romans to my attention.
15. Elgar eventually lost his Catholic faith and came round to Larkin's view. 'There is nothing but oblivion', he remarked towards the end of his life. See Andrew Walton's sleeve notes to *Elgar: The Dream of Gerontius* [EDG:3].
16. The vocabulary of real and notional assent is taken from Newman. See John Henry Cardinal Newman, *A Grammar of Assent* [GA].
17. There are several other poems where Larkin tries to excuse his own lack of altruism by a contentious reanalysis designed to show that altruism is

actually a disguised form of egoism. Indeed, he implies that his own position is more honest, first, because he is more clear-sighted, and second, because at least *he* – unlike the altruist – never pretends that his own position is morally superior or even laudable. For example, in 'Self's the Man' (if Larkin is not just assuming an ironized mask) he compares the time and effort Arnold puts into his family with his own self-concern, and comments:

> But wait, not so fast:
> Is there such a contrast?
> He was out for his own ends
> Not just pleasing his friends;
>
> And if it was such a mistake
> He still did it for his own sake,
> Playing his own game.
> So he and I are the same. [CP:117–18]

Similarly, the women (and possibly children) who see someone carried off in an ambulance whisper '*Poor soul* ... / ... at *their own* [my italics] distress' [CP:132–3] in contrast to the genuinely disinterested sympathy one might expect. Perhaps Larkin is implying disinterested sympathy is and must be a myth. If so, he is mistaken. A surprisingly popular conception of altruism holds that egoists want to satisfy their own desires but altruists don't. This is certainly wrong. Both the egoist and the altruist have desires they want satisfied, but in straightforward circumstances this is just a necessary condition for having a desire. A desire you did not want satisfied – even when it was not overridden by duty or some higher-order desire – simply wouldn't be a desire. The difference between an egoist and an altruist is really found in the different *content* of their desires. The happiness of others plays no part in an egoist's happiness, whereas the happiness of others *is* part of an altruist's happiness. This is all the difference there is between the two. To argue therefore that there is no difference between egoists and altruists because both have desires they want to satisfy, is to overlook the fact that one has *selfish*, and the other, *unselfish* desires. In the same way, sympathy for another's distress need not involve any thought about oneself undergoing the same distress, although this could happen on a particular occasion.

18. This point is not in tension with my remark in section III about the way the last verse channels Larkin back into his own life. The middle stanzas are private in the sense that they represent the unarticulated thoughts of a particular man. They are public in the sense that the content of the thoughts, being abstract, could be entertained by anyone. The last stanza is public in that it frequently mentions physical objects which are part of the objective realm. It is private in the sense that we know of objects' existence through perception, and perception, unlike thought, always implies a unique point of view. You and I can share the same thought at the same time, but we cannot both look at the same object from the same angle at the same time. Perception consequently emphasizes the separateness of persons in a way that thought does not.
19. I would like to thank Alison Mace for making this point to me.

20. 'Aubade' is one of the few poems – Plath's 'Daddy' is another – that seem to provoke a more than literary response. They somehow get through to people who normally think nothing of poetry. Others, who came expecting only to appreciate, turn away stunned and sickened. 'I remember reading it,' said one of Larkin's colleagues at the university, 'and it upset me so much it nearly ruined my holiday' [M:468–9]. The reaction is typical.

References

A John Milton, *Areopagitica and Of Education*, ed. George H. Sabine (Illinois: Harlan Davidson, 1951)

AEY Harry Chambers, ed., *An Enormous Yes: In Memoriam Philip Larkin (1922–1985)* (Calstock: Peterloo Poets, 1986)

AL *About Larkin: Newsletter of the Philip Larkin Society*

AOL C. S. Lewis, *The Allegory of Love: A Study in Medieval Tradition* (Oxford: Oxford University Press, 1953)

APL Simon Petch, *The Art of Philip Larkin* (Sydney: Sydney University Press, 1981)

AWJ Philip Larkin, *All What Jazz: A Record Diary* (London: Faber and Faber, 1970)

B Frederick Brown, *Flaubert: A Life* (London: Pimlico, 2006)

BAN Jean-Paul Sartre, *Being and Nothingness*, trans. Hazel Barnes (London: Methuen, 1958)

BBAB Humphrey Carpenter, *Benjamin Britten: A Biography* (London: Faber and Faber, 1993)

BMEC David Whittle, *Bruce Montgomery/Edmund Crispin* (Aldershot: Ashgate, 2007)

BJA *The British Journal of Aesthetics*

BL:I John Betjeman, *John Betjeman: Letters*, vol. I, ed. Candida Lycett Green (London: Methuen, 1994)

BL:II John Betjeman, *John Betjeman: Letters*, vol. II, ed. Candida Lycett Green (London: Methuen, 1995)

BS Peter Haining, *M. R. James – Book of the Supernatural*, Introduction by Sir John Betjeman (Slough: Foulsham, 1979)

BTQ John Daintith, ed., *The Bloomsbury Treasury of Quotations* (London: Bloomsbury Publishing, 1994)

C Samuel Taylor Coleridge, *Selected Poems of S. T. Coleridge*, ed. James Reeves (London: Heinemann, 1988)

CJ Immanuel Kant, *Critique of the Power of Judgment*, trans. and ed. Paul Guyer and Eric Matthews (Cambridge: Cambridge University Press, 2000)

CK Charles Kingsley, *Poems* (London: Macmillan, 1889)

CM M. R. James, *Count Magnus and Other Ghost Stories, The Complete Ghost Stories of M. R. James Volume I*, ed. S. T. Joshi (Harmondsworth: Penguin, 2005)

CP Philip Larkin, *Philip Larkin: Collected Poems*, ed. Anthony Thwaite (London: The Marvell Press and Faber and Faber, 1988)

CPPL P. French et al., eds, *Contemporary Perspectives in the Philosophy of Language* (Morris: Minnesota University Press, 1979)

CPSS Stevie Smith, *The Collected Poems of Stevie Smith* (London: Allen Lane, 1978)
CQ *Critical Quarterly*
CR M. R. James, *Casting the Runes and Other Ghost Stories*, Oxford World's Classics, ed. Michael Cox (Oxford: Oxford University Press, 1999)
CSB Robert P. Miller, ed., *Chaucer: Sources and Backgrounds* (New York: Oxford University Press, 1977)
CT Peter Bales, ed., *Challenges of Translation in French Literature: Studies and Poems in Honour of Peter Broome* (Bern: Peter Lang, 2005)

D James Joyce, *Dubliners*, ed. Robert Scholes (London: Cape, 1971)
DG Oscar Wilde, *The Picture of Dorian Gray* (Harmondsworth: Penguin, 1994)
DGE John Henry Cardinal Newman, *The Dream of Gerontius*, in Geoffrey Tillotson, ed., *Newman: Poetry and Prose* (London: Hart-Davies, 1957)

E *English: Journal of the English Association*
EA Michael Kelly, ed., *Encyclopedia of Aesthetics* (Oxford and New York: Oxford University Press, 1998)
ECH John Locke, *An Essay Concerning Human Understanding*, ed. Roger Woolhouse (Harmondsworth: Penguin, 1997)
ECP T. S. Eliot, *T. S. Eliot: Collected Poems 1909–1962* (London: Faber and Faber, 1974)
EDG Andrew Walton, sleeve notes to *Elgar: The Dream of Gerontius*, Naxos 8.553885–86
EN *Encounter*
EP Terry Whalen, *Philip Larkin and English Poetry* (London: Macmillan, 1986)

FBA W. H. Auden and Louis Kronenberger, eds, *The Faber Book of Aphorisms* (London: Faber and Faber, 1964)
FBTF Richard Bradford, *First Boredom, Then Fear* (London: Peter Owen Publishers, 2005)
FE Gustave Flaubert, *Flaubert in Egypt*, ed. and trans. Francis Steegmuller (Harmondsworth: Penguin, 1996)
FL:I Gustave Flaubert, *The Letters of Gustave Flaubert 1830–1857*, ed. and trans. Francis Steegmuller (London: Faber and Faber, 1981)
FL:II Gustave Flaubert, *The Letters of Gustave Flaubert 1857–1880*, ed. and trans. Francis Steegmuller (London: Faber and Faber, 1984)
FR Philip Larkin, *Further Requirements*, ed. Anthony Thwaite (London: Faber and Faber, 2001)
FS Gustave Flaubert and George Sand, *Flaubert–Sand: The Correspondence*, ed. and trans. Francis Steegmuller and Barbara Bray, based on the edition by Alphonse Jacobs (London: Harvill, 1993)
FSB *French Studies Bulletin*
FT Gustave Flaubert and Ivan Turgenev, *Flaubert and Turgenev: A Friendship in Letters*, ed. and trans. Barbara Bray (London: Athlone Press, 1985)

G Théophile Gautier, *Mademoiselle de Maupin*, trans. Helen Constantine, Introduction by Patricia Duncker (Harmondsworth: Penguin, 2005)

GA John Henry Cardinal Newman, *A Grammar of Assent* (New York: Image Books, 1955)
GB Christopher Isherwood, *Good-bye to Berlin* (London: Folio Society, 1975)
GDMM Stanley Sadie and John Tyrrell, eds, *The New Grove Dictionary of Music and Musicians*, 2nd edition (London: Grove, 1998)
GE T. J. Reed, *Goethe* (Oxford: Oxford University Press, 1984)
GS *Ghosts and Scholars 5* at www.users.globalnet.co.uk (accessed 25 March 2008)

HD M. R. James, *The Haunted Dolls' House and Other Ghost Stories, The Complete Ghost Stories of M. R. James Volume II*, ed. S. T. Joshi (Harmondsworth: Penguin, 2006)
HDO Bruce Montgomery/Edmund Crispin, *Holy Disorders* (London: Gollancz, 1945)
HJG Timothy Lustig, *Henry James and the Ghostly* (Cambridge: Cambridge University Press, 1994)
HJP *Hellas: A Journal of Poetry and the Humanities*
HSW William Hazlitt, *Selected Writings*, ed. and with an introduction by Ronald Blythe (Harmondsworth: Penguin, 1985)
HVCP Henry Vaughan, *Henry Vaughan: The Complete Poems*, ed. Alan Rudrum (Harmondsworth: Penguin, 1983)
HW Philip Larkin, *High Windows* (London: Faber and Faber, 1974)

ICV John Osborne, *Larkin, Ideology and Critical Violence* (London: Macmillan, 2008)

JBCP John Betjeman, *John Betjeman: Collected Poems*, ed. Andrew Motion (London: John Murray, 2006)
JC John Carey, review of Larkin's *Selected Letters*, *Sunday Times*, 25 October 1992
JP Sylvia Plath, *Johnny Panic and the Bible of Dreams and Other Prose Writings* (Harmondswoth: Penguin, 1990)

K John Keats, *John Keats: Poems*, ed. Gerald Bullett, Everyman's Library (London: Dent, 1974)
KACP Kingsley Amis, *Collected Poems: 1944–1979* (London: Hutchinson, 1979)
KAM Kingsley Amis, *Memoirs* (London: Hutchinson, 1994)
KEF Paul Guyer, *Kant and the Experience of Freedom* (Cambridge: Cambridge University Press, 1993)
KL John Keats, *Letters of John Keats*, ed. Robert Gittings (Oxford: Oxford University Press, 1985)
KTC Andrew Ward, *Kant: The Three Critiques* (Cambridge: Polity Press, 2006)

L Roger Day, *Larkin* (Milton Keynes: Open University Press, 1987)
LD Lionel Trilling, *The Last Decade: Essays and Reviews, 1965–75* (Oxford: Oxford University Press, 1982)
LE Lawrence Lerner, *Philip Larkin* (Plymouth: Northcote House, 1997)
LI Lionel Trilling, *The Liberal Imagination: Essays on Literature and Society* (Oxford: Oxford University Press, 1981)

LJ Philip Larkin, *Larkin's Jazz: Essays and Reviews 1940–84*, ed. Richard Palmer and John White, Foreword by Alan Plater (London: Continuum, 2001)

LKA Kingsley Amis, *The Letters of Kingsley Amis*, ed. Zachary Leader (London: HarperCollins, 2000)

LM Philip Larkin, *Philip Larkin: Letters to Monica*, ed. Anthony Thwaite (London: Faber and Faber / Bodleian Library, 2010)

LP Henry Longfellow, *The Golden Legend*, Part V, in *The Poetical Works of Longfellow* (London: Henry Frowde, 1906)

M Andrew Motion, *Philip Larkin: A Writer's Life* (London: Faber and Faber, 1993)

MC James Dolamore, ed., *Making Connections: Essays in French Culture and Society in Honour of Philip Thody* (Bern: Peter Lang, 1999)

MCP Louis MacNeice, *Louis MacNeice: Collected Poems 1925–1948* (London: Faber and Faber, 1949)

ME Jonathan Saville, *The Medieval Erotic Alba: Structure as Meaning* (New York: Columbia University Press, 1972)

ML Peter Dronke, *The Medieval Lyric* (Cambridge: D. S. Brewer, 1996)

MPG Trevor Tolley, *My Proper Ground: A Study of Philip Larkin and his Development* (Edinburgh: Edinburgh University Press, 1991)

MPM G. E. M. Anscombe, *Metaphysics and the Philosophy of Mind: Collected Philosophical Papers, Volume III* (Oxford: Blackwell, 1981)

MQ Thomas Nagel, *Mortal Questions* (Cambridge: Cambridge University Press, 1979)

MR Zachary Leader, ed., *The Movement Reconsidered* (Oxford: Oxford University Press, 2009)

MRJO Richard Holmes, 'M. R. James and Others', in his *Sidetracks: Explorations of a Romantic Biographer* (London: HarperCollins, 2001)

MT Bruce Montgomery/Edmund Crispin, *The Moving Toyshop* (London: Gollancz, 1946)

MW Dale Salwak, ed., *Philip Larkin: The Man and his Work* (Iowa: Iowa University Press, 1989)

N Gustave Flaubert, *November*, trans. Andrew Brown, Introduction by Nadine Gordimer (London: Hesperus, 2005)

NC Stephen Regan, ed., *Philip Larkin: Contemporary Critical Essays*, New Casebook Series (London: Macmillan, 1997)

NLO James Booth, ed., *New Larkins for Old: Critical Essays* (London: Macmillan Press, 2000)

NNP A. E. Housman, *The Name and Nature of Poetry* (Bromsgrove: Housman Society, 2006)

NOBEV Helen Gardner, ed., *The New Oxford Book of English Verse 1250–1950* (Oxford: Clarendon Press, 1973)

NS M. H. Abrams, *Natural Supernaturalism: Tradition and Revolution in Romantic Literature* (London: Norton, 1973)

OBD D. J. Enright, ed., *The Oxford Book of Death* (Oxford: Oxford University Press, 1983)

OBEV Sir Arthur Quiller-Couch, ed., *The Oxford Book of English Verse* (Oxford: Oxford University Press, 1900)

OBSV H. J. C. Grierson and G. Bullough, eds, *The Oxford Book of Seventeenth-Century Verse* (Oxford: Oxford University Press, 1968)

OCEL Margaret Drabble, ed., *The Oxford Companion to English Literature*, revised edition (Oxford: Oxford University Press, 1995)

OCM Percy Scholes, *The Oxford Companion to Music* (London: Oxford University Press, 1938)

OCPW James Joyce, *Occasional, Critical, and Political Writing*, ed. Kevin Barry (Oxford: Oxford University Press, 2000)

ODNB Tim Wales, 'Ketch [Catch], John [Jack]', in *The Oxford Dictionary of National Biography*, ed. H. C. G. Matthew and Brian Harrison (Oxford: Oxford University Press, 2004)

OED J. A. Simpson and E. S. C. Weiner, eds, *The Oxford Dictionary*, 2nd edition (Oxford: Clarendon Press, 1991)

OOR Andrew Swarbrick, *Out of Reach: The Poetry of Philip Larkin* (London: Macmillan, 1995)

OSR Geoff Dyer, *Out of Sheer Rage: In the Shadow of D. H. Lawrence* (London: Little, Brown and Company, 1997)

OTB Richard Church, *Over the Bridge* (London: Heinemann, 1955)

PALB M. W. Rowe, *Philosophy and Literature: A Book of Essays* (Aldershot: Ashgate, 2004)

PAP Alexander Pope, *The Poems of Alexander Pope*, ed. John Butt (London: Methuen, 1984)

PITT Barbara Everett, *Poets in their Time: Essays on English Poetry from Donne to Larkin* (London: Faber and Faber, 1986)

PL Stephen Regan, *Philip Larkin* (London: Macmillan, 1992)

PLIK Maeve Brennan, *The Philip Larkin I Knew* (Manchester: Manchester University Press, 2002)

PLO John Milton, *Paradise Lost*, ed. Alistair Fowler (London: Longman, 1989)

PLT George Hartley, ed., *Philip Larkin, 1922–1985: A Tribute* (Hull: The Marvell Press, 1988)

PLW James Booth, *Philip Larkin: Writer* (London: Harvester Wheatsheaf, 1992)

POA James Joyce, *A Portrait of the Artist as a Young Man*, ed. with an Introduction by Seamus Deane (Harmondsworth: Penguin, 1992)

PP James Booth, *Philip Larkin: The Poet's Plight* (London: Palgrave Macmillan, 2005)

PPE Maurice Merleau-Ponty, *Phenomenology of Perception*, trans. Colin Smith (London: Routledge & Kegan Paul, 1962)

PWS Sir Walter Scott, *Rockeby*, Canto II, section 11, in *The Poetical Works of Sir Walter Scott* (London: Macmillan, 1878)

R Plato, *The Republic*, ed. and trans. D. Lee (Harmondsworth: Penguin, 1987)

RB Al Alvarez, *Risky Business* (London: Bloomsbury, 2007)

RBSP Robert Browning, *Robert Browning: Selected Poems*, ed. Daniel Karlin (Harmondsworth: Penguin, 2004)

RO *Ratio: An International Journal of Analytic Philosophy*
RW Philip Larkin, *Required Writing* (London: Faber and Faber, 1983)

S Francis Steegmuller, *Flaubert and Madame Bovary* (London: Constable, 1993)
SB Gustave Flaubert, *Salammbô*, trans. J. C. Chartres (London: Dent, 1969)
SE Gustave Flaubert, *Sentimental Education*, ed. and trans. Robert Baldick (Harmondsworth: Penguin, 1975)
SH James Joyce, *Stephen Hero* (New York: New Directions, 1944)
SL Philip Larkin, *Selected Letters of Philip Larkin*, ed. Anthony Thwaite (London: Faber and Faber, 1992)
SOED Lesley Brown, ed., *The New Shorter Oxford English Dictionary* (Oxford: Clarendon Press, 1993)
SPM Louis MacNeice, *Selected Poems of Louis MacNeice*, ed. W. H. Auden (London: Faber and Faber, 1977)
SR Matthew Arnold, *The Complete Prose Works of Matthew Arnold*, ed. R. H. Super (Ann Arbor: University of Michigan Press, 1960–77)
STD Julian Barnes, *Something to Declare* (London: Picador, 2002)
SW Stephen Cooper, *Philip Larkin: Subversive Writer* (Brighton: Sussex Academic Press, 2004)

T Ludwig Wittgenstein, *Tractatus Logico-Philosophicus*, trans. D. F. Pears and B. F. McGuinness (London: Routledge & Kegan Paul, 1973)
THJ *The Historical Journal*
TIS Paul Auster, *The Invention of Solitude* (London: Faber and Faber, 1988)
TLF *Trésor de la Langue Française* (Paris: Cenre Nationale de la Recherche Scientifique, 1974)
TNP Al Alvarez, *The New Poetry* (Harmondsworth: Penguin, 1962)
TPL David Timms, *Philip Larkin* (London: Oliver and Boyd, 1973)
TRP Seamus Heaney, *The Redress of Poetry* (London: Faber and Faber, 1995)
TSA Gustave Flaubert, *The Temptation of St Anthony*, trans. Lafcadio Hearn, Introduction by Michel Foucault (New York: Random House, 2001)
TSV Colin McGinn, *The Subjective View: Secondary Qualities and Indexical Thoughts* (Oxford: Clarendon Press, 1983)
TT Gustave Flaubert, *Three Tales*, trans. Roger Whitehouse, Introduction by Geoffrey Wall (Harmondsworth: Penguin, 2005)
TWG Philip Larkin, *Trouble at Willow Gables and Other Fictions*, ed. James Booth (London: Faber and Faber, 2002)
TWT John Betjeman, *Tennis Whites and Teacakes*, ed. Stephen Games (London: John Murray, 2007)

VWCE Virginia Woolf, *Collected Essays* (London: Hogarth Press, 1966)

W Geoffrey Wall, *Flaubert: A Life* (London: Faber and Faber, 2001)
WECP William Empson, *William Empson: The Collected Poems*, ed. John Haffenden (Harmondsworth: Penguin, 2001)
WMP Winthrop Praed, *The Poems of Winthrop Mackworth Praed*, ed. Frederick Cooper (London: Walter Scott, 1886)

WR Duncan Wu, ed., *Romanticism: An Anthology with CD-Rom*, 2nd edition (Oxford: Blackwell, 2006)

WW William Wordsworth, *William Wordsworth*, ed. Stephen Gill, The Oxford Authors Series (Oxford: Oxford University Press, 1984)

WWR Arthur Schopenhauer, *The World as Will and Representation*, trans. E. F. J. Payne (New York: Dover Publications Inc., 1969)

YB Bevis Hillier, *Young Betjeman* (London: John Murray, 1988)

Index

Abrams, M. H., 122n.17, 157
aesthetic experience
  and blueness, 7, 33, 37, 41, 42, 43, 55
  contemplation, 14, 15, 27, 33, 35, 38–43, 46n.30, 73, 107–8, 109, 110, 113–15
  and detachment, 2, 117
  and inspiration, 3, 34, 55–6, 118, 119, 148–50, 152–4, 155, 164nn.12, 13, 196
  and loneliness, 3, 31, 33, 59, 73, 112, 150, 151, 152
  'poetic emotion', 148, 150–1
  and the self, 2, 8, 35, 36–8, 39–43
  and solitude, 24, 25, 31, 32, 35, 58, 60, 65, 98, 99, 105, 109–10, 112, 135, 150, 152, 153, 168
  see also creativity; imagination; perception; self/selfhood
aestheticism, 1–3, 5, 51, 72
  and cruelty, 53, 65, 66
  fin-de-siècle, 1, 51
  and politics, 50, 52, 64–5, 66, 68–9, 86n.14
  and sympathy, 65, 66, 67, 80, 203n.17
  see also beauty; emotion; sublime
alba (lyric song), 169, 170, 171, 172, 173
altruism/egoism, 202–3n.17
Alvarez, Al, 122n.17
Amis, Kingsley, 1, 45n.12, 94, 125, 128, 129, 144, 151, 162nn.3, 4, 180, 189
Andersen, Hans, 125
animism, 3, 112, 151, 152
Anscombe, G. E. M., 44n.5
Aquinas, St Thomas, 113, 122n.18
Arberry, A. J., 201n.4
Arnold, Matthew, 39, 40, 160
Arnott (later Bradshaw), Winifred, 79, 129
art
  l'art pour l'art, 49, 51, 122n.18
  and ethics, 51, 56, 66, 67–8
  Flaubert, 50, 56–7, 65, 71, 72–3, 74, 75, 83
  Larkin's attitude to, 1, 49, 51, 60, 71–2, 83, 119, 152, 200
  and love, 50, 56–7, 72–3, 73–4, 76–7, 153
  and religious attitude, 1, 49, 50, 51, 55, 152, 184, 188
  see also aesthetic experience; aestheticism; beauty; creativity; emotion
'aubade' (word), 168–9, 171–2, 201nn.2, 7
'Aubade'
  alliteration in, 193
  courage, 193–4
  darkness and light, 174, 177, 179, 180, 183–5, 192
  diction, 174–8, 180–2, 193
  fear of death, 173, 174, 177, 178, 179, 184, 189, 191–2, 193
  first-person perspective, 179, 187
  imagery, 178–9, 185, 187–8, 197–9
  narrator, 172, 173, 176–7, 178, 179, 191, 195, 198
  rhyme, 189–90, 202n.9
  rhythm, 176, 180, 181–2, 186, 199
  setting, 173
  simile, 174
  sky, 173, 178, 198
  structure, 176, 182–3, 202n.9
  symbolism, 172–4, 183–4, 187, 192, 195
  time, 185
  world of work, 194, 195–7
Auden, W. H., 69
Auster, Paul, 109–10

Barnes, Julian, 48, 51, 85n.6, 135
Barry, Kevin, 122n.18

Baudelaire, Charles, 2, 50, 167
beauty, 42, 49, 50, 55, 65, 66, 77, 79, 80, 81, 95, 114
  and awe, 2, 51, 67, 113, 115
  as goal of aesthetics, 113
  see also aesthetic experience; aestheticism; art; sublime
Bede, the Venerable, 143, 164n.9
Bedell, Jack B., 202n.11
Béranger, Pierre-Jean, 86n.10
Berlioz, Hector, 201n.7
Betjeman, John, 103, 125, 137–8, 144, 148
Bible, the, 184, 202n.14
Bizet, Georges, 172
Bock, Frederick, 201n.4
Booth, James, 33, 45nn.10, 14, 46nn.19, 22, 24, 26, 27, 121n.3, 122n.15
Bouilhet, Louis, 52, 71, 74, 77, 81
Bowman, Deborah, 14
Bowman, Ruth, 51, 60
Bradbury, Saville, 92
Bradford, Richard, 91
Bradshaw (née Arnott), Winifred, 196
Brecht, Bertolt, 69
Brennan, Maeve, 82, 97, 117, 142, 188, 196
Brett, R. L., 164n.14
Brezhnev, Leonid, 63
Britten, Benjamin, 100
Brown, Frederick, 77
Browning, Robert, 103–4, 198
Bulwer Lytton, Edward, 95

Cawein, Madison, 201n.4
Charles I, King, 100
Chaucer, Geoffrey, 170
Chesters, Graham, 85n.4
Chevalier, Ernest, 74
childhood, Larkin's, 96, 185–6,
children, Larkin's attitude to, 57, 62, 75–6, 87n.16
Chin, Marylin, 201n.4
Church, Richard, 46n.33
Clark, Lawrence Gordon, 147
Coghill, Neville, 170
'Coleman, Brunette' (Larkin's pseudonym), 78, 80, 96, 129
Coleridge, Samuel Taylor, 22, 34, 35, 46n.29, 86n.14, 151, 157
Colet, Louise, 48, 50, 72, 74–5, 77, 82, 85n.2, 122n.18
Commanville, Caroline (Flaubert's niece), 70, 87n.18
Commanville, Ernest, 70
Conan Doyle, Sir Arthur, 95
Conquest, Robert, 1, 10, 175
consciousness
  and aesthetic experience, 35, 39–43, 85n.10
  disembodied, 20, 21, 45n.14
  and indexicals, 11–13, 18
  limits of, 7, 42
  poetic imagery, 9, 40–2, 111–12, 143, 152
  and point of view, 17, 18, 45n.13
  self-consciousness, 7, 12, 13, 22, 42, 44 n.8, 53
  see also aesthetic experience; creativity; death; indexicals; perspective; self/selfhood
Constant, Benjamin, 122n.18
consumerism, 26–7
Cooper, Stephen, 32, 33, 46n.19
Cornford, Frances, 133, 155
Coster Greene, Bella da, 161
Cousin, Victor, 85n.2, 122n.18
Cox, C. B., 103, 190
Crabbe, George, 147
creativity, 2, 3, 5, 33, 34, 36, 55–6, 85n.10, 110, 117, 118, 151, 152, 153, 154, 199
  and dissolution/loss of self, 35, 36–8, 39–43
  inspiration, 34, 55–6, 119, 148–50
  and loneliness, 3, 31, 33, 59, 73, 112, 150, 151, 152
  love and marriage inimical to, 73–4
  'poetic emotion', 148, 150–1
  poetic muse, 3, 118, 119, 148–50, 152–3, 154, 155, 164nn.12, 13, 196
  and property, 116–18
  and sexuality, 2, 3, 5, 76–9, 92, 149–50, 152–4

creativity – *continued*
and solitude, 24, 25, 31, 32, 35, 56, 57, 58, 59–60, 65, 98, 99, 105, 109–10, 112, 135, 150, 151, 152, 153, 168
see also aesthetic experience; aestheticism; imagination; self/selfhood; sexuality; supernaturalism
creepy, *see* supernaturalism
Cripps, Stafford, 53
'Crispin, Edmund' (Bruce Montgomery's pseudonym), *see* Montgomery
Cumberland, Duke of (Ernest Augustus), 101

Davenant, William, 169, 173, 195, 197
Davie, Donald, 98
Day, Roger, 14
Dean, Jeffrey, 201n.3
death, 3, 32, 117, 130, 135, 167–204
fear of, 43, 61, 116, 130–1, 170, 174, 177, 180, 181, 184, 189, 191, 192, 193
poetic imagery, 131, 136, 143, 173, 178–9, 182, 187, 198
see also nothingness; the past; self/selfhood; supernaturalism
de Chirico, Giorgio, 175
Derrida, Jacques, 119
Dhomhnaill, Nuala Ni, 201n.4
Dionysius the Areopagite, 185
Donne, John, 201n.4
Dronke, Peter, 201n.3
Dryden, John, 152
Dyball, Ian, 46n.32

Egerton, Judy, 117, 153, 175
egoism/altruism, 202–3n.17
Elgar, Edward, 121n.4, 188–9, 195, 202n.15
Eliot, George, 167
Eliot, T. S., 69, 143, 185
Eliphaz the Termanite, 159
Elizabeth, Queen of Bohemia, 141

emotion, 12, 42, 76, 81, 96, 193–4
anger and rage, 12, 60–1, 62, 79, 85n.10
and art, 67–9, 148, 150, 160
awe, 2, 51, 67, 113, 115
depression, 60–1, 199
happiness, 43, 49, 57, 99, 203n.17
imagination and, 67–8, 69, 81
misanthropy, 61, 62, 64
'poetic emotion', 148, 150–1
sympathy, 65, 66, 67, 80, 81, 203n.17
Empson, William, 170, 171, 172, 173
Enright, D. J., 184, 199
Epicurus, 189
Ernest Augustus (Duke of Cumberland), 101
Escarbagnas, Marquise d', 58
Everett, Barbara, 1, 92, 121n.9, 142, 164n.9
Exall, Jane, 78

Flaubert, Achille (writer's brother), 87n.18
Flaubert, Achille-Cléophas (writer's father), 87n.18
Flaubert, Anne-Justine (writer's mother), 82, 87n.18
Flaubert, Gustave, 2, 4, 48–87
on art and beauty, 50, 56–7, 65, 71, 83, 122n.18
on art and love, 72–3, 74, 75
Bouvard and Pécuchet, 53
The Candidate, 52
career choice, 70–2
Le Château des coeurs, 52
on creativity, 58–9, 76–8
eroticism, 77–8
feminine element, 81–2
hatred of life, 60–1, 64, 76
'Herodias', 85n.8
Larkin's interest in, 48–9, 51
Madame Bovary, 52, 53, 54, 76, 79–80, 125
November, 52, 79
political stance, 63, 65, 68
Romanticism, 52–3
'St Julian Hospitator', 55, 85n.8
Salammbô, 53, 66, 76

Sentimental Education, 53, 68
'A Simple Heart', 80, 85n.8
The Temptation of St Anthony, 52, 53, 77
and women, 79–80, 81–3
freedom, 2, 35, 37, 42, 43, 92, 106–7, 108, 110, 113, 114–15, 118, 173
see also aesthetic experience; creativity; self/selfhood
Freud, Sigmund, 202n.13
friendship, 64, 75, 105
see also love and marriage

Gautier, Théophile, 49–51, 65, 85n.3, 122n.18
George III, King, 101
George IV, King, 101
ghost stories, 125, 128, 129, 130, 131, 135, 136, 140, 147, 153, 154, 155, 158, 159, 160–1
see also M. R. James; mysticism; supernaturalism
ghostly, *see* supernaturalism
Goethe, J. W. von, 42, 124
Grimshaw, John Atkinson, 162n.6
Gross, Miriam, 59
Gunn, Thom, 97
Gunner, Colin, 63
Guy the Gorilla, 85n.10
Guyer, Paul, 122n.20

Hani, Ibn, 201n.4
Hardy, Dr (Flaubert's doctor), 81
Hardy, Thomas, 4, 125, 135, 158, 160, 162n.2
Hartley, Jean, 79
Hazlitt, William, 66, 67, 68, 69, 86n.14
Heaney, Seamus, 45n.10, 182, 183
Hébert, Caroline, 'Julie' (Flaubert's nurse), 85n.9
Herbert, George, 102
Herbert, Juliet, 82
'Here'
aesthetic experience, 8, 27
cityscape, 25–6
and consciousness, 11, 12, 13, 17, 45n.13
description of Hull, 25–31
dissolution of the self, 8, 35, 37–8
dreamlike quality, 21–2, 36
grammatical form, 23–4, 27, 28–9, 31–2
imagination, 17–18, 19, 22, 33, 34, 35
impersonal perspective, 16, 19, 20, 22, 33, 37, 41
indexicals, 8, 9, 11–13
landscape, 11, 18–19, 22, 26, 29, 32, 33, 36, 38–9, 41
metaphor, 23
movement, 24–5, 28, 31
narrative method, 13
narrator, 7, 8, 9, 14, 15, 16, 19, 20, 21, 27, 30, 37, 44n.3, 45nn.13, 14
philosophical themes, 7, 8
point of view, 12, 16–17, 19, 20, 22, 24, 41
realism, 7, 21, 33
reference, 7–12
rhythm, 27–8
seascape, 33, 34, 36
symbolism, 9, 33–8
tense, 24
travel, 14–16, 17, 18–19, 20, 44n.3, 45n.16
Hewett, Kitty (Larkin's sister), 87n.18
Holmes, Richard, 153
Housman, A. E., 124–5, 159–60, 161
Howard, Richard, 201n.4
Hughes, Noel, 51
Hughes, Ted, 201n.4
Hull, 10–11, 16, 20, 22, 45n.15, 58, 59, 117, 173
description of, in 'Here', 25–31
Hulse, Michael, 121n.8
Husserl, Edmund, 47n.35

Iles, Norman, 56
imagination, 7, 16–18, 19, 22, 51, 66–7, 68–70, 135–6, 144, 145, 178, 194, 195, 196
and emotion, 67–8, 69, 79, 96, 114
and the feminine, 78, 80, 97–8, 119, 154
impersonal, 33, 35–6, 37
and magic, 18, 21

imagination – *continued*
poetic, 17–18, 22–3, 33, 34, 35, 80, 111–12, 142–3, 164n.14
and religious attitude, 51
and time, 24
see also aesthetic experience; creativity; perspective
indexicals, 8, 9, 11–13, 18, 44n.2, 87n.15
see also consciousness; perspective; self/selfhood
inspiration, *see* aesthetic experience; creativity
Isherwood, Christopher, 22

James, Clive, 91, 121n.11, 122n.14
James, Henry, 125, 155, 158
James, M. R., 124, 139–41, 152, 155–6, 159, 160–1
influence on Larkin, 125–9, 130–6, 138–9, 143–7, 151, 162 n.1
sexuality, 153–4
see also ghost stories; supernaturalism
Jenkins, Nicholas, 44n.2
Johnson, Samuel, 168, 201n.2
Jones, Monica, 57, 82, 83, 119, 133, 160
Joyce, James, 4, 5, 52, 69, 112, 113, 115, 122n.18, 150, 156
'Julie' Caroline Hébert (Flaubert's nurse), 85n.9

Kant, Immanuel, 3, 46n.31, 111, 113–14, 122nn.18, 19, 20
Kaplan, David, 44n.2
Keats, John, 151, 159
Keney, Richard, 201n.4
Kermode, Frank, 48
Ketch, John (Jack), 100, 101, 146, 164n.10
Kingsley, Charles, 128

Lalo, Edouard, 172
Larkin, Eva (writer's mother), 82
Larkin, Philip
works
'Absences', 18, 33, 36–7, 99
'Afternoons', 140
'Ambulances', 186–7, 202–3n.17
'Ante Meridian', 99, 129
'Aubade', 1, 2, 3, 4, 165–204 (*see also detailed analysis above*)
'Ballade des Dames du Temps Jadis', 167
'Best Society', 1, 85n.10
'Bridge for the Living', 19, 20, 31
'Broadcast', 140, 141
'The Building', 141, 178, 187
'The Card-Players', 99, 141, 142
'Church Going', 136–8, 139, 158, 163n.8, 191, 202n.12
'Days', 136
'Deceptions', 81, 135, 158, 184
'Deep Analysis', 119, 148–9
'Dockery and Son', 13, 22, 57–8, 61, 107, 179, 202n.12
'Dry-Point', 2
'Dublinesque', 54, 135
'Dying Day' (later, 'Going'), 135
'Essential Beauty', 173
'The Explosion', 142
'Faith Healing', 81, 202n.12
'Femmes Damnées', 2, 167
'Friday Night in the Royal Station Hotel', 141, 142, 157, 158, 184
'Ghosts', 130
A Girl in Winter, 81
'Going' (earlier, 'Dying Day'), 135
'Going, Going', 15, 135, 136, 160
'Heads in the Women's Ward', 81
'Here', 2, 3, 4, 6, 7–47 (*see also detailed analysis above*)
'High Windows', 37, 47n.34
High Windows, 2, 91, 117, 121n.4, 141, 142, 143, 162n.1, 177, 178, 187, 192
'Homage to a Government', 190
'How Distant', 135
'I Remember, I Remember', 15
'If, My Darling', 2
'The Importance of Elsewhere', 9
The Less Deceived, 1, 2, 9, 52, 81, 131, 187
'The Life with a Hole in it', 71–2
'Livings', 2, 3, 4, 33, 88–123, 141, 142, 143, 145, 146, 147, 152,

153, 154, 158–9, 164n.10 (*see also detailed analysis below*)
'Love Songs in Age', 81
'MCMXIV', 135, 158
'Money', 2
'Mother, Summer, I', 2, 97
'Negative Indicative', 2, 92–3, 94–5, 96
The North Ship, 1, 10, 53, 81
'The Old Fools', 141
Preface to *A Rumoured City*, 10, 19
'Reference Back', 81
'Round another Point', 87n.17
'Sad Steps', 107
Selected Letters, 1, 2, 151
'Self's the Man', 202–3n.17
'Send No Money', 57
'Show Saturday', 180
'Solar', 2, 178, 184
'The Story of an Occurrence and a Disoccurrence' (later, 'Whatever Happened?'), 131–2, 134, 150
'Sympathy in White Major', 2, 91
'To the Sea', 202n.12
'Traumerai', 168
'The Trees', 182
Trouble at Willow Gables, 50
'Vers de Société, 1, 57, 141, 168, 172, 180, 202n.12
'Waiting for Breakfast', 119, 149, 164nn.12, 13
'Water', 2
'The wave sings ...', 2, 202n.9
'Wedding-Wind', 81, 140
'Whatever Happened?' (earlier, 'The Story of an Occurrence and a Disoccurrence'), 131, 132, 140
'When first we faced ...', 153
'The Whitsun Weddings', 13, 15, 20, 22, 202nn.9, 12
The Whitsun Weddings, 2, 9, 24, 81, 141, 187
Larkin, Sydney (writer's father), 96
La Rochefoucauld, François de, 184
Lawrence, D. H., 13, 51, 66, 69
Lefanu, Sheridan, 125, 141
Lerner, Lawrence, 169, 171, 172, 185
Leroyer de Chantepie, Marie-Sophie, 80
lesbianism, Larkin's interest in, 5, 50, 51, 78
see also imagination; sexuality
Levi, Peter, 14
Lévy, Michel, 62
Lewis, C. S., 170
'Livings'
aesthetic experience, 92, 110, 111, 112, 113–15
alienation, 105–6
diction, 110
freedom, 92, 106–7, 108, 110, 113, 114, 115, 118
imagery, 98–9, 111–12
imagination, 111–12
metaphor, 98
narrators, 91, 93–4, 95, 96, 98, 104, 105, 106, 107, 108, 110, 111, 112, 118, 121n.12, 147, 152, 153
nature, 98, 107, 114
poetic form, 98, 100–4
seascape, 97, 108, 112, 152
settings, 99–104, 121n.2
sexuality, 92, 118–19
sky, 93, 95, 107, 108, 110, 111, 122n.21
solitude, 98, 112
stars, 108, 112, 114, 145
symbolism, 107–8, 122nn.15, 17
use of blanks, 95, 121n.4
Locke, John, 44n.9
Longfellow, Henry, 128
Longley, Edna, 1, 85n.5
Longley, Michael, 201n.4
love, 12, 153, 170, 172–3, 186
and art, 50, 56–7, 72–3, 73–4, 76–7
and marriage, 72–3, 73–4, 75
see also art; creativity; sexuality; women
Lowell, Robert, 157
Lucian, 59
Lustig, Timothy, 164n.11
Lynam, 'Skipper', 125

Mace, Alison, 203
Mackereth, Betty, 82
Macmillan, Harold, 26
MacNeice, Louis, 169, 172, 174, 197
Mallarmé, Stéphane, 4

Maugham, Somerset, 72
Maupassant, Guy de, 71
McGinn, Colin, 44nn.2, 9
Merleau-Ponty, Maurice 43
Merton, Thomas, 201n.4
Methuen, Lord, 101, 121n.7
Middleton, Thomas, 99
Miller, Robert P., 201n.3
Miller, Vassar, 201n.4
Milton, John, 148, 184, 202n.14
Modernism, 86n.14
Monmouth, Lord, 100
Montgomery, Bruce, 51, 61, 128, 129, 136, 144, 148, 162nn.4, 5
Moore, George, 85n.6
Motion, Andrew, 16, 19, 32, 116, 194, 195
Movement poetry, 2, 34, 167, 168
Murdoch, Iris, 125, 155, 162n.3
Murphy, Richard, 108
muse, *see* creativity
Musset, Alfred de, 201n.7
mysticism, 4, 51, 80, 145, 152
  see also supernaturalism

Nagel, Thomas, 44n.7, 87n.15
Napoleon, 101
narrator
  in 'Aubade', 172, 173, 176–7, 178, 179, 191, 195, 198
  in 'Dockery and Son', 13, 107
  in 'Here', 7, 8, 9, 14, 15, 16, 19, 20, 21, 27, 30, 37, 44n.3, 45nn.13, 14
  in 'High Windows', 37
  in 'Livings', 91, 93–4, 95, 96, 98, 104, 105, 106, 107, 108, 110, 111, 112, 118, 121n.12, 147, 152, 153, 147
  in 'Unfinished Poem', 130–1
  in 'The Whitsun Weddings', 13, 20
Newman, John Henry, Cardinal, 188, 202n.11
Newton, Isaac, 100–1
nothingness, concept of, 8, 11, 54–5
  and blueness, 41, 42, 54, 55, 157
  see also aesthetic experience; death; poetic imagery; self/selfhood

O'Neill, Michael, 46n.29
Opie, Iona, 75
Opie, Peter, 75
Orr, Harry, 202n.14
Orwell, George, 69
Osborne, John, 8
Ovid, 76

past, the, 3, 93, 94, 108, 158, 159
  see also death; indexicals; self/selfhood; supernaturalism
pastiche, 103, 104, 129, 132, 143, 147
pastoral, 21, 28–9
Paulin, Tom, 122n.15
perception, 18, 153, 203n.18
  aesthetic, 38–40, 56, 111–15
  see also aesthetic experience
perspective
  first-person/subjective, 8, 11, 12, 13, 16, 18, 19, 20, 21, 45nn.14, 18, 46n.19, 179
  and imagination, 17–18, 22, 35–6, 41, 42, 96, 119
  impersonal, 16, 18, 19, 20, 22, 24, 33, 35, 37, 45nn.14, 18, 46n.19
  spectator's, 57–8
  subjective/objective, 11, 12, 13, 23, 87n.15, 203n.18
  third-person, 45 n.18, 187, 191
  see also consciousness; indexicals; narrator; self/selfhood
Petch, Simon, 9, 16, 91, 95, 121n.3
Phillips (music publisher?), 168
philosophy, 3–4, 7, 8, 36, 70, 179, 189, 192
Pinter, Harold, 69
Plath, Sylvia, 160, 172, 201n.4, 204n.20
Plato, 148
Plomley, Roy, 196
poetic devices
  alliteration, 32, 99, 105, 182, 193
  assonance, 32, 99
  metaphor, 23, 98, 111, 141, 151, 178
  rhyme, 23, 64, 98, 102, 189–90, 202n.9
  rhythm, 23, 27–8, 98, 103, 148, 180, 181–2, 199, 202n.9
  simile, 98, 111, 174, 178

symbolism, 2, 33, 34, 35–6, 54, 95, 107, 143, 148, 149, 156–7, 175, 179, 197
poetic subject matters
blueness, 7, 33, 37, 41, 43, 55, 157
cityscape, 19, 25–6, 30–1
death, 32, 131, 136, 143, 173, 178–9, 180, 182, 184, 187, 190, 191, 193, 198, 199, 202n.9
landscape, 9, 10, 11, 14, 18–19, 22, 23, 24–6, 32, 33, 36, 38–9, 41, 45n.12, 111, 130, 134, 135, 147, 175
movement, 8, 19, 20, 21, 24–5, 26, 28, 31, 33, 37, 174, 181
railways, 13, 14, 15–16, 20, 45n.16
sea/seascape, 10, 11, 19, 22, 32, 33, 34, 36, 96–7, 98, 112, 128, 152
sky, 32, 34, 35, 37, 41–2, 43, 47n.34, 55, 93, 95, 97, 107, 110, 111, 173, 174, 178, 198
time, 24, 25, 112, 130, 135, 177, 185
travel, 14–16, 17, 18–19, 20, 24
point of view, *see* perspective
Poittevin, Alfred le, 74, 77
politics
and aestheticism, 50, 51, 64–5, 66–70, 86n.14
Flaubert, 53, 62, 63, 65, 68–9
Larkin's conservative outlook, 62, 63–4, 68–9
Pope, Alexander, 181
Pradier, James, 50
Praed, Winthrop, 102–3
primitivism, 3, 99, 109, 112, 141, 143, 151
see also animism
Pritchard, William, 189, 190
Proust, Marcel, 50, 69, 181
Punch and Judy shows, 101, 132, 146, 163n.7, 164n.10
Pym, Barbara, 117, 134

Quiller-Couch, Arthur, 169

Ravel, Maurice, 172
realism, 7, 14, 19, 20, 21, 22, 33, 35, 46n.19
Regan, Stephen, 26, 33, 46n.19
religious attitude, 49, 51, 55, 99, 152
see also aesthetic experience; beauty; emotion; sublime
Ricks, Christopher, 170, 171
Robinson, Agnes, 201n.4
Robinson, Henry Crabb, 122n.18
Romanticism, 1, 35, 52, 53–4, 96, 134–5, 151–2, 157, 161, 172
Rossen, Janice, 8
Russel, Nick, 125–6, 128
Russell, Lord, 100

Sade, Marquis de, 65
Sainte-Beuve, Charles, 66
Salwak, Dale, 129
Sand, George, 58, 61, 62, 63, 64, 79, 80, 81
Saville, Jonathan, 201n.3
Schelling, Friedrich von, 122n.18
Schiller, Friedrich, 7
Scholes, Percy, 201n.3
Schopenhauer, Arthur, 3, 40, 122n.18
Schumann, Robert, 168, 201n.1
Scott, Walter, 128
self/selfhood
and aesthetic experience, 2, 4, 8, 35, 36–8, 38–43, 115
and consciousness, 7, 8, 11, 18, 20, 35
dissolution/loss of, 2, 8, 22, 35, 36–8, 39–43, 122n.21, 177
and nothingness, 8, 11, 54–5
and poetic imagination, 22–3, 33
self-consciousness, 7, 12, 13, 22, 42, 44n.8, 53
see also aesthetic experience; consciousness; creativity; death; freedom; the past; perspective
self-knowledge, 42, 108, 115
sexuality
and creativity, 2, 3, 5, 76–9, 92, 149–50, 152–4
homosexuality, 77–9
masturbation, 76, 78
pornography, 66, 78
prostitution, 65, 77, 78

sexuality – *continued*
see also aesthetic experience; art; creativity; freedom; lesbianism; love; women
Shakespeare, William, 59, 66, 87n.14, 122n.17, 169, 173, 198
Shapiro, Karl, 201n.4
Sitwell, Edith, 201n.4
Sitwell, Osbert, 201n.4
Smith, Stevie, 171, 172
Sorbonne, 122n.18
Stalin, Joseph, 68
Steegmuller, Francis, 48, 83, 85n.1
'Steel, Byron' (Francis Steegmuller's pseudonym), 85n.1
Steele, Timothy, 201n.4
Strang, Patsy, 48–9, 131, 132, 150, 152, 153
sublime, 2, 3, 33, 113–15
see also aesthetic experience; art; beauty; emotion; religious attitude
supernaturalism, 2, 4, 112, 124–64
creepy, 3, 4, 126, 142, 143, 144, 148, 150, 151, 152, 154
ghostly, 124, 130, 133, 137–8, 140, 143, 160, 162n.1
'poetic emotion', 148, 150–1
superstition, 4, 124, 129, 130, 133, 137, 138, 141, 142, 152
uncanny, 112, 124, 130, 152, 157, 158
see also creativity; ghost stories; M. R. James; mysticism
Sutton, Jim, 33, 35, 51, 56, 61, 64, 66, 73, 145, 151, 152
Swarbrick, Andrew, 169, 171, 195, 196, 197, 198

Tennyson, Alfred, Lord, 147, 202n.9
Thatcher, Margaret, 53
Thwaite, Ann, 87n.16
Thwaite, Anthony, 87n.16, 103, 170, 197
time, 8, 9, 24, 101
poetic imagery, 24, 25, 112, 130, 135, 177, 185
see also indexicals; the past
Tolley, Trevor, 174, 202n.10
Tolstoy, Leo, 57, 125
Trilling, Lionel, 69, 86n.13

uncanny, *see* supernaturalism

Victoria, Queen, 100, 108
viewpoint, *see* perspective
Villon, François, 167

Wagner, Richard, 172
Wallace, Robert, 201n.4
Walton, Andrew, 202n.15
Walton, William, 201n.4
Ward, Andrew, 122n.19
Warren, Robert Penn, 201n.4
Whitman, Walt, 66
Wilde, Oscar, 51–2
William IV, King, 101
Wittgenstein, Ludwig, 42, 167, 189, 191
women, 49, 153, 154, 167, 177, 188
Flaubert's attitudes to, 56–7, 72, 76–7, 79–80
and imagination, 78, 79–82, 97–8, 154
Larkin's relationships with, 78–83, 118–19
see also beauty; creativity; lesbianism; love and marriage; sexuality
Woolf, Virginia, 124, 158
Wordsworth, Dorothy, 86n.14
Wordsworth, William, 12, 34, 35, 36, 67, 86n.14, 157, 181

Yeats, W. B., 4, 53, 69, 85n.6, 121n.17, 141

Zola, Émile, 69